ISO Standards for Computer Graphics:
The First Generation

To Joyce (1949-1989)

ISO Standards for Computer Graphics:
The First Generation

D.B. Arnold
Dean, School of Information Systems, University of East Anglia, Norwich

D.A. Duce
Deputy Head of Systems Engineering Division, SERC Rutherford Appleton Laboratory

Butterworths
London Boston Singapore Sydney Toronto Wellington

PART OF REED INTERNATIONAL P.L.C.

First published 1990

© Butterworth & Co. (Publishers) Ltd., 1990

British Library Cataloguing in Publication Data

Arnold David. B.
   ISO standards for computer graphics: the first generation
   1. Computer Systems, Graphic displays
   I. Title II. Duce, David A.
   006.6
   ISBN 0-408-04017-3

Library of Congress Cataloguing-in-Publication Data

Arnold, David B.
ISO standards for computer graphics: the first generation / D.B. Arnold, D.A. Duce.
   p.   cm.
Includes bibliographical references.
ISBN 0-408-04017-3
1. Computer Graphics—Standards. I. Duce, David A.
II. International Organization for Standardization. III. Title
T385.A76   1990
006.6'0218--dc20   89-25455
                            CIP

Printed and bound in Great Britain by Courier International Ltd, Tiptree, Essex

Series Preface

Writing the preface for a book is an enjoyable challenge. Writing the preface for a series of books is another matter entirely. When the series of books will be written over the next five to ten years, and will include titles and subjects not yet known to us, it is indeed a major undertaking.

We can, however, describe our plans and goals for these books, as well as our philosophy for the structure of the series. The nature of our contributions to the content of graphics standards and management of graphics standards projects in both national and international committees will be reflected in this series. The goal of efficient production of quality work which guides us in the committees will also shape these volumes.

The first step to assure the quality of volumes in this series is to select authors with outstanding qualifications. Our authors are wherever possible the editors of the ISO standard or may be closely associated with the management of the standardization project they describe. In other cases a member of the committee which developed the standard will normally be involved. Having been part of the decision making process they can describe not only the standard, but also the reasons why alternatives were rejected.

All of the volumes will deal with some aspect or example of computer graphics standards. We will interpret the definition of computer graphics rather broadly, so that some of the work of committees other than ISO/IEC JTC1/SC24 will be covered. In fact, where there is no related ISO standard, even *de facto* (product based) "standards" will be included, where there is realistic expectation of a standardization project in the technical area, based, at least in part, on the material covered.

Standards are nor renowned for their readability. Volumes in this series will be more readable than their corresponding standard for several reasons. They will be able to present the material in a more natural order. There will be more explanatory text and greater use will be made of figures and examples. However, all the material from the underlying standard will be covered in a rigorous manner, but since some standards will be 2 to 3 times the length of the book, some of the detail may not be included and the texts will complement and act as tutorial material for the standards they describe. The level of detail will allow decisions as to the applicability of particular standards and assessment of different implementations of the standards to be made.

The liberal use of figures and examples will make these volumes suitable for use as formal or private textbooks. The usage is fostered by the inclusion where appropriate of questions and problems to test comprehension of underlying concepts. A comprehensive index and tabular information makes each volume an indispensable reference source.

You may know that the graphics standards committee decided to produce separate standards (or at least sections of standards) describing first semantics and then appropriate syntaxes for accessing the functionality. In the case of applications programming interfaces such as GKS, GKS-3D and PHIGS, the syntax definitions are in terms of bindings of the functionality to Fortran, Ada, Pascal and C.

For our volumes we have taken a different approach. We believe that, at least initially, any given application programmer (or system implementor) will be interested in accessing the semantics of one standard through/from a single programming language. Thus the semantics of a standard such as PHIGS are described in terms of a programming language such as Ada.

Our approach is efficient for the first encounter of a programmer with a functional (semantic) standard in a particular programming language environment. However we intend to pursue consistency in two dimensions. Suppose a programmer is asked to use a given semantic standard (such as GKS-3D) in a different language environment (for example, C rather than Pascal). We will as far as possible keep the organisation of volumes on a given semantic standard common across different languages. We will also keep the way in which the concepts are presented as consistent as allowed by the capabilities of the different programming languages. This will eliminate the unlearning of old approaches, and the confusion caused by different ways of achieving common results.

We will also seek consistency along the other axis, that is, for all bindings of semantic standards to Fortran, as an example. Thus the style used in the description of the Ada binding of GKS will also be employed in the description of the Ada binding not only of PHIGS, but also of the CGI. In this way, the migration to a different functional capability within the same programming language environment will require minimum acquisition of new skills.

Beyond consistent treatment within all bindings of a given semantic standard and all bindings to a particular programming language, there are other aids to consistency. The major one is uniform graphics style or design for all volumes. However as series editors we will endeavour to provide a quality and completeness which will not only be uniform, but also very high.

As stated above, we do not yet know all the volumes that will be included in the series. However some of the early volumes are clearly defined. There will be an overview of graphics standards as we know them today, including description of the historical development, the standards making process and a reference model which shows their interrelationships.

There will be a volume on the principles of language bindings and the generation of language bindings of extensions to standards, either registered or local to installations. This volume will also include sections on the testing and implementation of standards. A volume giving a very thorough coverage of all aspects of the Computer Graphics Metafile and its encodings will be among the early offerings.

Volumes on GKS-3D (which includes GKS as a proper subset), PHIGS and CGI each expressed in terms of Fortran, Ada, Pascal or C are planned. The set of semantic standards is likely to be extended with an imaging system interface and a window management system interface. Although there are currently no ISO projects on bindings to other languages, the set of languages will probably be augmented in the future, with Lisp, Prolog, Mumps and Cobol all as possible future projects. These innovations will be covered by volumes in the series as and when appropriate. Other subjects include the Computer Graphics Interface (CGI) and its data stream encodings, Product Description Standards, Videotex, SPDL (a standardized page description language) and standardized font architecture.

Fortunately these standards will not appear simultaneously. However, as soon after the appearance of the standard as practical, a corresponding volume will be added to the series. Appearance prior to publication of the standard would raise the possibility that the volume did not fully reflect the adopted standard.

Our ultimate goal is to satisfy you, the reader. If your experience with this volume convinces you to buy another volume in the series when you need to understand another graphics standard then we will be pleased. If you think of this series as the definitive explanation of graphics standards we will be satisfied. However with the timescale for the production of the series there are opportunities to incorporate changes in the style and role. If you feel that particular changes would have made the volume even more useful, let us know. Trying to produce the best quality document in the light of public criticism is an integral part of the standardization process and we would be more than happy to receive suggestions — who knows, we may even produce a response document!

B.J. Shepherd   David B. Arnold
Colleyville   University of East Anglia
Texas   Norwich
USA   England

Preface

The authors of this book have collectively over 20 years of experience in the design and production of International Standards for computer graphics. The subject has come a long way since activities started in the U.S.A. in the late 1960's and the Seillac I workshop in May 1976 which marked the start of serious work to formulate standards.

The first International Standard for computer graphics was the Graphical Kernel System, GKS, which was published by ISO in August 1985, almost 10 years after design work first started. There are now three standards at the application programming interface level, GKS, GKS-3D and PHIGS, there is one standard for the transfer of picture description information, CGM, and a standard for the transfer of device data, CGI, is nearing completion. Completion of CGI can be seen as the completion of a family of standards, covering the common requirements of application program interface, data transfer and device interfaces. Language bindings for these standards to the common programming languages are also completed or are nearing completion. Thus users of computer graphics now have available a family of standards (now commonly called "The First Generation") and it is timely to step back, see what has been achieved, why the standards have changed during development, and look at where we should be going next. These are the functions this book sets out to fulfil.

The authors of this book first came together to start drafting in February 1989, having worked independently up to that point. One of the most significant events in the development of standards took place in February 1979 at the Mathematical Centre in Amsterdam, when the authors of the GSPC Core proposal and the DIN GKS proposal came together under the skilful chairmanship of Paul ten Hagen and Bob Hopgood to try to resolve the significant differences in thinking between the two groups and to establish a way forward. It was the realization of this ten year perspective that gave the book its shape; namely a compare and contrast approach to the significant features of the family of standards. We hope that the historical exposition will lead to a deeper understanding of how and why the standards have turned out the way they have.

The standards described in this book are largely specified in natural language. The specifications were developed in English; subsequently French and other, translations have been made. The problems of ambiguity in natural language are well-known. Perhaps the most appropriate example of the potential for misunderstanding is the phrase "tabling a document", whose meaning is well-known to any English-speaking committee member. Unfortunately, although instantly understood, the interpretations may vary widely. To an American "tabling a document" implies that it will not receive discussion. It is "held in abeyance", presumably on a table at the back of a meeting. To an Englishman, however, "tabling a document" implies that, despite its late availability, the document will be available for discussion at the meeting, but only by distribution around the table where the members of the committee sit. There are many (hopefully apocryphal) stories of the trans-Atlantic disputes this phrase has caused. It is however a salutary lesson for those engaging in any international work. The problems do not arise where translation is obviously required; they arise where translation is obviously not required.

This was again brought home to the authors when the first draft of this book was sent out for comment. In English it was perfectly reasonable to have designated the first part of the book "The Pitch" (meaning the part of a cricket ground where wickets are pitched - the field of play). However, as Barry Shepherd pointed out, the primary meaning of the word to an American (a con man's sales presentation) is rather different! Hence the part title was changed to 'The Field' which we hope carries appropriate connotations in both languages.

The lack of a common understanding of natural language is an impediment to the development of standards and it is partly for this reason that there is interest in the application of formal description techniques in the development process. The mathematical basis of such techniques offers a basis for a common understanding. Chapter 11 and Annex D have been included to give a flavour of approaches currently being explored.

We have tried to be exact in our treatment of the technical material of the various projects. However it is very difficult to write anything unambiguous in natural language and it is often necessary to read the whole to obtain complete information rather than rely on dipping into sections. In particular we have tried to acknowledge where projects have published full standards and where documents are still under definition. The reader should refer to Table 14.1 for the best information we have as to the exact status of the work. For any project not yet completed the content is open to some change. In fact even where a standard is published the opportunity for interpretation inevitably exists. All the standards committees can hope to achieve is a minimisation of the possible degree of interpretation.

Where a project is not yet complete to final publication the level of change may be substantial. Indeed one of our objectives in reviewing the development of the standards is to quantify the level of changes which have occurred during processing. In this volume the two standards with the highest possibility of change are the Computer Graphics Interface standard (CGI) [103] and the Reference Model for Computer Graphics [130]. For the CGI the level of change of functionality is now expected to be small. However, changes to the description of the functionality will be substantial and the way in which the functionality is delivered may well vary considerably. In particular, since the CGI (a document of several hundred pages) has at least two further editions before becoming an ISO standard it is important that the descriptions included in this book are viewed as predictions of the eventual content. A later volume in the series will provide detailed information on the actual content of the eventual standard when it is completed.

A project of this nature is never the work of the authors alone. There are many people who have given us support and encouragement and constructive comment. We would particularly like to thank Bob Hopgood and Barry Shepherd for reading and commenting upon an early draft of this volume. Needless to say, any errors in the volume are the sole responsibility of the authors. Thanks are also due to Fiona, Philip and William who spent long days on the beach at Cromer whilst the finishing touches were put to this volume, and to Tony Arnold who kept us fed and watered during a hard week's worth of writing in February!

David B. Arnold
David A. Duce
Norwich

Contents

Part 1
The Field

1
Introduction

1.1 Motivation

The definition of "standardization" as drafted by ISO is:

> "The activity of establishing, with regard to actual or potential problems, provisions for common and repeated use, aimed at the achievement of the optimum degree of order in a given context."

The underlying motivation for standardization in Information Technology (IT) is to protect the investment in increasingly expensive IT by extending the useful life of systems. This extension is achieved by building into the design of the system as much independence from the particular technology and the particular supplier of that technology as possible, leading to *portability* at both the software and hardware levels. There are many types of portability, each of which is important in particular circumstances and all of which are potential money savers.

In the field of computer graphics the following types of portability may be defined:-

* Applications Portability – the ability to move a suite of applications programs from one system configuration to another with minimum (preferably no) work in adapting the code. Within this overall objective it should also be possible to maintain the "look and feel" of the application so that an operator would be familiar with the operations required, but at the same time any investment in hardware should be reflected by corresponding improvements in system performance. The evolution of hardware is discussed in Chapter 2.

* Graphics Package Portability – the ability to use the same range of graphics facilities in a variety of situations. This is typically a combination of the host machine independence and device independence listed below, but also needs to reflect how thorough the implementation of the system is in simulating any features which the underlying hardware and devices do not supply directly. Without such simulation the real level of portability must be the lowest common denominator amongst the sets of hardware between which the system is to be portable.

- Host Machine Independence. A graphics package which is host independent is able to run successfully on many underlying computer systems, from a variety of suppliers. In practice this may well mean that a supplier has implemented the system on a variety of hardware rather than supplying a system which can genuinely be moved between machines. The success of the supplier in containing the extent of the changes required for successful mounting on new hardware will dictate the level of portability achieved. Also to be considered here are factors of relevance to portability of algorithms, but not specific to the graphics, in particular the number systems used on particular machines which will dictate the accuracy of computations etc.

- Device Independence. This covers the ability to use the same code to control a wide range of graphics devices and implies a careful structuring of the graphics package implementation to isolate the parts of the code which are specific to a particular display or input device in a small proportion of the overall system. Substitution of this small portion of code then allows the addition of a different device to the repertoire of devices supported by a graphics package.

- Programming Language Independence implies that the same facilities should be available from all common programming languages. In practice this is likely to mean providing common functionality in all the relevant languages, but the concept can be taken further in implementation terms by using common subroutine linkage mechanisms between languages. Ideally the system should have the same "feel" in any programming environment, involving the use of similar control structures for example.

- Programmer Portability is primarily a question of education. By using agreed ranges of functionality in many languages and agreed terminology for common graphics concepts, the lessons learnt in using a 2D graphics package in Fortran for example, are still relevant when moving to a 3D system in Ada. In such circumstances there will of course be additional lessons to be learnt, but the approach remains one of attempting to minimize the additional effort of adapting to new circumstances.

- Operator Portability is similarly involved with education. In this case however the effort has to be put into adopting a uniform approach over a number of applications, which amounts to adoption of a house style for interactive systems. This has numerous advantages where personnel are expected to switch between several applications packages, but also for the marketing side of a company's operations in that the distinctive style becomes associated (if done well) with a company image for well designed products. The Apple Macintosh interface is a good case in point.

All of these aspects of portability, with the possible exception of the last, are potential candidates for standardization. Even the last is likely to be the subject of at least in-house standards.

However for graphics standards, or indeed for any standards, to be agreed there must be a consensus on good practice, drawing upon the accumulated expertise in the graphics community to define the exact functionality to be incorporated into systems. As part of this process the agreements must be documented and discussed for potential ambiguity of interpretation or incompleteness of specification. This process can take a great deal of time and effort and requires the involvement of a wide range of expertise, partly to provide the wide perspective on the interpretations of the documents and partly since graphics as a technical area is involved increasingly in almost every application of information technology. In the next section we take a brief look at the history of the graphics standardization process, which has its origins in the 1960's, in particular since an important part of understanding what is now provided for within the first generation of graphics standards is to understand the environment in which particular decisions were taken and the reasoning behind the decisions.

1.2   A brief history of graphics standards making

1.2.1 Early history

The standardization of computer graphics has a history that goes back to the late 1960's. As soon as interactive computer graphics started to reach a significant market following the introduction of the first Tektronix storage displays, the portability of computer graphics programs became a real issue. A number of packages acquired the status of 'de facto' standards (examples were Tektronix' Plot-10, Cambridge University's (and subsequently the Computer Aided Design Centre's) GINO-F and Culham Laboratory's Ghost), but they were all variously flawed at that time.

The important developments from which all else has grown happened in the 1970's; they were

- the establishment (in 1972) of the Graphics Standards Planning Committee (GSPC) by ACM SIGGRAPH, and

- the Seillac I workshop (held in May 1976) called by Richard Guedj (France) under the auspices of IFIP WG5.2.

- following the proposal that GINO-F should be adopted as an international standard, a meeting of international experts decided that no known computer graphics system could be considered suitable for a standard.

The Seillac I meeting [45] really marked the beginning of the formal moves to achieve a set of standards for computer graphics by consensus amongst experts in the field. At this meeting there were discussions on the objectives to be met by a standard, what types of applications it should support (including or excluding for example image processing or high quality typesetting) and, probably most importantly, discussion on where a standard should fit into the current practice of assembling graphics systems. This discussion focussed on the level at which the standard should be defined.

Typical configurations of the "best practice" systems at that time consisted of a device independent "front end" driving one or more device specific "back ends" (termed variously "code generator" or "device driver") (figure 1.1). The front end was driven by the applications program via a set of (normally Fortran) subroutine calls, whilst the back end would typically be a single entry point routine, which for portability, would supply any of the features not directly supported on a device, within the limits of portability supported by the system. The back end would typically have portions of code specific to the requirements of interfacing to a particular operating system and would thus be both device and machine dependent.

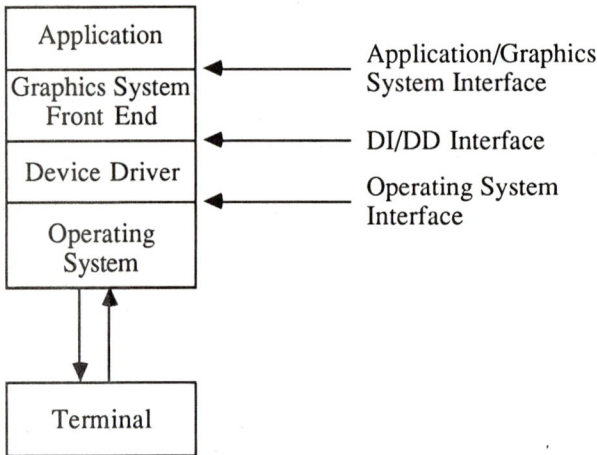

Application

Graphics System Front End

——— Application/Graphics System Interface

——— DI/DD Interface

Device Driver

——— Operating System Interface

Operating System

Terminal

Figure 1.1 Structure of a device independent graphics system

This overall architecture was recognized as giving rise to two principal contenders for standardization. The first is the application/front end interface and the second the Device Independent/ Device Dependent (or DI/DD) interface between the front and back ends. The decision taken at Seillac was that the first step should be to standardize a kernel graphics system on top of which applications-orientated graphics packages would sit. It was generally agreed that any standard would specify a set of virtual input and output facilities which would be realized in terms of the functions of particular graphics devices.

It was recognized that one of the problems with existing packages was that they did not distinguish between transformations used to view a picture and those used to construct the object or model to be viewed. The separation of modelling and viewing was an important outcome of Seillac I, and it was resolved that a kernel graphics system would only use transformations for viewing a previously constructed model. It was felt that the modelling subsystem might be very much dependent on the application, though it was recognized that it ought to be possible to design modelling subsystems for large classes of applications.

Other agreements reached concluded

- that virtual graphics devices should be used for both input and output

- that virtual input devices would be based on string, locator, pick and valuator input primitives with less agreement about choice and stroke.

- that there was less agreement over the range of output primitives to be used with little agreement beyond the need for lines and some form of text, with markers considered another potential candidate.

There was immediate controversy over the vexed question of whether "current position" was a useful concept to include in the expected standard. This concept was widely used in existing systems, but although simple use was relatively consistent, there were major differences in the interpretation of "current". Figure 1.2 illustrates one problem – where is the current position when the coordinate system is transformed halfway through a picture – is the current position left in the old coordinate system, transformed to the new coordinate system, set to a default, or something else. This problem illustrates the major areas of difficulty in achieving genuine standards:

- Terms in common usage are often assumed to mean the same thing to all participants in a discussion. This assumption has been proved dangerous on many occasions and is the reason that considerable effort was put into the glossary section of graphics standards quite early on in their development.

- If the concept of current position was to be used in the standard system there was probably no "right way" of including it. The decision would be made by the opinions of the experts present at discussions. When the people involved in discussions change, the balance of such opinions may change and if old decisions are not to be constantly revisited mechanisms have to be invented to record and document decisions in a way which does not encourage instability.

- It was felt important that a standard should specify what should be done, but not how, but these two are at times difficult to separate. In the case of current position the mechanism is merely a shorthand to describe the start point of each primitive, but is unfortunately ambiguous. The solution adopted in this case (but not in such a strong form at Seillac I) has been to make the start point explicit in each output primitive's specification and not specify whether current position may be used by an implementation internally in order to compress the required communications within the graphics system.

The activities generated by Seillac I developed into the efforts of the International Organization for Standardization (ISO) (and subsequently into joint efforts with the International Electrotechnical Commission (IEC), see Section 4.2.2) which are now the predominant source of standards in computer graphics. Initially several countries indulged in national efforts to produce proposals. In the light of the decisions taken at Seillac groups in several countries began work on designing a standard system. The first national standard was the Norwegian GPGS-F, subsequently revised to produce IDIGS.

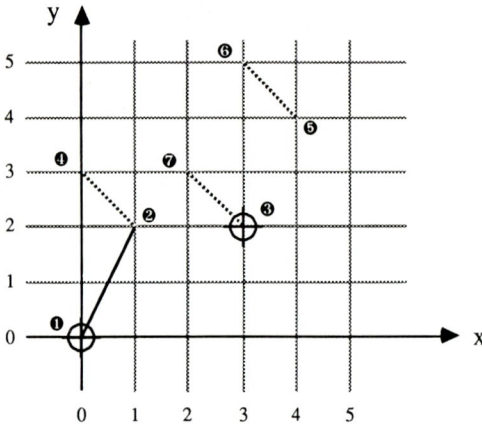

- ❶   Original Origin and Current Position
- ❷   Draw(1,2)
- ❸   Translate(3,2)
- ❹   Drawby(-1,1)
- ❺   (1,2) in new coordinates
- ❻   (-1,1) from new point (1,2)
- ❼   (-1,1) from new origin

Figure 1.2 Problems interpreting current position

The GSPC sat until 1979, when it produced its final "Core" proposal [19]. The important thing about the Core was that it was only a proposal. It had several serious problems that made it an unsatisfactory basis for the development of really portable software. The significant problems with the Core were:

- it was only ever a proposal for a standard: for example one area that was never properly reviewed was the requirement of conformance, and also GSPC was not a formal standards making body;
- it was specified in terms of abstract functions with no proposed mappings of those functions into any existing programming language (see Chapter 9), so that the names by which functions of the package are called from application programs might well differ from implementation to implementation;
- it retained the ("traditional" but lamentably ill-defined) concept of current position; and
- its model of graphical input was not well developed or symmetrical.

Notwithstanding these drawbacks, it did represent a real conceptual advance on anything previously published, and many of its concepts survive in the graphics standards work now in progress. A large number of implementations of the Core were made, and they were at one time quite widely available commercially.

The third proposal developed at this time was the Graphical Kernel System (GKS) developed within the DIN group (the standards body of the Federal Republic of Germany). Whereas Core was a 3D system, GKS contained 2D functionality, which was simpler to specify, but would only ever address a fraction (but probably a majority) of users.

1.2.2 Activities within ISO

The first formal meeting of WG2 (the graphics working group) was held in Bologna in September 1978. The meeting received reports of the GSPC and DIN activities and a statement from Norway that they intended to propose IDIGS (a successor of GPGS-F) as a Norwegian standard. An Editorial Board was set up to compare the various proposals and recommend changes so that the proposals might converge or at least be compatible.

The Board met in Amsterdam in February 1979, chaired by Paul ten Hagen (WG2 Convenor) and Bob Hopgood [46]. The meeting considered GKS version 3 [6] and a draft of the 1979 Core report. IDIGS was not available. The Board recommended changes to both GKS and Core to bring them closer together. Some of the recommendations are discussed later in this book. The recommendations were subsequently discussed by DIN and GSPC at a joint meeting held in Boulder, Colorado.

It June 1979, it was recommended that the GSPC work should be passed to the formal American standards body, ANSI. The first meeting of the ANSI graphics Working Group, X3H3, was held in September 1979. In December 1979, GSPC Core was accepted as the starting point for the work of X3H3.

The next ISO working group was held in Budapest in October 1979. GKS Version 5.0 [7] was presented, which incorporated many of the

Editorial Board recommendations. Revised versions of the Core and IDIGS were also presented. The working group eventually decided that resources were not available to evaluate more than one proposal at the same time and it was agreed that the formal steps necessary for work on GKS standardization would be initiated.

GKS was reviewed internationally at four working group meetings prior to publication as an international standard (ISO 7942) on 15th August 1985, the first ISO standard for computer graphics programming. Chapters 5 to 8 examine the development of some of the changes to GKS that took place over this period. The version numbers of the documents considered at each meeting are listed in Table 1.1 for reference.

GKS is defined independently of programming languages. Standardization of language bindings proceeded in parallel with the Fortran, Pascal and Ada bindings reaching DP status (see Chapter 4 for an explanation of the stages in the standardization process) two years after GKS, in 1984.

Work on a metafile standard was approved in early 1983 and the metafile for the storage and transfer of picture description information (CGM) was published as ISO 8632 in 1987 [85]. Various Addenda to the standard are now being progressed to enhance the scope and functionality of the metafile.

As technical work on GKS drew to a close attention turned to the standardization of 3D graphics. Some experts wished to extend GKS in an upwardly compatible manner, whilst others, notably from the USA, wished to produce a new system, PHIGS (Programmer's Hierarchical Interactive Graphics System), a system which incorporated modelling as well as viewing functions. It was agreed at the Gananoque (Canada) meeting in 1983 that approval should be sought to launch both projects. Final text for both GKS-3D and PHIGS was produced in 1988. GKS-3D was published in 1988 [15] and publication of PHIGS [16] took place early in 1989. Language binding standards for GKS-3D and PHIGS are also being produced.

Table 1.1 GKS versions

Meeting	GKS Version
Editorial Board 1979	3 [6]
Budapest 1979	5.0 [7]
Tiefenbach 1980	5.2 [8]
Melbourne 1981	6.2 [9]
Abingdon 1981	6.6 [10]
Steensel 1982	7.0 [11]
(Output document)	7.2 [12]

Production of a lower level device interface standard (CGI) [103], started formally within ISO in 1985 and is now nearing technical completion although the length of time taken to final publication should not be underestimated (perhaps two years) and has always been longer than expected for the other standards.

It has long been felt that a suitable reference model for computer graphics would have accelerated the process of achieving consensus on the individual standards and a project to standardize a reference model for computer graphics was finally spawned following on from discussions held at the working group meeting in Timberline, Oregon, in 1985.

If standards are to be meaningful, it is important to know what is required for a product to conform to a standard and to know how conformance can be established. The work on defining a standard for conformity testing of implementations of graphics standards and the establishment of conformity testing services is described in Chapter 12.

There are some kinds of entities, for example linetypes, for which it is convenient and appropriate to be able to extend the range of standardized values outside any particular standard. A Registration mechanism has been set up which enables this to be done. The procedures were published in 1988 [132]. This work is described in Chapter 13.

The status of all current projects in SC24 is described in Chapter 14.

1.3 Applicability of first generation ISO standards

As hinted at above there were some discussions at Seillac I over the types of application which should be addressed in graphics standards and about the areas of graphics functionality which should be covered. There was agreement even then that a number of related standards would be required to cover the complete subject area known as Computer Graphics.

When the standardization exercise was begun it was anticipated that 90% of the benefits of standardization could be achieved for 90% of the users by standardizing a small two dimensional interactive kernel graphics system. Amongst the applications areas whose primary needs would be met were:

- business graphics;
- planar finite element analysis;
- drafting;
- simple statistical charts;
- cartography;
- CAD for circuit design.

Many applications requiring 3D graphics have handled 3D in the application and used a 2D graphics system to output the projection onto 2D. This has allowed applications to take advantage of specific characteristics of the graphics associated with that application. Nevertheless, it was felt that by a simple extension to 3D most of the additional requirements of applications like:

- Computer Aided Architectural Design;

- Finite Element Analysis;

would also be satisfied. It was noted that standardized modelling functionality would be of value in these areas and the view was that this should be provided on top of the kernel graphics system.

In reviewing this list of application areas in 1989, it must be remembered that what we might view as the "primary requirements" of an application area now may be very different from those expected in 1976 and is heavily conditioned by knowledge of what can be available at the leading edge of technology. Standards are often quoted as being "concerned with standardization of the best of current practice", which is by definition not at the leading edge of the hardware technology. Standards are however directly concerned with the best of current practice when it comes to engineering systems which are robust and adaptable so as to give long product lifetime. The ways in which "primary requirements" may have altered would affect for example the expected text support for business graphics where at the start of the standardization exercise high quality text systems were not to be widely available on PCs for another 10 years, or in the area of colour support where sophisticated colour rendering on an interactive three dimensional CAD system was still thought to be 20 years away (and is still, for most purposes, in the future).

While the first generation of standards addresses many of the requirements of users of graphics systems across a wide range of applications, it is freely acknowledged that some legitimate uses, which would commonly be thought of as "Computer Graphics", are not addressed. Amongst these are:

- Image Processing applications. The successful processing of images was not commonplace before the wide availability of raster devices. Raster devices were far from commonplace when ISO standardization activities started in 1978. This has resulted in a set of standards which do not address raster graphics functionality at the applications level and therefore do not contribute to the more advanced graphics functionality for full image processing systems. The CGI has gone furthest towards meeting the requirements of this community and new work currently proposed is expected to address the requirements for image processing more directly.

- Window Management. There is an uneasy interrelation between graphics and window management currently, caused mainly by underlying assumptions as to the responsibility for management of physical resources. Graphics standards were initially developed at a time when the full physical resources on each display would be available to a single application, whereas window management systems are based on the approach of dynamic partitioning of a set of resources between tasks. Graphics systems have in general assumed therefore that a particular configuration of resources will be available for a complete session, whereas many windowing systems will dynamically change the availability of resources for any particular application during a run, and with the responsibility for adapting to the new resource level being placed on the application rather than the display management system. However, much work is being done to try and address this mismatch and elementary interworking is already available from many manufacturers.

- High quality typesetting. The quality of text facilities available on modern systems far exceeds that expected to be widely available in the original timeframe for the standards' development. Consequently the current text facilities are neither simple enough for convenient novice use nor sufficiently sophisticated for control of high quality typesetters for example. The whole area is currently being re-examined.

- High performance graphics systems, both from the point of view of specialized accelerators for particular operations (which are not normally directly visible to the application and therefore beyond the scope of the API standards) and also from the point of view of production of high quality graphics with photo realism. This last application is expected to be addressed at least partially by new proposals, but for the first generation of standards was felt to be beyond the requirements of the vast majority of users (particularly in 1976!!)

Chapter 14 describes the future directions expected for computer graphics standards development and includes some projects which are designed specifically to examine the current generation's shortcomings in many of the areas listed above.

1.4 The structure of the book

The rest of this book will concentrate on standards that are (or are expected to be) outcomes of the ISO computer graphics working groups.

This book surveys the whole area of these standards, adopting a "compare and contrast" style, with a view to helping the reader to understand how the standards interrelate and where features are different, explaining why this has arisen and what the implications are. Later volumes in the series will adopt more of a tutorial style and address the questions of how a particular standard should be used and, where the standard is the subject of a language binding, illustrating the concepts using one of the standardized bindings.

This book is divided into five Parts

- Part 1 ("The Field"), including this chapter, describes the general background to the standards work, hardware and software environments in which the standards originated, a reference model for the interrelationships between the various standards and the process of getting the necessary international agreements.

- Part 2 ("The Players") compares and contrasts the ways in which pictures can be described and interactive systems built in the various standards, by examining four different aspects – output primitives, coordinate spaces and viewing, storage mechanisms and input – in turn.

- Part 3 ("The Rules") examines the role of language bindings and data encodings in defining the exact appearance of functionality in particular programming or communications environments.

- Part 4 ("Refereeing") describes the measures taken to try to ensure the effectiveness of the standardization process. It includes chapters on; formal specification, which has been a steady theme within graphics standardization attempting to improve the accuracy of the descriptions of standard functionality; Validation and Testing, which seeks to enforce both that claiming conformance to a standard offers some guarantee of usefulness to the user and that the implementors are justified in making the claim; and finally a chapter on Registration of Graphics Items, which is a procedure instigated to allow the range of standardized facilities to be extended.

- Part 5 ("The Result") which is an attempt to describe the current status of projects and the likely future directions.

The book concludes with four annexes giving firstly a bibliography of sources of more information on the standards, secondly a glossary of the abbreviations used within the standards, thirdly contact addresses for standards-promoting organizations, and finally an example of a formal specification of part of GKS.

2
Architectural Concerns

2.1 Evolution of underlying hardware models

Prior to about 1968, most of the applications of computer graphics used hardcopy output devices, such as pen plotters and microfilm recorders. The characteristics of these devices had a significant influence on the architecture of the graphics packages used to drive the devices and on the range of facilities available to the graphics applications.

Interactive graphics applications really began with the invention of vector refresh devices during the 1960's. These devices were very expensive and at least initially of rather low display capacity. Frequently these operated using a dual processor architecture where one processor (the display file compiler) created a set of machine instructions for the other processor (the display processor) to execute (figure 2.1). The continual execution of the display program was used to maintain a flicker free display, requiring about 30 complete executions of the display instructions every second. To change a displayed picture the display program would be edited such that on the next execution, 1/30th of a second later, a revised picture could be displayed. The arrangement involved dynamic assembly and editing of the display program and had the advantage that local processing power within the display could be exploited to control the interactions with the operator. The device could also store previously prepared picture parts helping to reduce the communications bandwidth required to update the display from a remote host.

As indicated in Chapter 1 the introduction of the first Tektronix direct view storage tubes, coupled with the advent of time-sharing systems, revolutionized the availability of graphics, making graphics available for the first time to a very wide range of applications. At the same time as the storage tube was spreading the availability of graphics it was also changing the nature of graphics systems. Since storage tubes involved a technology which did not use a continual refresh cycle it became much more difficult to make incremental changes to the display. Items could be added but the screen had to be completely cleared and the image redrawn in order to remove an item. By eliminating the possibility of selective erasure, storage tube technology forced a style of program control structure which was far less capable of supporting genuinely interactive interface design than the vector refresh technology which had previously dominated the development of interactive techniques.

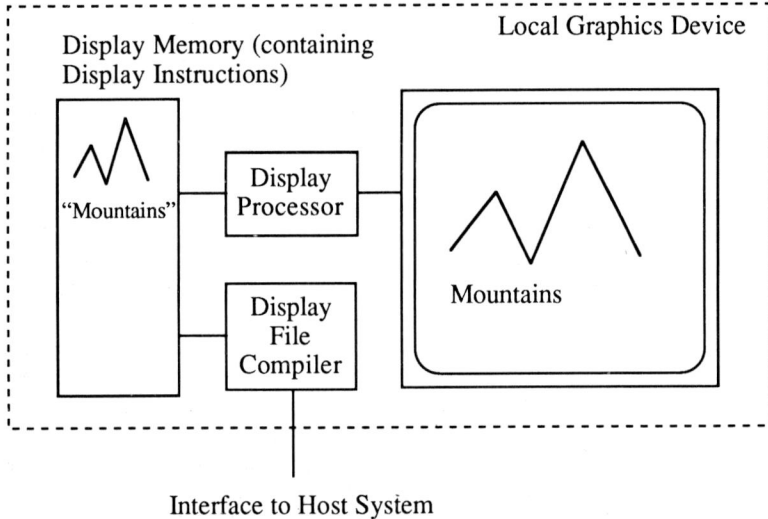

Figure 2.1 Schematic of vector refresh display architecture

It was precisely because vector refresh technology required the availability of local processing power that it allowed the local manipulation of picture parts and the local processing of inputs. It could therefore support interfaces that made extensive use of prompting, echoing (defined as information on the significance of input actions in the context of the display) and feedback (defined as information on the significance of input actions in the context of the application domain). But it was also this requirement for local processing power which gave rise to the very high price tag associated with interactive graphics.

The interactive techniques developed on vector refresh technology could only be emulated on the much cheaper (and therefore more widely available) storage tubes by developing software layers which simulated the same actions and by accepting the degradation of performance which was inherent in the greatly reduced price tag. Different interactive techniques and program control structures tended to be developed for applications using storage tubes.

In attempting to reconcile these differences by providing a uniform range of functionality across the range of devices then available the software suppliers of the early 1970's structured their systems such that the code controlling a particular device was separated from the code which handled an applications program's request for particular graphical effects. Such an approach could also be used in developing systems to control the wide range of plotters which were already available then. This led to the sort of software structuring for portability referred to in Chapter 1, but also had some fundamental consequences for the concerns which drove the standardization process and for the actual functionality provided. In particular the concepts of workstation control, deferral and update control had to be generalized, and concerns over the overhead of some simulations which might be required by strict conformance to all aspects of the documented functionality led to some "allowed variations". In this last category for example the prevalent technology in 1975 could be seriously slowed down if forced to render all text at the same quality as that achievable on fast high quality vector refresh displays. Factors upwards of 100 to 1 could be demonstrated on quite simple interactive dialogues, by the choice of the quality of text used, which would turn a highly interactive system into a system with a minute's reaction time, completely invalidating the objectives and benefits of an interactive system.

The other architectural impact which has had a major impact on the way in which graphics systems are programmed has been the development of the low cost raster refresh device. This has distinctly different characteristics in a number of ways which are important to those attempting to define device independent graphics systems. The image is again refreshed from a stored description 30 times a second and changing the stored description will again cause an effectively instantaneous update to the display. However the image is stored as a number representing the colour at every point on the screen (figure 2.2), rather than as the collection of graphics objects which need to be drawn to recreate the picture. Thus although there is a certain amount of inherent processing power within the graphics system, unlike the vector refresh display, there is very little information to allow what is displayed in the image to be associated with parts of the applications' database and interaction is of a different type. In addition there is no automatic availability of local storage for predefined picture parts etc., and the manipulations which can be performed on the stored picture description are different from those available on a vector refresh display.

2.2 Software architecture

Chapter 1 introduced some of the concerns of the graphics systems implementors in providing a consistent functionality over the evolving range of devices available in the early 1970's. These concerns led to layered implementations of graphics systems which had a number of characteristics. In this section we elaborate on a typical structuring of implementations and the consequent design decisions and potential problems for efficient interaction.

2.2.1 Typical layered model

Many implementations of graphics systems can be conveniently mapped onto a layered model of the software structure (figure 2.3). This model would have the following components:-

*   The application layer, which is the application specific code and calls the graphics system in order to produce output and interact with the operator of the graphics device.

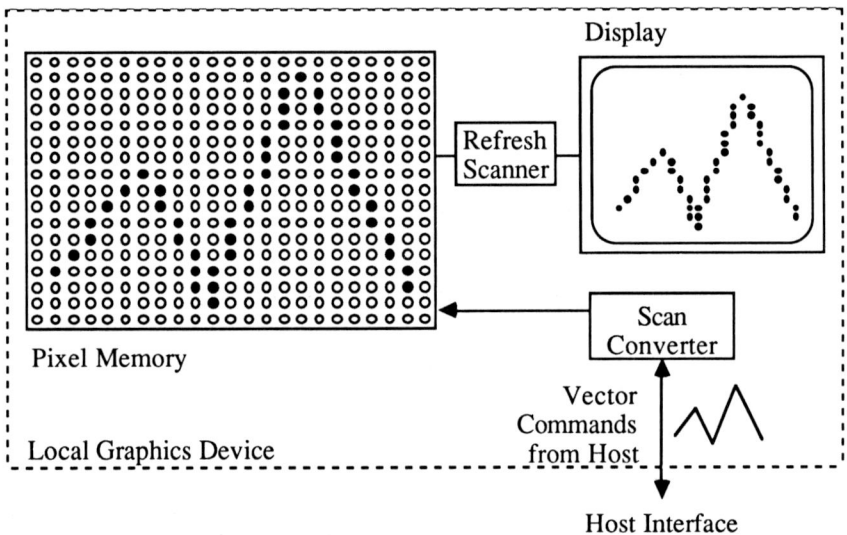

Figure 2.2 Schematic architecture for basic raster devices

*   The graphics system front-end, which contains the device independent code. This code handles all aspects which are not dependent on the particular device selected for this interactive session. It may also contain a very large amount of software used to simulate the capabilities of intelligent devices with local storage, etc. when less capable devices are provided in a particular system's configuration.
*   The graphics system back-end, which is the code which translates the application's requests for particular graphics effects into the device specific protocol to be sent to the device.
*   An operating system level, which provides the transport mechanisms for transferring the coded protocol to the device.

- At the device level there may be a level of device software (or possibly firmware) used to control the local intelligence and storage facilities.

- At the lowest level there are the hardwired facilities of the device, which reflect the most efficient operations which the device can handle.

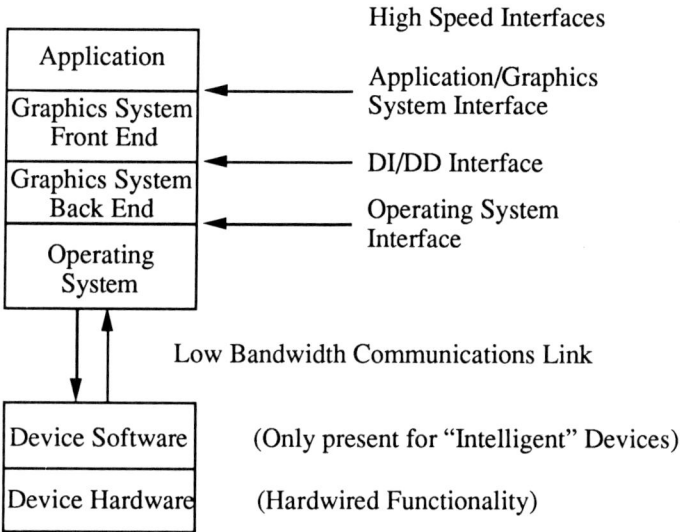

Figure 2.3 Layered model of graphics system functionality

At the time when the standards work was being initiated the link between the operating system and the device would be typically a low speed RS232 connection, with 1200 baud considered a luxury. The other alternative, a DMA connection between a host machine and a general purpose dedicated mini (e.g. a DEC PDP 7 controlling a single device), was very expensive and as such not the primary market for standards. Where Direct Memory Access was not available speeds of up to 19200 baud might be provided to the more intelligent devices. There was thus both a wide variety of potential speeds and a very severe potential bottleneck to the graphics communications. In these circumstances the mapping of the graphics functionality to particular locations in the system architecture could be crucial in determining the viability or otherwise of an application.

2.2.2 Implications of the layered model

The main components that need to be considered for efficient matching of the graphics facilities to particular layers in the system are those which involve the storage of graphics data and the types of responses available for interactive use. Efficient interactive use in this case, due to the potential bandwidth problem and the prevalence of timeshared hosts, has to be considered as that class of operation which was supportable on the local dedicated hardware.

The major storage facilities involved are the provision of segmentation, or other application-defined graphics objects, and the use of fonts. With the description of a complete font typically taking perhaps 10K bytes it is fairly obvious that having the information on the wrong side of a low speed link will lead to very slow operations. Just to transport the whole font description across a 1200 baud line would take a couple of minutes and operations which changed fonts during an interactive session would be liable to major delays. In addition even for intelligent devices in the mid 1970's there would often have been insufficient local storage to handle local descriptions of this size and individual character shapes would have had to have been loaded as and when required. Thus selection of device independent fonts was very impractical and situations in which software design led to clogging of the communications could easily be set up, and frequently were by inexperienced programmers.

Similar situations could also be found in the handling of stored graphics objects like segments, but in this case there were rather more complex decisions to be made to try and balance the amount of information required on the local side of the communications link with the requirements for interaction at a meaningful level with applications related data. Thus loading of a set of segments representing one view of an engineering design might allow interactions locally for a particular set of operations, but a more complete or merely different view might be required if a different set of operations was to be performed. For example an architectural application might define segments which described the pipework involved in a building, and store these locally, but not predefine the wiring at the same time since the application would expect a major switch if the designer was to move to wiring problems and the extra use of local device storage would not be justified while the designer was working on the piping.

The designer of an interactive application thus needed to be aware of both the implementation strategy for the graphics support package and the underlying device's capabilities before being able to make efficient use of the overall system. In addition the graphics package implementor had some very difficult design decisions to make in the area of device independence and portability of applications. It can be argued that the difficulty of making these decisions about the division of functionality between the device dependent and device independent parts of the system led to the decision to standardize the Applications Programmer Interface first (see below), but it is also reflected in the facilities provided to the applications programmer for control of the timing of updates, etc. The implementor of the standard graphics support package must also still take decisions about the mapping of the support of the standardized functionality onto the various parts of the system.

2.2.3 Design choices for the DI/DD interface

An implementor of a graphics support package has to determine the level of device independence to be supported by the package and make choices about the means by which device independence will be provided. A decision to reduce all graphics devices to a lowest common denominator makes the device dependent part very small and therefore very easy to implement for new devices, but reduces the potential to exploit new devices to the full. In contrast assuming the need to exploit expensive devices to the full may lead to the definition of a rich functionality at the DI/DD interface in order to access the device's capabilities. The implication is then that the device dependent back-end must in all cases be capable of at least simulating the functionality and the back-end code increases in size and complexity. Various alternative strategies involving use of predefined classes of device and/or negotiation at run time about the functionality supported at the device level have also been implemented [39].

The difficulty of standardizing the decisions about what should be provided above and below the DI/DD interface is reflected in the complexity of the proposed standard for this area (CGI) which is expected to permit a very wide range of possible standard interfaces, by adopting an approach of defining a toolkit for the assembly of standardized DI/DD interfaces. Whether this interface also corresponds to the position of a potential communications bottleneck is a philosophical question which is largely unanswered, although there is a definite statement that the underlying model in the CGI is of a generator and interpreter of a linearly encoded CGI data stream (figure 2.4).

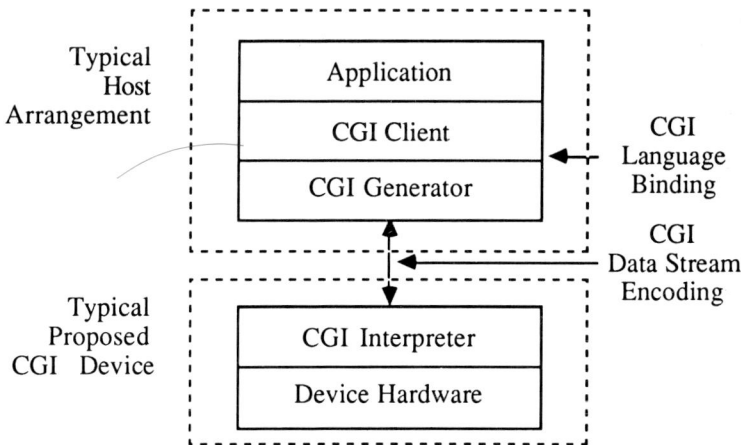

Figure 2.4 CGI generator/interpreter model

Whilst a single DI/DD interface is very common amongst implementations of graphics support packages, there may be more than one internally defined interface. For example the GKS workstation interface is a potential candidate for explicit definition, as well as the workstation to device interface, which could be more correctly classed as the DI/DD interface (figure 2.5). Whilst complicating the definition process this approach allows more possible choices for the places at which the simulations required for device independence can be contained and helps support the benefits of modular software engineering techniques.

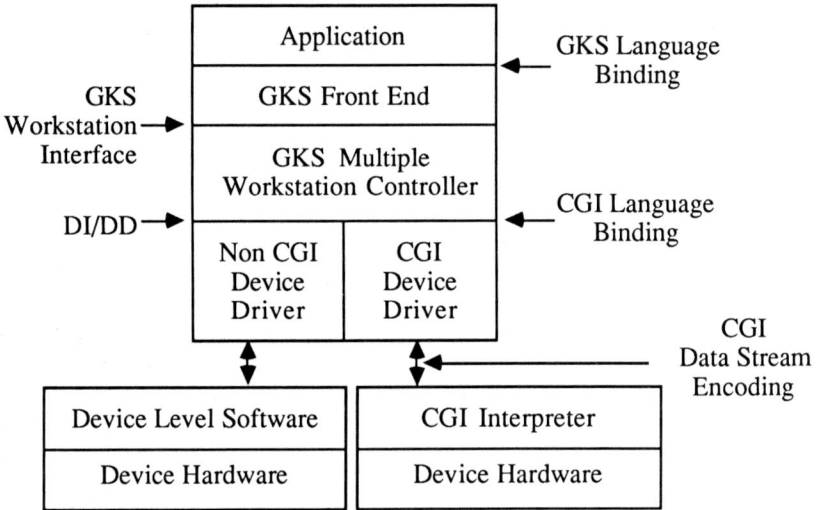

Figure 2.5 System with multiple internal interfaces defined

2.3 Update, deferral and regeneration control

The difficult interactions between the wide variety of potential divisions of labour between the dedicated and shared parts of the interactive system, and between the device independent and device dependent parts of the system, led to the conclusion that a good graphics support package would provide mechanisms for the application to control to some degree the timings of when particular updates to a display were undertaken. For example an application which was about to delete a number of pieces of graphics information from a display, where the display did not support selective erasure, would probably wish to prevent the graphics package from completely redrawing the display until all the items to be deleted had been identified and then carry out the deletions in one batch. However where the device did support selective erasure the implementation would be likely to be simplified if the deletions were forwarded to the device without batching.

In order to facilitate control at this level several mechanisms were introduced in the first generation of standards, to allow an application to determine the level of support for dynamic update of the display, to batch changes and to control when actions which would implicitly specify the need to redraw the display should be carried out.

These facilities are not described in this book but are left to the individual standard specific volumes, partly since their use is very context dependent and partly since this is an area in which implementations vary widely dependent on the particular combinations of hardware being used. It is also expected that revisions of the current standards will adopt a very different approach to these problems given the changes in the power of hardware available dedicated to any particular interactive application.

2.4 Future trends in architectures

2.4.1 Computational power and storage

Hardware has obviously moved on a long way since the mid 1970's and many of the features which were regarded as only available for the highly privileged few in research laboratories are now common features on personal machines. The computational power which is available for an individual's application is typically of the same order as would have been regarded as sufficient for a mainframe system and the storage capacities of average machines has risen by at least two orders of magnitude. In these circumstances it might well be assumed that none of the concerns of system efficiency held by the pioneers of standardization in interactive graphics in the mid-70's could possibly have any relevance to the systems of today.

Whilst the technology used to support applications may now offer a completely different level of performance, the same levels and interfaces still exist. What was a fundamental concern in the efficiency of a mainframe has now become of concern to the PC user and many of the concerns which drove the earlier standards decision making remain relevant at the level of implementation practice even on larger machines or in networked environments. However the end user of an application mounted on a "mainframe system" (if such a concept still exists) will be progressively less likely to see the inner workings of the graphics support environment and it is likely that the partitioning of functionality between different standards will change in future revisions of the set of graphics standards, with concerns which affected the API standards' functionality in the future being reflected in lower level standards like a revision of the proposed device interface standard (CGI).

It is an inescapable conclusion that whilst systems' power continues to rise, there is a compensating increase in the demands placed on the systems as their capabilities become understood by the users. For example in considering the major circumstances giving rise to concern over work sharing between different parts of the system in the mid-1970's the use of fonts and segments were particularly highlighted. Since that time the advent of raster displays, in many cases storing images of several megabytes, means that novel applications in the image processing area may well find that the bandwidth and manipulations required are placing different and even larger communications demands on the systems. It is therefore rash to predict that constraints will be totally removed due to increasing hardware capability.

2.4.2 Device ranges and graphics functionality

One area in which the complexity should go down however is in the variety of constraint placed on the system design by the variety of classes of interactive graphics devices. The very different nature of interaction with a vector or raster refresh display and the different control structures involved in using unintelligent terminals, were major concerns with the first standards. However increasing power of vector refresh displays is leading to larger numbers of vectors being available in colour, with the associated potential for full colour shading, whilst in raster devices the increasing power not only means better displays, but also more dedicated hardware handling the equivalent of the vector refresh display list. Thus the differences are becoming less relevant at the device level.

Similarly the days of the unintelligent device are numbered and it is likely that all devices will be assumed capable of supporting local processing when the current standards are revised.

The availability of full colour rastered images and potential applications using them has begun to be reflected in the facilities provided in the standards, but there is still some way to go before the range of functions appropriate to raster devices can be directly accessed through the graphics standards and this is likely to be the subject of further work within ISO/IEC.

By the time the results of this further work are available it is, of course, inevitable that other developments will have changed the underlying constraints and that a different set of concerns will be the current challenge. However it is likely that the increasing performance of personal workstations will lead to more commonality of supported functionality at the "device" level and therefore that the fundamental problems of the discrepancies between particular display technologies will be very much less important to system performance and have substantially less impact on the range of functionality available at the API.

3
A Reference Model

3.1 Introduction

The purpose of this chapter is to present a reference model for the first generation of graphics standards which provides a framework within which the relationships between the standards can be described. Because of the piecewise development of these standards, there are areas in which the fit is less than perfect. This is in part a consequence of the diversity of requirements for graphics standards, which are difficult to accommodate within a single framework. It is also due to the extended development time for standards and the consequent changes in external constraints (for example display architecture), personnel and ideas which have influenced the projects' directions. In addition the understanding of computer graphics has deepened considerably during the development of the first generation standards, and it is now clearer how certain areas fit together.

It is important to appreciate that this chapter describes a reference model constructed for the purposes of this book. It is NOT being standardized in this precise form. The status of the SC24 Computer Graphics Reference Model project is addressed later in this chapter.

There are five types of standards in the current family:

- *Application Program Interface (API) Standards* - these define a programming interface for applications programmers. GKS was the first to be developed, and was later followed by GKS-3D and PHIGS.

- *Metafile and Archive Standards* - these standards define representations of graphics for storage and transfer between systems. These are fundamentally file format and file transfer encoding standards. The Computer Graphics Metafile (CGM) and Part 2 *et seq* of PHIGS (which describes the PHIGS archive file) are of this type. The Addenda which have been proposed to both GKS (and GKS-3D) and CGM to address more fully the metafile requirements of GKS (and GKS-3D) also fall into this category.

- *Device Interface Standards* - the requirement for a standard at this level (the DI/DD interface) was acknowledged at Seillac I, but is only now beginning to bear fruit with the CGI project. This project essentially covers the requirements for sequential protocols to graphics devices and the interface to the device driver software which produces the sequential protocols. The CGI is in part a toolkit to allow a range of device types to be defined and controlled.

- *Language Binding Standards* - API and device interface standards are defined independently from particular programming languages. Each standard characteristically has an attached language binding standard which states how the functionality should be accessed from a variety of programming languages.The encoding parts of Metafile and Archive standards are really analogous to language binding standards even though they are usually included as parts of a multipart standard. They describe different methods for encoding the abstract functionality defined by the functional description part of the standards.

- *Framework Standards* - this type is typified by the standardization of a reference model for computer graphics, conformance criteria and the registration of graphical items.

A question often asked is what is the relationship between the graphics standards and window managers and between User Interface Management Systems (UIMS) and the graphics standards. Figure 3.1 shows the broad relationship between these entities.

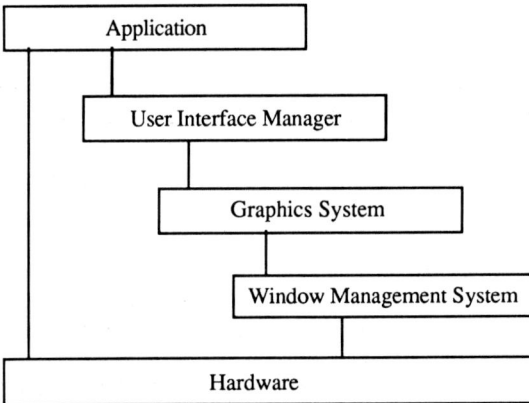

Figure 3.1 Relationships between different software layers

The intention of the diagram is to show that the graphics system is at a higher level of abstraction than a window management system (which essentially manages physical resources such as screen real-estate and physical input devices) and at a lower level of abstraction than a UIMS (which is concerned, *inter alia*, with dialogue management). Graphics systems can use the facilities of a window management system and a UIMS can use the facilities of a graphics system.

It has to be said that these relationships are not universally accepted, especially for UIMS which are still very much a topic of research [205]. In addition debate continues as to whether or not a window management system should be capable of operating as a client of a device interface standard.

The next section describes a simple reference model for computer graphics standards.

3.2 Fundamentals

Computer graphics standards can be discussed in terms of the following fundamental notions:

(1) *Output primitives*: graphical output is defined in terms of basic building blocks or atomic units, which are called output primitives. Points, lines and areas are examples of output primitives, which may or may not appear in any particular system.

(2) *Primitive aspects*: when an output primitive is displayed on a graphics device it will have a particular appearance, for example lines may be displayed with a particular colour and solid or dotted linetype. Those properties of a primitive which characterize its appearance when displayed are termed *aspects*.

(3) *Primitive attributes*: attributes are essentially parameters of a primitive which control the values of properties of the primitive, for example its aspects.

(4) *Output model*: an output model describes how output primitives are created from information supplied, and how they are displayed on output devices.

(5) *Coordinate systems and clipping*: graphical output has to be described to the graphics system in some coordinate system and presented to a display device in its coordinate system. It is accepted that the user of a graphics system should be able to define graphics in a coordinate system relevant to the application and this is unlikely to be the coordinate system used by the one or more output devices being addressed. A graphics system may therefore involve a number of coordinate systems and will define transformations between them. Clipping is the operation of restricting graphical output to a particular region in a coordinate space and is commonly linked in the API standards with the specification of coordinate systems.

(6) *Input primitives*: interactive programs need to be able to accept graphical and non-graphical input. Input primitives are the basic units of input made available by the graphics system.

(7) *Input model*: an input model describes how input primitives are related to physical input devices, the degree of control provided to the application (for example selection of the way in which input values are echoed to the device's operator). Control is provided through input device attributes.

(8) *Storage*: graphical information may be stored for a variety of purposes, for example for transfer to another application program. The state of the information being stored, and the point in a system at which information is retrieved, are key considerations.

It is also useful to distinguish four levels of abstraction in order to describe the current family of graphics standards. The intention of these different levels will become clearer as the various standards are described. The following loose descriptions will suffice as an introduction.

(1) *Application*: at this level applications-related information is composed into abstract graphics related to the application.

(2) *Virtual*: at this level, the graphical output to be displayed is described in terms of output primitives.

(3) *Logical*: this level lies below the virtual level and assembles the information necessary to render a primitive on a particular device.

(4) *Physical*: this level is associated with a particular output device and collection of input devices. The physical level does not necessarily correspond to real devices, for example a pen plotter or tablet; there could be further layers of system between the physical level and real hardware, for example a window management system. The distinguishing feature therefore is that the graphics system intends no further graphical refinement of the data.

The level structure is illustrated in figure 3.2.

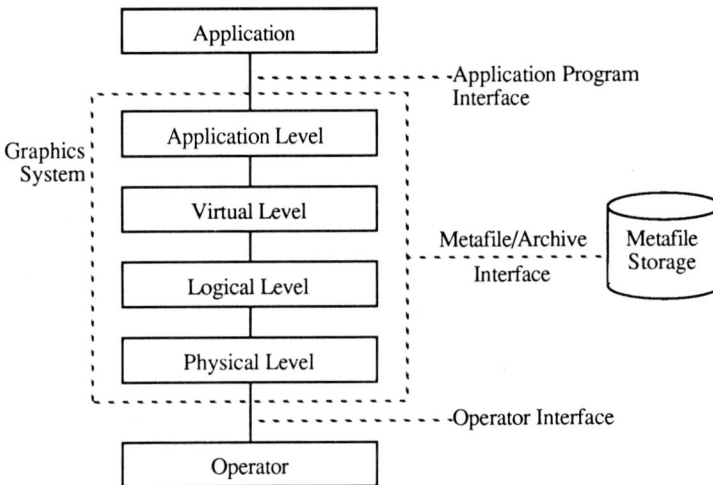

Figure 3.2 Reference model level structure

The application program interface is the interface between the application and the graphics system. There are also interfaces to metafiles and archives and to the operator. In this context only, "operator" does not necessarily mean human operator, it is the user of the graphics system at the bottom end as it were, which might be a window management system, for example.

Using these notions as a framework, the current family of standards is briefly described, in order to convey the flavour of each standard and the ways in which they are related. These descriptions necessarily give a broad-brush treatment of each standard; many details are omitted, but the reader should gain a sufficient grounding in each in order to understand the later chapters.

3.3 Application Program Interface standards

3.3.1 General

The Graphical Kernel System (GKS) [13] is a system for two-dimensional graphics and provides no support for three dimensions. The Graphical Kernel System for Three Dimensions (GKS-3D) [15] is an extension of GKS to provide basic functions for computer graphics programming in 3D. The Programmer's Hierarchical Interactive Graphics System (PHIGS) [16] is a set of functions for computer graphics programming in environments requiring rapid modification of graphical data that describes geometrically related objects. PHIGS provides modelling functionality as well as viewing functionality.

A central concept in each standard is the idea of a *workstation*. This is an abstraction from physical device hardware, providing zero or one display surfaces for graphical output and zero or more input devices. Graphical output may be directed to more than one workstation simultaneously. Workstations essentially encompass the logical and physical levels in the model, as shown in figure 3.3. This use of the word workstation predates its widespread use in describing a configuration of hardware incorporating personal computing power for applications software. The use here is however in line with the word's definition in the graphics standards, in which it is used to describe an abstract level of refinement of the graphics data, and an associated set of graphical capabilities.

3.3.2 Primitives, aspects and attributes

GKS provides six basic output primitives: polyline, polymarker, fill area, text, cell array and generalized drawing primitive (GDP). These primitives have a rich set of aspects, allowing a high degree of control over the way primitives are rendered on displays.

GKS-3D and PHIGS provide the same basic primitive set as GKS, except that they are extended to work in three dimensions. Text, fill area and cell array remain planar primitives, but can be positioned in an arbitrary plane. Polyline and polymarker become genuine 3-dimensional primitives with no constraints on the positions used in the function call.

One additional primitive has been added to both GKS-3D and PHIGS, fill area set, which specifies a set of fill areas all of which will be rendered together as a single entity. It will be seen later that this idea is taken considerably further in the proposed device interface standard, CGI (see Section 5.3).

A further primitive has been added to PHIGS, annotation text relative, whose purpose is to facilitate labelling of objects.

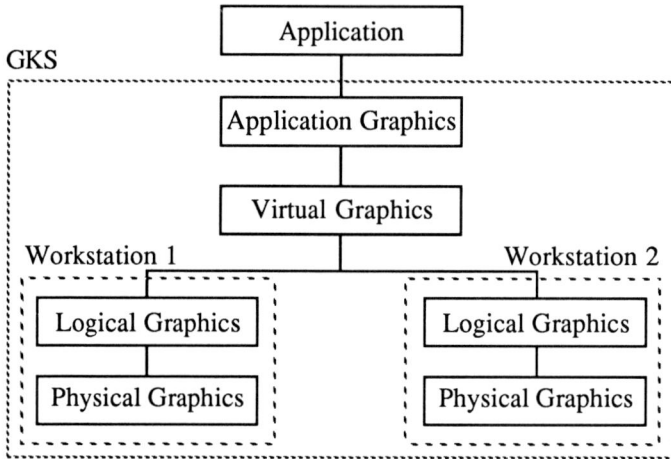

Figure 3.3 Mapping levels onto workstation model

The appearance of primitives on the display surface of a workstation is controlled by their aspects. GKS distinguishes two types of aspects, workstation independent aspects which have the same value on all workstations on which the primitive is displayed, and the workstation dependent aspects which may have different values on different workstations.

The values of aspects are controlled by attributes. For workstation independent aspects, there is one attribute per aspect. For workstation dependent aspects, two methods of specification are possible, *bundled specification* and *individual specification*. Bundled specification uses a lookup table approach. A single attribute for each primitive, the primitive index, controls the values of all the workstation dependent aspects of the primitive. Primitive indices are workstation independent. Each workstation has its own bundle tables. For individual specification there is one attribute per aspect, and that attribute has the same value for all workstations.

A set of *aspect source flags* controls the mode of specification of each aspect. Some aspects may be specified individually, whilst others are specified by a bundle.

The virtual level corresponds to primitives with attributes bound. The logical level corresponds to primitives with aspects bound (fully determined) and the physical level to rendered primitives. In GKS, there is one virtual level for the whole system, but each workstation has its own logical and physical levels; this will become clearer when coordinate systems are described below.

GKS-3D provides the same mechanisms for appearance control as GKS. PHIGS also provides the same mechanisms. More is said about this in Section 3.3.5.

3.3.3 Coordinate systems

In GKS, output primitives are specified in a cartesian world coordinate (WC) system. Transformation to the coordinate space of the display device is accomplished in two stages. First, world coordinates are transformed to an intermediate coordinate system, called *normalized device coordinates* (NDC), by a window to viewport mapping termed a *normalization transformation*. A second window to viewport mapping, the *workstation transformation*, transforms these coordinates to *device coordinates* (DC).

GKS allows multiple normalization transformations to be defined, one of which may be selected at any point in time. The purpose of the normalization transformation is to facilitate the composition in NDC space of pictures defined in different world coordinate system spaces. The workstation transformation may be set differently for different workstations, thus allowing different regions of NDC space to be displayed on different workstations.

The virtual level corresponds to NDC space. In terms of coordinate systems, the logical level corresponds to the coordinate system of the workstation and the physical level to the coordinate system of the output device.

Graphical output may (optionally) be clipped to the viewport of the selected normalization transformation and (compulsorily) to the window of the workstation transformation.

Coordinate systems in GKS-3D and PHIGS are more complex as will be seen in detail in Chapter 7. At the virtual level, GKS-3D has a 3D normalized device coordinate system, NDC. PHIGS has a corresponding coordinate system which is called *world coordinates*. A viewing transformation is inserted between the virtual coordinate space and the workstation transformation. The view transformation is defined in two stages, first a *view orientation transformation* changes the coordinate system to one whose origin and axes have a convenient relationship to the object to be viewed. This coordinate system is called *View Reference Coordinates* (VRC). The second transformation, the *view mapping transformation*, transforms VRC into *Normalized Projection Coordinates* (NPC) and is typically a parallel or perspective transformation. The workstation transformation maps NPC coordinates to device coordinates.

There is an optional *view clip* to a region in NPC space.

Each primitive has a *view index* associated with it which partitions the output into a number of sets. Different views can be specified for each view index. This allows, for example, the titling on a display to be output using a parallel projection, while the 3D objects associated with the titles can be viewed in perspective. The views corresponding to different view indices are specified in workstation dependent view bundle tables.

The virtual level in GKS-3D and PHIGS corresponds to NDC or WC space respectively, with view indices bound to primitives. The logical level corresponds to primitives with workstation dependent view representations applied.

GKS-3D and PHIGS provide support for Hidden Line and Hidden Surface calculations at the workstation. Each primitive has an index associated with it which the workstation can use to provide different types of rendering depending on the index.

The physical coordinate system in GKS-3D and PHIGS, DC, is a 3D coordinate system. Thus in these standards, all coordinate systems are 3D.

At the application level, GKS-3D provides similar facilities to GKS, notably multiple world coordinate systems (3D), which can be transformed to NDC by normalization transformations.

PHIGS is more complicated at the application level. PHIGS provides a *centralized structure store* (CSS) which contains data from which graphics is generated by a process called *traversal*. Structures consist of sequences of structure elements. This is explained in Section 3.3.5. Positional information in CSS is described in a cartesian coordinate system called *modelling coordinates* (MC).

Each structure has a global and local modelling transformation which are concatenated to produce the transformation to be applied to map modelling coordinates into world coordinates. Structures and hence modelling transformations can be nested, thus providing a mechanism for constructing complex objects from simpler parts.

Modelling clipping regions may be defined in modelling coordinates as the intersection of a collection of half-spaces. These regions are then transformed to world coordinates and combined, using standardized or implementation dependent combinators, to produce a composite modelling clipping region.

3.3.4 Input

GKS specifies a set of logical input devices onto which real input devices can be mapped. The data that can be entered into an application program by the operator are divided into six different types, and six classes of logical input devices are defined corresponding to these. The types are: LOCATOR, STROKE, VALUATOR, CHOICE, PICK and STRING.

Logical input devices may operate in one of three possible modes: REQUEST, SAMPLE and EVENT.

Some degree of control over logical input devices is provided to the application program through device initialization functions. These enable the application program to define the initial value for the device, the prompt and echo type (for example a LOCATOR device may be echoed as a rubberband line, tracking cross etc.), the area of the display to be used for displaying the echo and further device dependent data.

The input models in all three standards are very similar. Both GKS-3D and PHIGS extend the logical input devices by allowing 3D LOCATOR and STROKE devices as well as the six logical input classes defined in GKS. PICK input in PHIGS is extended to relate the graphical object picked to the path through the CSS which led to traversal of the structure element from which it was generated.

3.3.5 Storage

In GKS there is a segment store associated with each workstation (Workstation Dependent Segment Store - WDSS) in which segments consisting of sets of GKS primitives and associated attributes can be stored. Associated with each segment is a set of attributes which control visibility, highlighting, priority for output and detectability by a PICK device. There is also a segment transformation such that the primitives in the segment can be scaled, rotated, translated and sheared etc.

Primitives that are not stored in segments (primitives outside segments) cannot be highlighted, made invisible or picked and cannot be transformed.

There is also a workstation independent segment storage (WISS) which is used as a central library, though it is regarded as a special type of workstation in terms of the functions which control it.

Segments stored in WISS can be copied to other workstations in a number of ways. Segments cannot be edited.

Segment storage takes place in NDC space. The level model is rather inadequate for describing segment storage in that the state of the objects in segment storage corresponds to the virtual level as attributes are fully determined and·bound, but different segments may be stored on different workstations, so the global flavour of the virtual level is lost. It is perhaps easiest to think of WISS at the virtual level, being accessible to all workstations at the logical level, and WDSS at the logical level, being associated with particular workstations.

The segment storage in GKS-3D is identical to that in GKS except for the extension to three dimensions.

Storage in PHIGS is at the application level. PHIGS has a centralized structure store (CSS) which has greater functionality than segment storage. A structure consists of a sequence of structure elements which can represent both graphical and non-graphical data. Thus it is possible to keep application data associated with graphics in the same database. PHIGS provides facilities for editing as well as creating structures held in CSS.

Particular features of PHIGS are:

(1) *Hierarchy*. Structures can call other structures and the same structure may be called more than once from a higher level.

(2) *Modelling.* As described in Section 3.3.3, structure elements contain positional information in modelling coordinates. Modelling coordinate systems can be nested, providing a convenient method for describing complex hierarchically structured objects in terms of simpler components.

(3) *Editing.* Labels can be placed in structures and there is a structure element pointer. Consequently, it is possible to move around a structure and edit it after initial creation.

Graphical output is generated in PHIGS by a process called *traversal*. Traversal is conceptually a continuous process keeping each workstation's display surface up to date with respect to the information in the CSS.

The display of graphics on a workstation is initiated by *posting* a structure to the workstation. The structure posted is the root of a structure network which will be traversed. More than one structure network may be displayed on a workstation by posting the appropriate root structures.

During traversal, structures inherit attributes, modelling clipping volume and modelling transformations from the calling structure. A root structure inherits a set of defaults. When a structure has been completely traversed, control reverts to the calling structure and the attributes, transformations etc. are reset to those in force on entry to the substructure. A substructure can therefore have no effect on the calling structure.

PHIGS essentially provides the same mechanisms for appearance control as GKS, but it is important to realize that attributes are only bound to primitives when the CSS is traversed. The appearance of a primitive can be changed by editing the structure store.

One other point of difference concerns the control of visibility, highlighting and detectability, which in GKS and GKS-3D are controlled by segment attributes. In PHIGS they are controlled for each primitive through a NAME SET attribute associated with the primitive. A filter mechanism is provided on each workstation which controls the relationship between NAME SETs and visibility, highlighting and detectability. This gives a very flexible mechanism for controlling these entities, for example, the heating system or electrical system of a house could be selectively displayed by merely changing filters, if the primitives corresponding to objects in these systems have appropriate NAME SET attributes.

3.3.6 Environment

The three standards, GKS, GKS-3D and PHIGS have many architectural features in common. Of particular importance is the way in which state information is handled. Each of the standards has a set of state lists which contain information about the current state. In GKS, for example, the main state lists are the GKS State List and the Workstation State List. There is a separate Workstation State List for each open workstation. The GKS State List contains the current settings of attributes, normalization transformation, etc. Entries in the state list are set by GKS functions. A Workstation State

List records the current state of the workstation, for example bundle table entries and the workstation transformation.

There are also description tables which describe the capabilities of an implementation of the standard. The GKS Description Table, for example, records the maximum normalization transformation number supported. There is a description table for each type of workstation supported by the implementation which defines characteristics of that workstation type, for example, whether the workstation is monochrome or colour, the maximum display space size, the number of character heights supported and the range of linetypes supported.

GKS-3D and PHIGS have similar state lists and description tables. All of the standards provide a set of inquiry functions to access all the information contained in the state lists and description tables. This enables an application program to discover the properties of the workstations it is using and to tailor its behaviour accordingly.

GKS and GKS-3D are not single systems, both are divided into a two-dimensional set of levels. In the output dimension the levels are:

(0) Minimal Output: bundle table entries cannot be changed, only one workstation in use at a time.

(1) Bundle table entries can be defined, multiple workstations and Workstation Dependent Segment Storage added.

(2) Workstation Independent Segment Storage added.

The input levels are:

(a) No input facilities.

(b) Only REQUEST mode input.

(c) Full input.

Implementations have to conform to one of these levels. A minimal implementation of either standard is Level 0a, whilst a full implementation is Level 2c.

3.4 Metafile and archive standards

3.4.1 The Computer Graphics Metafile (CGM)

The Computer Graphics Metafile for the storage and transfer of picture description information (CGM) [85] enables pictures to be recorded for long term storage, and to be exchanged between graphics devices, systems and installations.

Pictures are described in CGM as a collection of elements of different kinds, representing, for example, primitives, attributes and control information. CGM is a multi-part standard. Part 1 defines the available elements, the structure of the metafile and the order in which elements may appear. Parts 2-4 of the standard define three representation schemes, or encodings, for the abstract syntax of the elements. Part 2 is a character encoding aimed at compactness and transferability across networks. Part 3 is a binary encoding aimed at minimizing the processor effort involved in generating and/or interpreting the metafile. Part 4 is a clear text encoding aimed at a metafile that can be read and edited by people. Encodings are discussed in Chapter 10.

A CGM is structured as a series of levels:

(1) *Metafile*. A metafile consists of a metafile descriptor followed by a number of picture descriptions. The former contains information valid for the whole metafile, for example, the precision of real and integer quantities in the metafile. Picture descriptions are self-contained.

(2) *Picture*. Pictures are bounded by picture delimiters. A picture starts with a picture descriptor which contains information about how this particular picture is stored. This is followed by the picture body which contains the definition of the picture.

(3) *Picture body*. The elements at this level are essentially primitive and attribute elements describing the graphical content of the picture.

CGM elements are split broadly into seven classes:

(1) metafile descriptor elements;

(2) picture descriptor elements;

(3) control elements;

(4) graphical primitive elements;

(5) attribute elements;

(6) escape elements;

(7) external elements.

CGM only allows 2D pictures to be described.

CGM provides a total of 19 graphical primitive elements; the main additions compared to GKS are polygon set, rectangle, circle, circular arcs, ellipse and elliptic arcs.

Aspects of primitives may be defined by either individual or bundled attributes, determined by aspect source flag settings. CGM does not provide elements for specifying bundle table entries. CGM in this respect is at the virtual level in the four level model. Attributes are bound to primitives, but aspects are not.

Colour handling is an extension of the mechanism used in GKS. Colour in GKS is specified by indices into a colour table on each workstation. Two colour specification modes are provided in CGM, *indexed*, which is equivalent to the GKS mechanism and *direct*. In direct mode, the parameters of the colour specification elements are RGB triples. This mode is effectively saying that colour is part of the virtual picture.

GKS includes a metafile definition in Annex E to the standard, which is adequate for the purposes of GKS. A decision was taken at an early stage that the requirements for metafiles were more general than those arising from GKS and so metafile standardization became a separate project. This raises the question of the relationship between GKS and CGM.

Two types of metafile may be distinguished:

(1) a *static picture capture metafile*, which records information from which a static picture may be reconstructed;

(2) an *audit trail metafile*, which records the process (i.e. sequence of function invocations) by which a picture is generated and may contain dynamic information.

CGM is a picture capture metafile; GKS metafile is an audit trail metafile.

CGM is suitable for use as a GKS metafile only for the lowest output level, level 0. Certain control capabilities are necessary for GKS support and not included in CGM. CGM does not allow any picture structure to be represented, for example segments. An addendum to CGM, CGM Addendum 1 [86], is under development to extend CGM to cater for all output levels of GKS. Some of the contents of Addendum 1 are discussed in later chapters of this book. The principal elements added in Addendum 1 include:

(1) segmentation support;

(2) capabilities needed for dynamic picture regeneration, for example, elements to set bundle table entries;

(3) device viewport control.

It is interesting to note that the capabilities being added to CGM now effectively belong to lower levels in the reference model; device viewport control, for example, pertains to the relationship between the logical and physical levels. CGM is intended as a metafile for the capture (representation) of static pictures. One of the difficulties with GKS is that it does not have a clearly defined notion of picture and hence it is somewhat difficult to see what should be captured. The relationship between CGM and GKS is discussed in detail in the paper by Brodlie et al [91].

An addendum to GKS [14] is also being developed which will allow a CGM metafile to be written in the sense indicated by GKS (i.e. as an audit trail). This will use the elements defined in the CGM and CGM Addendum 1, with a few additional elements defined in the GKS Addendum, but with a somewhat different structure affecting which elements are allowed to appear in which parts of the metafile, to that for a static picture capture metafile.

A second Addendum to CGM is also being processed. This Addendum will apply principles similar to those of the first addendum to address the requirements for static picture capture of 3D pictures.

3.4.2 PHIGS archive files

Parts 2 and 3 of PHIGS define an archive file format for storage and transfer of PHIGS structures and structure network definitions from the CSS. Part 2 describes the file format and Part 3 a clear text encoding. This encoding is constructed using the same techniques as employed by CGM.

Like CGM, an archive file is a collection of elements. Two levels are discernible in the archive file:

(1) *Archive*: an archive file contains an archive file descriptor, which like the metafile descriptor contains information valid for the whole file.

(2) *Structure*: Structures are delimited by BEGIN STRUCTURE and END STRUCTURE elements. The archive file elements in between represent the structure elements in the structure. In this there is a one-to-one correspondence between structure elements and archive file elements.

There are seven classes of archive file elements:

(1) *Delimiter elements*: delimit significant entities within the archive file, for example, structures.

(2) *Archive file description elements*: describe the functional content, default conditions, identification and characteristics of the archive file.

(3) *Output primitive elements*: represent the structure elements describing output primitives.

(4) *Attribute elements*: represent the structure elements describing attributes of output primitives.

(5) *Modelling transformation elements*: represent the structure elements describing modelling transformations.

(6) *Miscellaneous elements*: represent the structure elements which facilitate the usage of structures. These include label elements, the execute structure element (through which one structure refers to another structure).

(7) *External elements*: represent structure elements which communicate information not related to the content of structures.

The archive file is at the application level.

3.5 Device interface standards - CGI

There is currently only one project at this level, "Interfacing techniques for dialogues with graphical devices", commonly called the Computer Graphics Interface, CGI [103]. This specifies the exchange of information between the device independent and device dependent parts of a graphics package. As the standard is currently at the stage of second Draft Proposal (see Section 4.2.4 for an explanation of the stages of processing an ISO standard), it is probable that further technical changes will occur before standardization is completed, and hence the information given in this book about CGI may become invalid.

Whilst the CGI has been defined primarily on the basis of providing support for a suitable DI/DD interface for the standard APIs it is also considered reasonable that other clients requiring DI/DD interfaces may be supported by CGI. For example the raster part of CGI provides some additional functionality for clients supporting applications with rather more raster functionality required than GKS or the other APIs could currently provide.

Unlike the CGM which only has to handle graphical output, CGI has to handle both output and input and it is assumed that the device is on-line and capable of supporting dynamic interaction graphics. The current CGI draft is in six parts.

- Part 1: *Overview, profiles and conformance*. This part gives an overview of the whole standard. Profiles, which are essentially definitions of the CGI functions and minimum support requirements for a particular purpose, are defined to meet common requirements, for example, the various categories of workstation recognized by GKS. This part also contains the conformance statements for CGI.

- Part 2: *Control, negotiation and errors*. This part defines the functions concerned with virtual device and error control. This functionality is concerned with management of the graphics image and the inter-relationship of the graphical and non-graphical parts of the interface. Virtual device control allows the client of the interface to initiate and terminate sessions of dialogue. Coordinate space control allows for the establishment of coordinate information, placement of the picture on the view surface, and management of clipping. Negotiation is the process of establishing the capabilities of the device the client will use. This involves interrogation of the facilities provided and selection of those to be used. Error handling is necessarily different to functional standards and CGI provides the ability to turn off error reporting and detecting.

- Part 3: *Output and attributes*. This part describes output primitives and their associated attributes and some related control functions. The output primitives of CGI and CGM are very similar. Bundled and individual specification of aspects is supported and aspect source flags control which mode is used for which aspect of a particular primitive.

- Part 4: *Segments*. This part describes how primitives and their associated attributes may be grouped into segments. A set of functions for creating, modifying and manipulating segments is described. The segment model is close to the GKS model.

- Part 5: *Input and echoing*. The CGI input functionality is designed to support the input models of the application program interface standards. CGI provides the six input classes of GKS together with a raster class and generalized input class. An additional operating mode, ECHO REQUEST, and associated functions are provided to enable an input device associated with one CGI device to be echoed on another device. Control functions are provided to initialize and deallocate devices and to tailor their characteristics.

- Part 6: *Raster*. This part describes functions for creating, modifying, retrieving and displaying information stored as pixel data below the level of CGI. Non-displayable bitmaps may be created and deleted, and bitmaps selected for drawing and display. Client created bitmaps are not displayable, but these can be combined with a displayable bitmap. Any bitmap may be selected as the drawing bitmap. The drawing bitmap is the destination bitmap for the rendering of output primitives. Raster operation functions include the BitBlt (RasterOp) operation. Bitmap data held by the client as arrays of colours can be moved to a CGI bitmap using the PIXEL ARRAY function and bitmaps may be retrieved by the client using the equivalent inquiry function.

It will be apparent from this brief description of CGI that CGI functionality spans several levels in the reference model. Coordinate data is generally supplied in Virtual Device Coordinates. This is roughly the same coordinate space that CGM operates in. A device viewport can also be specified, which is the region of the device drawing space into which the VDC extent is mapped. The concept of VDC extent is explained in Chapter 6.

CGI essentially receives from the client a description of graphics at the virtual level. The display and manipulation of the graphics is controlled by information at the logical and physical levels. The raster functionality in CGI is at the physical level.

This spanning of several roles is also evident from the envisaged range of implementations of CGI functionality. Not only does the profiling mechanism allow systems designers to construct specifications for a very wide range of situations, but also there are a variety of ways of invoking the functionality being envisaged. As we shall see below, invocation through programming languages is expected, but linear data encodings of the CGI functions are also proposed in the three forms standardized for the CGM (character, binary and clear text). Currently the first two of these exist as early drafts for comment [104,105].

3.6 Language binding standards

As noted earlier, the application program interface standards are defined independently of particular programming languages. In order to standardize usage from a particular programming language, a binding has to be specified for the standard to the language. API standards are normally described in programming languages as collections of procedures or subroutines with associated datatypes. Language binding standards are multipart standards. Each standard defines the interface for a particular API standard. The parts of the standard give bindings to particular programming languages. A consistent numbering scheme for parts is used across all the standards as shown in Table 3.1.

The correspondence between APIs and language bindings is shown in Table 3.2. The development of the C bindings has had to be delayed to await the definition of the underlying ISO programming language standard. It would obviously be impossible to define an ISO standard binding to a non-standard language.

Table 3.1 Standard part assignments for multipart language bindings

Part Number	Language
Part 1	Fortran
Part 2	Pascal
Part 3	Ada
Part 4	C

The parts of a language binding standard may progress at different rates through the standardization process. Language bindings are discussed in detail in Chapter 9. The status of the standards is described in Chapter 14.

For CGI two types of language binding are envisaged: procedural bindings following the same general approach as the API standards, and single entry point bindings, following a commonly used technique for writing device drivers. The device driver is accessed through a single routine, a parameter of which specifies the particular driver function required at a particular invocation. At the time of writing, working drafts for Fortran and C procedural bindings exist [116,117] for the first DP functionality (with working drafts due at any time), but little work has yet been reported on bindings to other programming languages. A project has been approved for a single entry point binding, but there is as yet not even an initial draft document for this standard.

Table 3.2 Number of language documents corresponding to API standards

API Standard	Reference Number	Language Binding
GKS	[110, 111]	ISO 8651
GKS-3D	[112-115]	ISO 8806
PHIGS	[118-121]	ISO 9593

3.7 "Framework" standards

3.7.1 Reference model

Broadly speaking a Reference Model is a framework within which relationships between standards can be described and relationships to other fields of standardization addressed. Each of the graphics standards is based around a number of concepts, and the relationships between these concepts form a reference model for that standard. Much of the discussion in standards meetings centres around concepts and their relationships. GKS was the first computer graphics project to be approved; CGM was the second. Since the time that the CGM work started, the need for a more formal reference model has been felt, in order to clarify and establish relationships between the evolving family of standards.

This is seen for example in the issues that arise because CGM is a picture capture metafile, the metafile in GKS Annex E is an audit trail metafile and GKS has no explicit concept of picture. The relationship between PHIGS and CGM also raises interesting questions: what does it mean to capture a picture in PHIGS by a CGM metafile? Does it make sense to input a picture defined by a CGM to PHIGS?

The best-known example of a Reference Model is probably the 7-layer model for Open Systems Interconnection (OSI) [131].

A reference model project for computer graphics has been approved, but there is as yet no universal agreement on the form a reference model for computer graphics should take, or indeed what is expected of a reference model for computer graphics. It is easy to slip across the dividing line between formal description techniques and reference models or reference models and API or metafile and archive standards themselves. Some of the early activities are reported in the paper by Carson and McGinnis [138]. At the time of writing an interim draft of the Reference Model [130] had just been proposed which is based on four levels of abstraction roughly as described here, but given the early stage of this work and the instability this project has displayed to date, it is inappropriate to discuss it further here.

3.7.2 Registration

There are a number of graphical entities that can be found in a bewildering number of varieties, for example the set of all "useful" marker types. Rather than delay the standards in progress by trying to get agreement on extensive lists of such elements for each standard in turn, a small number of elements is mandated in each standard and value ranges are reserved for further elements standardized by Registration. An example is linetypes. GKS mandates the meanings for linetypes given in Table 3.3.

Table 3.3 GKS standard linetypes

Linetype Number	Meaning
1	solid line
2	dashed line
3	dotted line
4	dashed-dotted line

Linetype values <0 are available for implementation dependent linetypes; values ≥5 are reserved for Registration. The value 0 is an invalid linetype value.

The Registration mechanism initially deals with the following kinds of elements:

(1) generalized drawing primitives;

(2) graphical escape function definitions;

(3) linetypes;

(4) marker types;

(5) hatch styles;

(6) text font appearance (excluding broader issues being addressed by ISO/IEC JTC1/SC18);

(7) prompt and echo type definitions;

(8) error messages.

The mechanisms provide, by default, for the extension of each relevant graphics standard in each of these areas. Thus, for an extra linetype, Registration will define the appearance of the linetype, allocate a linetype number for GKS, CGM and other standards to which it applies. Language bindings are included in the Registration of generalized drawing primitives and escape functions (see Chapter 13). New categories are likely to be added to the above list as a result of the CGI project, for example, application profiles.

Registered items are recorded in a Register of Graphical Items, which is maintained by a Registration Authority. The US National Institute of Science and Technology (formerly the National Bureau of Standards) has been approved as the Registration Authority. Procedures are being defined for the registration of graphical items and these are being published in an ISO technical report [132]. Items for incorporation in the register are voted on by ISO/IEC JTC1/SC24.

3.7.3 Conformity testing of implementations

The existence of standards raises the issue of how certain can one be that an implementation of the standard adheres to the standard. At the present time, the only practical approach to this question is through methods of *falsification*, which make systematic efforts to demonstrate that an implementation is incorrect. This approach is followed extensively in programming languages, where a compiler is subjected to a large suite of test programs designed to uncover likely errors in implementations. This approach is followed for conformity testing for graphics standards also.

There is a deep issue underlying this discussion and that is how should conformance for a graphics standard be defined? Should a conforming implementation implement exactly what is in the standard? Are any forms of extension allowed? What can be done in certifying layered implementations by multiple manufacturers?

There is currently a project in SC24 to produce a standard for conformity testing [129]. The purpose of the project is twofold: first to specify the characteristics of standardized test sets for use in determining the conformance of implementations of graphics standards and second to provide directions to developers of functional standards concerning conformance rules.

The project recently advanced to DP stage, with an aggressive timescale for resolving comments. With a major review due to turn the recent draft into DIS text by the end of the year it is inappropriate to describe its content further.

4
The Process of Standardization

4.1 Standards bodies

Standards are defined and ratified by a number of institutions world wide. This book concentrates on those standards produced through the International Organization for Standardization (Organisation Internationale de Normalisation), whose standards are normally adopted as National Standards by the members of the organization either explicitly through the appropriate national process, or implicitly by using the ISO standard for work in a particular area in preference to producing a National Standard.

This chapter therefore concentrates on a description of the ISO process and its relation to the national processes of some of the major contributors to the international graphics standards work. Brief descriptions are also included of some of the other standards making bodies which the reader might encounter. Since many outsiders find the various committee designations rather confusing we have included some reference to whereabouts within a particular organization the reader might expect to find work on a particular topic being processed.

Graphics standards are long documents (typically 400 to 600 pages) and so may take more time to develop than standards in other areas of information processing. Furthermore, up to now, each standard has been the first in a particular area, a factor that contributes to the time it takes to develop consensus.

4.2 The ISO process

Graphics standardization has been undertaken by ISO on the basis of international review of successive versions of documents through a number of rounds each of which is intended to bring the proposed standard closer to acceptance on the basis of consensus. The sections which follow show how the process of achieving consensus is managed and who is involved in the discussions. It is important when talking about the various projects to be clear that informally many proposals or other non-standard systems are talked of as if they were standards, long before they have achieved consensus within the international standardization organizations.

4.2.1 Overview

Each proposed ISO standard is assigned an ISO reference number quite early in the processing (at the time of being registered as a Draft Proposal (see below) or sometimes even earlier) and this number will be associated with the eventual published document. The number once assigned is kept through all the stages of processing. It is therefore possible for successive drafts of a standard to have different committee document numbers, but the same ISO reference, possibly with a version number attached. The reference number is a four (or in the near future five) digit number which is normally prefixed by one of ISO, DIS or DP, which indicate the stage in the processing which the document has reached (see below).

Any ISO standards project is assigned to a particular technical committee (TC) responsible for standards in quite a broad area. That committee in turn will normally be organized as a number of Sub-Committees (SC's), each consisting of working groups (WG's) one of which will be tasked with the project's progression. The members of Sub-Committees are national standards-making bodies. There are two important categories of membership, Participating Members (P-Members) who are voting members of the SC and Observer Members (O-Members) who do not have voting rights. Each working group will normally be responsible for a number of projects processed in detail by a group of international experts in a Committee called the Rapporteur Group (RG).

Rapporteur Groups are charged with progressing a specific project between SC meetings, under the overall technical coordination of the WG to which the project is assigned. RG's normally meet during WG meetings and frequently between WG meetings also.

Drafting Committees may be appointed by WG's to prepare clean output documents following a WG meeting, in accordance with agreements identified by the WG.

Editing Committees can be appointed by an SC secretariat in consultation with the SC chairman and WG convenor, to consider and process comments received during ballots and prepare responses to comments and revised text.

At the Rapporteur Group and Working Group levels experts are involved as individuals, although there is an expectation that they will take into account the likely attitudes of their National Bodies when discussing technical alternatives. At the Sub-Committee level participants are involved as National Body representatives. There are around 1900 ISO technical committees, subcommittees, and working groups.

4.2.2 Computer graphics committee designations

Information Technology (IT) now encompasses such a broad range of activities that IT standards cut across the territory traditionally reserved for different standards-making bodies. One step in the rationalization of the standards scene took place in the last quarter of 1987 with the formation of ISO/IEC JTC1, the first Joint Technical Committee (hence JTC1) of the International Organization for Standardization and the International Electrotechnical Commission (IEC). JTC1 has responsibility for "Standardization in the field of Information Technology". There is close cooperation between ISO/IEC and the International Telegraph and Telephone Consultative Committee (CCITT), but this is less important in the graphics area than in open systems networking areas. These organizations are discussed further in section 4.4.

JTC1 first met in November, 1987, succeeding ISO/TC97 (Technical Committee 97, which had been responsible for Information Processing Standards). Until late 1987 graphics work had taken place in Working Group 2 (called "Computer Graphics") of Subcommittee 21 (called "Open Systems Interconnection") of TC97 (called "Information Processing"). After that time all computer graphics standards projects were assigned to a new Sub-Committee, SC24. The official designator of the new graphics Sub-Committee is therefore *ISO/IEC JTC1/SC24*.

The P-Members of SC24 are Australia, Austria, Belgium, Brazil, China, Czechoslovakia, Denmark, France, German Democratic Republic, German Federal Republic, Hungary, Italy, Japan, Netherlands, Sweden, Switzerland, UK, USA and USSR. The O-Members are Bulgaria, Canada, Finland, Iceland, Republic of Korea, India, Iran, Philippines, Portugal, Poland, Singapore, Turkey and Yugoslavia.

The terms of reference of SC24 are currently:

• Standardization of methodologies for computer graphics programming.

• Standardization of functional specifications of computer graphics facilities (including those needed for image processing, graphical databases and graphical user interfaces).

• Standardization of programming language bindings for computer graphics functional definitions.

• Standardization for graphical information exchange, including computer graphics metafiles and computer graphics device interfaces.

• Methods and procedures for testing and validation of implementations of computer graphics standards.

• Specification techniques for computer graphics standards.

• Standardization of procedures for the registration of graphical items and administration of those parts of the procedures for which the Sub-Committee is responsible.

The work of this new Sub-Committee has been divided up between five working groups.

- Working Group 1 (SC24/WG1, "Architecture")
- Working Group 2 (SC24/WG2, "Application Programming Interfaces")
- Working Group 3 (SC24/WG3, "Metafiles and Interfaces")
- Working Group 4 (SC24/WG4, "Language Bindings")
- Working Group 5 (SC24/WG5, "Validation Testing and Registration")

Since all documents being processed by ISO have committee numbers it is often desirable to know whereabouts in the system the documents are likely to be discussed. All documents have a reference N xxx and readers may well come across references to ISO/IEC JTC1/SC24 documents (e.g. ISO/IEC JTC1/SC24 N177, which is a draft of the Reference Model for Computer Graphics), which are often referred to loosely as SC24 N xxx (e.g. SC24 N177).

Each of the standards projects is assigned to a working group for the bulk of its processing, but international review and balloting takes place at either the SC24 or the JTC1 level and therefore the documents of most public interest usually have at least SC24 numbers and often JTC1 numbers, as well as the ISO (latterly ISO/IEC), DIS or DP number referred to above.

4.2.3   Other JTC1 committees

Included in JTC1 as separate Sub-Committees are Character Sets and Information Coding (SC2), which covers teletext, videotex, picture and image coding, audio coding, and facsimile; Networking Services (SC6); Text and Office Systems (SC18), which covers office document architecture, office document interchange format, integrated text and graphics content architectures, page description languages, and font naming and description; Open Systems Interconnection (SC21), which covers OSI architecture and reference models, data bases, operating systems, virtual terminal, and file transfer; and Programming Languages (SC22).

4.2.4   Stages in processing ISO/IEC standards

New Work Item (NWI).   In ISO, a new project is started when a Sub-Committee (like SC24) or a member body (like ANSI or BSI) drafts a New Work Item proposal and submits it to JTC1 for a three-month letter ballot. Each P-Member has one vote to decide if it accepts the definition of the work item, if it supports the work item, and if it will commit resources to work on it. To be accepted at least five national bodies must commit to work on the project. An NWI is often accompanied by a base document; DIN provided the GKS base document, ANSI provided the base documents for the CGI and CGM NWI's.   After an NWI is approved, the project will be assigned to a Working Group of SC24. This stage can take five to eight months.

Working Drafts (WD) and Rapporteur Groups.   From the base document, the SC24 Working Group prepares one or more working drafts (WD's) that are circulated for comment by SC24 National Bodies. This comment period is usually three months. SC24 Working Groups manage their projects by creating Rapporteur Groups (subgroups of the WG) who may hold meetings in between the meetings of the WG, by assigning Rapporteurs to lead them, and by assigning Document Editors for each international standard being developed. It can take 6 to 18 months to get an acceptable complete Working Draft, depending on how complete the base document is and how much consensus there is among SC24 National Bodies.

Draft Proposal (DP).   When the working draft is essentially complete and most major issues have been resolved, SC24 can register the document as a Draft Proposal. This is accomplished by resolution at an SC24 meeting or by a three-month SC24 letter ballot. If successful, an ISO number is assigned to the proposed standard (for example, CGM is ISO 8632; at the draft proposal stage, it was known as DP 8632). At the time when a draft proposal is first registered other numbers may be reserved for known future projects. For example at the time the GKS-3D abstract functional specification was first registered as DP 8805, 8806 was reserved as the number for the multi-part language binding standard for GKS-3D, with part numbers being reserved for each of the four languages being standardized for GKS.

Immediately upon registration, the same document is usually circulated for a three-month DP approval and comment ballot among SC24 National Bodies. National Body comments must be responded to either by an editing committee, by SC24 during a meeting, or by the appropriate SC24 WG during a meeting. The output of this stage is a new document and a Disposition of Comments indicating how each National Body's comments were resolved. If the document changes substantially in the process, additional DP cycles, requiring two-month ballots within SC24, may be needed. It is the goal of SC24 that this stage not take more than 12 to 14 months, but this has not always been achieved.

Draft International Standard (DIS). When consensus has been reached (that is, the document is considered technically stable) and the DP has been put into a format acceptable to ISO/IEC, it is circulated by the ISO Central Secretariat for a six-month combined voting ballot by the National Body members (P-Members) of both JTC1 and SC24. The document is now called a Draft International Standard and its designator is changed accordingly (for example, CGM was DIS 8632). The DIS stage can take 9 to 12 months after the text is received by ISO Central Secretariat, assuming that no second DIS ballot is required.

International Standard (ISO).   Comments from the DIS ballot must be responded to either by an editing committee appointed by the SC24

Secretariat (and typically including the Document Editor and the Rapporteur in charge of the standard), by SC24 during a meeting, or by the appropriate SC24 WG during a meeting. If the document is technically changed in a substantial way as a result of the DIS vote, another DIS ballot (only three months, this time) will be required. In general, multiple DIS rounds are to be avoided; that is why a graphics standard will not reach the DIS stage if SC24 still has technical concerns about the content of the standard. The final International Standard text is then submitted to the ISO Central Secretariat by the SC24 Secretariat. This is then presented to ISO/IEC Councils who take a final ballot to ensure that all National Bodies are satisfied that the ISO/IEC procedures have been followed in the production of the International Standard and that the document is suitable for publication. It can then be published by ISO. One final time the designator changes form (for example, CGM is known as ISO 8632:1987 – the addition of the date reflects the ISO rule that all standards are considered for revision every five years and new versions may result).

Addenda. A mechanism exists for enhancing a standard prior to the five year review. This is done by publishing an Addendum to the standard. Addenda are progressed through similar phases to standards themselves, Working Draft (WD), Proposed Draft Addendum (PDAD), Draft Addendum (DAD) and Addendum (AD). Up to three addenda are permitted to a standard; beyond this a full revision is required.

4.3   National bodies

4.3.1 Introduction

While similar in intent to the ISO process, national processes differ in many particulars, in the time scale for each stage, and in the voting procedures. A list of contact addresses for the national bodies participating in graphics standards development is included in Annex C and those interested in finding out more about the particular processes relevant to their own country are advised to contact their national organization. The standards-making process in the USA is briefly discussed. This is rather unusual within the graphics standards making national bodies in that there is parallel production of both a National Standard and the ISO version. In the case of GKS this led to slight, but significant, differences between ISO GKS and the American National Standard for GKS. Some effort has been made to try to make sure that this situation does not recur.

4.3.2   ANSI

The American National Standards Institute is the coordinating organization for America's federated standards system. Its membership includes over 900 companies and 200 trade, technical, professional, labour and consumer organizations. It was founded in 1918 and has headquarters in New York City.

ANSI does not itself develop standards, but, in cooperation with its members, it identifies what standards are required, provides a set of model procedures that standards-writing organizations may follow to attain industry-wide standards by consensus, and makes the resulting national and international standards available for purchase by industry, government, and the public.

ANSs and FIPS   ANSs are developed and used voluntarily. In the information processing field however, many ANSs are adopted as Federal Information Processing Standards through the National Institute of Science and Technology. FIPS are mandatory for government use and contracts. Once adopted as a FIPS, a standard will carry a great deal of influence in dictating procurement requirements by US government agencies.

X3, X3H3 and CBEMA   X3 is the standards development committee accredited by ANSI for information processing.   The committee is administered by CBEMA, the Computer Business Equipment Manufacturers Association, located in Washington, D.C.   X3 has about 30 technical committees, each with about 15 to 80 members. Within X3, technical committee X3H3 is responsible for all computer graphics standards.   X3H3 prepares the US comments on each stage of the processing of proposed standards and forwards them to ANSI via X3 for submission to SC24. Currently more than 100 participants, representing about 70 companies, regularly attend X3H3 meetings.   Represented on X3H3 are such industry stalwarts as AT&T, CalComp, Digital Equipment Corporation, Evans and Sutherland, Hewlett-Packard, IBM, Intel, National Semiconductor Corporation, Prime, Tektronix, Texas Instruments, Unisys, and Wang.   Also active are large end users like Boeing, General Motors, Hughes, and McDonnell Douglas, and governmental organizations like NIST, Los Alamos National Lab, and Sandia National Lab.

US TAGs A US Technical Advisory Group or TAG is the X3 counterpart of an ISO committee. X3H3 is the TAG for SC24 (graphics); X3 is the TAG for JTC1.

A proposed ANS is progressed through a number of stages, similar to those of a proposed ISO standard.

SD-3   To start a new graphics standards project, X3H3 must draft and approve a project proposal (or SD-3), which must be approved by SPARC (Standards Planning and Requirements Committee - the Committee which oversees all the technical committees of X3) and is then subject to a vote of X3. This stage can take six months or more.

Working Drafts   X3H3 prepares a series of working drafts that are circulated and commented upon by X3H3 members. For graphics, this stage typically takes several years.

dpANS and public review When X3H3 believes that the proposed standard is sufficiently stable, it votes to forward the draft for public review in order to solicit opinions from outside the committee. Six to ten months from the first X3H3 ballot on public review to the start of the public review period is typical.

The initial public review period for X3 draft standards is four months; subsequent public review periods are two months. After each public review, X3H3 prepares responses to the comments and, if substantial technical changes are made to the document, a new public review begins. This stage can take eight months or more depending on the number of public review cycles. Most X3H3 standards require at least two public reviews before final approval.

Final Approval by the Board of Standards Review When X3H3 has approved a public review response that results in no more technical changes, X3 ballots on forwarding the dpANS to the ANSI Board of Standards Review for acceptance as an ANS. The BSR does not judge technical merit but must be assured that procedures were followed. Publication can take six to nine months, primarily to get the document into an acceptable ANSI format.

4.3.2 BSI

The British Standards Institute is funded by government grant, and a mixture of sales of standards documents, licensing and industry sponsorship. In contrast to the ANSI process in the graphics standards area there has been no recent attempt to define national standards other than by direct adoption of the appropriate ISO standard. The ISO DIS GKS text was adopted as a British Standard (BS 6390), but this has now been superseded by ISO 7942. With the long development time to reach a full IS status there has however been an attempt to make the content of earlier stages of ISO standardization officially available to the public by producing the DIS text of each standard as a Draft for Development (DD). This is produced with a BSI cover and explanation of the status of the work and allows interested companies to begin to develop products based on the standard two to three years before the final text is available, but with confidence in the technical stability of the functional specification.

The equivalent of ISO/IEC JTC1 within the BSI organization is IST/- which has a committee IST/21 corresponding to JTC1/SC21, which until October 1988 had a "Panel" on computer graphics, the equivalent to the old SC21/WG2. With the formation of SC24 and the change in status of Graphics Standards work within ISO a new committee has been formed, but unfortunately since IST/24 already existed this new committee has been designated IST/31. This changed status for computer graphics standards work means that participants in the main committee (IST/31) must be nominated by organizations. Individual experts will now contribute at the level of "Panels" which are being established to correspond to each of the SC24 Working Groups, with the exception of WG1. WG1's functions are expected to be picked up by a combination of IST/31 action and assigning tasks to the other panels.

4.3.3 Other national bodies

The organization of graphics work within the BSI is much more typical of the processing by most National Bodies than the ANSI processing, which duplicates many of the ISO processes. The German Federal Republic standards body, DIN, and the French and Dutch counterparts (AFNOR and NNI) have played leading roles in the development of the early standards in computer graphics. Addresses for all the national bodies which are P-members of ISO/IEC JTC1/SC24 (Computer Graphics) are included in Annex C.

4.4 Other standardization bodies

4.4.1 Other world-wide organizations

In addition to the International Organization for Standardization (ISO), two other international organizations have world-wide responsibilities for standardization work in the Information Technology area. These are the International Electrotechnical Commission (IEC) and the International Telecommunications Union (ITU). There are corresponding bodies to all three organizations within Europe, the European Committee for Standardization (CEN), the European Committee for Electrical Standardization (CENELEC) and the European Conference of Postal and Telecommunications Administrations (CEPT). The European bodies are discussed in Section 4.4.2.

ISO consists of the national standards bodies in its member countries, IEC consists of the national electrotechnical committees in its member countries and the ITU is an intergovernmental organization which in May 1988 had 166 member countries.

IEC is responsible for the entire field of electrotechnology. ISO covers fields apart from electrotechnology. Information Technology (IT) crosses many boundaries and the formation of the first Joint Technical Committee of ISO/IEC in 1987 has already been mentioned, together with the procedures under which JTC1 operates. IT also features in the work of the ITU and so it is appropriate to discuss briefly the way ITU operates and the relationship with ISO/IEC.

The purposes of the ITU are:

- to maintain and extend international cooperation for the improvement and rational use of telecommunications of all kinds, as well as to promote and to offer technical assistance to developing countries in the field of telecommunications.

- to promote the development of technical facilities and their most efficient operation with a view to improving the efficiency of telecommunication services, increasing their usefulness and making them, so far as possible, generally available to the public;

- to harmonize the actions of nations in the attainment of those ends.

As far as standards for information technology are concerned, the important parts of the ITU are the International Consultative Committees. One of these, the International Radio Consultative Committee (CCIR) studies and issues Recommendations on technical and operating questions relating to radiocommunications. The second is the one that is important for IT standards, the International Telegraph and Telephone Consultative Committee (CCITT) which studies and issues Recommendations on technical operating and tariff questions relating to telegraphy and telephony.

CCITT operates in a very different way to ISO/IEC. In CCITT the principal way to approve a document is at a Plenary Assembly. Plenary Assemblies are held every four years. They draw up lists of technical subjects, questions relating to telecommunications, study of which should lead to improvements in services. These questions are then referred to Study Groups which are composed of experts from different countries. CCITT has 15 such Study Groups. Several of these groups have terms of reference which include the impact of networks on telecommunications provision and *vice versa*. The Study Group recommendations are submitted to the next Plenary Assembly. If approved, the Recommendations are published in a book of recommendations. Interestingly the 1980 edition was 6,000 pages whilst the 1988 edition ran to 20,000!

When ISO/IEC JTC1 was formed, it was recognized that the base of common work between ISO and IEC also extended into the work of CCITT. There is a good spirit of cooperation between ISO/IEC and CCITT in activities in areas such as Telematics, Message Handling Systems, Office Document Architecture, Directory Services, Open Systems Interconnection Services and Protocols, Public Data Network Protocols, Data Interfaces and ISDN. This has led to the production of informal guidelines to foster cooperation between JTC1and CCITT, including an informal approach to the coordination of their respective work programmes.

At the present time, the areas of overlap between ISO/IEC and CCITT do not specifically include computer graphics, but as higher bandwidth networks become available and interest in multi-media services grows, this situation may well change. Certainly there is a growing need for consideration of the networking services necessary to support distributed graphics applications and this does overlap with the interests of CCITT.

4.4.2 European organizations

Within Europe, standardization is dealt with by CEN and CENELEC. CENELEC is responsible for the electrotechnical field and CEN for all other fields. CEN is made up of the national standards bodies of 18 EEC and EFTA member states (Austria, Belgium, Denmark, Finland, France, Germany, Greece, Iceland, Ireland, Italy, Luxembourg, Netherlands, Norway, Portugal, Spain, Sweden, Switzerland and the United Kingdom). CENELEC is made up of national electrotechnical committees of European countries. CEN and CENELEC are intrinsically independent bodies, but there is a close working relationship between them and together they make up the Joint European Standards Institution.

The role of European standardization has been steadily increasing owing to the contribution standardization has to make to the preparation of the Internal Market foreseen for 1992. Essentially the aim is to replace national standards in Europe by European Standards.

The European equivalent of ITU is CEPT, which maintains relations with CCITT. Since 1984 there has been an Information Technology Steering Committee (ITSTC) which is made up of representatives from CEN/CENELEC and CEPT and coordinates European Standardization in IT and data processing.

CEN/CENELEC try hard to promote the implementation of ISO/IEC standards and avoid duplicating work being done elsewhere. They are also concerned with the harmonization of national standards and have the ability to prepare new European Standards where no standards exist.

There is an agreement between CEN/CENELEC members that when work is started at a European level, they will not publish a new or revised national standard on the same subject that would endanger the progress of the European project.

CEN/CENELEC produce three kinds of documents:

- *European Standards* (EN): these are totally harmonized documents and are implemented nationally by the publication of a national standard identical in presentation and content.

- *Harmonization Documents* (HD): these apply to less stable situations, but require withdrawal of conflicting standards. They do not otherwise demand implementation and allow agreed national deviations.

- *European Pre-Standards* (ENV): these are used as guidelines or indications of the expected European Standards or Harmonization Documents and are primarily relevant to fast moving technologies. They have an initial validity of three years. After two years members are asked whether the ENV should become an EN, be prolonged for a further two years (once only), be withdrawn or be replaced by another ENV. ENV's are not binding and conflicting national standards need not be withdrawn.

GKS has been adopted as an EN (EN 27942).

Another aspect of European standardization concerns conformance certification of IT products and services. There have to be mechanisms for:

(1) agreeing the requirements for standards;

(2) testing for conformance with these requirements;

(3) certifying that the requirements have been satisfied.

Item (1) is covered by the Joint European Standards Institute. Items (2) and (3) are the subject of a Memorandum of Understanding between CEN/CENELEC members for the establishment of a European Committee for IT-Certification (ECITC). All CEN/CENELEC countries except Iceland, Luxembourg and Spain have signed the Memorandum (although Spain has announced that it will participate in the scheme). The Memorandum commits members to monitoring and promoting a European System of IT Testing and Certification. The objectives of the scheme are:

(1) to test IT products for conformity to standards;

(2) to issue harmonized European IT certificates of conformity.

The scheme is based upon existing national certification structures and the idea is that any national certification body (based upon a test report from an accredited testing laboratory) will be recognized by any other country which participates in the scheme, thus eliminating the need for repeated testing and certification of the same candidate implementation in different countries.

Recognition arrangements are currently being negotiated for the European Testing and Certification for Office and Manufacturing Protocols (ETCOM) under this scheme.

There is already a harmonized European Certification Scheme (CENCER) which covers the IT products for which CEN alone is the responsible body. This scheme provides national recognition of harmonized European test reports and certificates. The first products handled under the scheme were Pascal compilers. GKS is now covered by this scheme.

A very useful source of information on CEN/CENELEC activities is the Esprit Information Exchange System Newsletter, *iesnews*, published by DG XIII of the Commission of European Communities.

4.4.3 Industry organizations

In addition to Standards promulgated by the formal standards-making bodies, there are several bodies within the industry which generate industry standards. Within Europe, the most important of these is the European Computer Manufacturers Association, ECMA. The motivation for the establishment of ECMA came at the end of the 1950's when the growing use of computers originating from different manufacturers revealed the need to standardize programming languages and input/output codes to enable data and programs generated for one machine to be used on another. National standards bodies had very little interest in these areas at that time and so industry took a lead. ECMA is a non-profit-making organization whose main aims are:

- To study and develop, in co-operation with the appropriate national and international organizations as a scientific endeavour and in the general interest, methods and procedures in order to facilitate and standardize the use of data processing systems.

- To promulgate various standards applicable to the functional design and use of data processing equipment.

Membership consists of ordinary and associate members; ordinary membership is open to "companies which in Europe develop, manufacture and market data processing machines or groups of machines used to process digital information for business, scientific, control or other similar purposes".

It is ECMA's stated intention that proposals should be drafts to be considered by other organizations, for example ISO/IEC and CCITT. There are close relations between ECMA and ISO/IEC and ECMA is a liaison member of JTC1. ECMA representatives sit on SC's within JTC1.

Open Systems Interconnection (OSI) offers the possibility of connecting together heterogeneous equipment so that interchange of information between the systems is freely possible. Standards in the OSI area seem inevitably to offer a large number of options and to cope with this situation, groups of users have come together to decide which options should be chosen to ensure that their requirements to communicate are satisfied. Such groups of options have become known as *Application Profiles*. Typical examples are the Manufacturing Automation Protocol (MAP), which was initiated by General Motors, and the Technical Office Protocol (TOP), initiated by Boeing. Such profiles are becoming important in graphics, especially for interchange standards such as CGM. A CGM profile will be incorporated in version 3 of MAP/TOP.

Application profiles are also known as *Functional Standards*, the idea being that if function X is required, then use Standards A,B, C, ... in the manner described in the Functional Standard. Within Europe Functional Standards are promulgated by CEN/CENELEC. Functional Standards have been drafted by the European Workshop on Open Systems (EWOS). This body was created in December 1987 by the major supplier and user organizations: Cooperation for Open Systems Interconnection in Networking in Europe (COSINE), ECMA, European MAP Users' Group (EMUG), Open Systems Interconnection Technical and Office Protocols (OSITOP), Reseaux Associes pour la Recherche Européenne (RARE) and Standards Promotion and Applications Group (SPAG) in conjunction with CEN/CENELEC. The aim of EWOS is to reach consensus on functional profiles and corresponding test specifications in order to allow inter-working between various computer systems on the basis of international standards. The technical work of EWOS is carried out by a number of Expert Groups which report to the Technical Assembly. The latter meets four times a year. The results of EWOS are submitted to the formal CEN/CENELEC ratification procedures for conversion to ENV's.

The first EWOS proposals were released in January 1989; three concern profiles for the Office Document Architecture Standard (ODA ISO 8613), the fourth addresses a profile for File Transfer and Management (FTAM). Although there is no specific graphics work within EWOS at this moment, this may well develop in the future, especially given the adoption of CGM as a mechanism for including graphics within ODA documents.

4.5 Summary

This Chapter has attempted to describe the more important of the standards-making bodies and the processes which they operate. It will have become apparent that the standards-making process is a complex one and seems inevitably to be very time-consuming. This is particularly disadvantageous in a fast-moving subject such as IT where the requirements for a standard may well be significantly changed by advances in technology which occur whilst the standard is being developed. GKS fell into this trap to some extent in that raster graphics technology was considered unimportant when the standardization process started, but was the dominant technology for interactive devices by the time GKS was published. This means that standards do have to have a sound conceptual basis that will withstand fluctuations in technology.

It will also be clear that there is ample scope for producing incompatible standards, just because of the shear volume of work going on and the difficulties of being and keeping aware of all relevant activities. SC24 has liaisons with other groups both within ISO/IEC and with organizations outside.

Partly in an attempt to circumvent the lengthy timescales involved in formal standards making, other bodies such as the Open Software Foundation are springing up which are promulgating *de facto* standards. Whilst there is something here to be applauded, it remains the case that there is a requirement for "official" standards, not least because users increasingly ask for guarantees that products conform to unambiguously defined functionality. Achieving this is aided by consideration of draft definitions which is not normally achievable in short timescales with a wide range of technical expertise.

Part 2
The Players

5
Output Primitives and Attributes

5.1 Introduction

In the Seillac I discussions reported in Chapter 1 we highlighted the lack of agreement reached over the range of output primitives to be included in a standard for the Application Program Interface. The following sections show how quickly the various proposals evolved to produce the range of primitives which were finally standardized in GKS and have subsequently been further elaborated in the device level standards.

5.2 Pre Editorial Board output primitives

The first English language version of GKS (GKS Version 3 [6]) already included the POLYLINE, POLYMARKER, STRING and DRAW primitives. The notable features were the lack of reliance on the Current Position concept; the total absence of raster primitives and the inclusion of the DRAW primitive, which has subsequently evolved into the GENERALIZED DRAWING PRIMITIVE of ISO 7942.

Core '77 [18] however was heavily reliant on the concept of current position (CP) and included primitives which were defined in both 2 and 3 dimensions. Since the primitives used the concept of current position it was necessary to provide a MOVE primitive, which has the effect of resetting the current position without producing a visible effect. The functions MOVE_ABS_2, MOVE_ABS_3, MOVE_REL_2, and MOVE_REL_3 define movements in absolute terms or relative to the current position, and these forms of parameterization were also included for the LINE_REL_2, POLYLINE_ABS_2, and MARKER_ABS_2 (etc.) functions. The other output primitive was the TEXT function, whose attributes bore a strong similarity to those of GKS today, but whose definition included display starting at the current position. Interestingly Core '77 includes three different text display qualities (LOW_QUALITY, MEDIUM_QUALITY, and HIGH_QUALITY), reflecting the accuracy with which the individual characters are to be rendered and clearly the forerunners of STRING, CHARACTER and STROKE precisions in GKS.

GKS Version 3 and GSPC Core '77 adopted very different approaches to controlling the visual appearance of output primitives on a display device.

GSPC Core '77 associated *attributes* with output primitives which defined the general characteristics of the primitive. Attributes associated with primitives were static in the sense that the attributes associated with a primitive could not be changed after the primitive had been created. The primitive attributes were: COLOUR, INTENSITY, LINE WIDTH, LINESTYLE, FONT, CHARSIZE, CHARSPACE, CHARPLANE, CHARQUALITY and PICK-ID. If a particular attribute value was not supported by a particular device, it was permissible to simulate the effect of that value using other values for that attribute, other attributes and other primitives. A particular dashed linestyle could be simulated by a sequence of MOVE and solid LINES, for example. The essence of this approach is that the application specifies a precise appearance and the system does the best it can to reproduce that appearance.

GKS Version 3 took a different line. The central idea here was that of a *pen*. Output primitives were drawn with a particular pen number. The properties colour, thickness of a line, linetype and intensity, were attributes of the pen which could be set by a SET PEN REPRESENTATION function. There were separate functions to set text quality, text font, character spacing and character size. The marker type with which a POLYMARKER primitive was displayed was a parameter of the POLYMARKER function.

Pen representations could be set differently for different workstations and this gave a very nice mechanism for tailoring the appearance of output primitives to the capabilities of the particular workstation on which the output was to be displayed. Thus if a monochrome rather than a colour workstation was used, linestyle might be used to achieve differentiation between primitives on the former, whilst colour might be used with the latter. With the approach taken in Core '77, the application program would need substantial changes to move to a different output device, or the application programmer would have to rely on the implementation handling requests for different colours on a monochrome device in such a manner as to achieve satisfactory differentiation between primitives.

The GKS pen concept was also used to good effect in the graphical supplement to the NAG numerical algorithms library [29]. For example the user of a contouring routine could specify that every fifth contour was to be highlighted. The writer of the contouring routine was not concerned with how this should be done; the contouring routine would insert a call to select a particular pen at the start of each contour, and the user of the supplement was provided with a pen definition routine to define representations for each pen used.

5.3 Post Editorial Board developments

Following on from the Editorial Board meeting in 1979 [46] (see Section 1.2.2), Core '79 [19] had been expanded to include the POLYMARKER_ABS_2, (etc.) functions and the TEXT attribute model had been elaborated considerably to include CHARJUST, the forerunner of GKS' TEXT ALIGNMENT, redefinition of the QUALITY's as precisions and inclusion of a CHARPATH.

Also included in the report was a sub-committee report on proposed extensions for raster graphics. This report included a POLYGON primitive, with a variety of fill styles and two colour models (RGB and HLS). The interior of the POLYGON was defined using the odd/even rule for the number of intersections of a ray to infinity from the point under test (as in GKS) and there was a single closed boundary. One of the options for rendering the POLYGON was "patterned", which used a PIXEL ARRAY definition to tile the interior.

Meanwhile GKS 5.2 [8] had also expanded the range of primitives and included two primitives in the raster area, FILL AREA and PIXEL ARRAY. FILL AREA was a simple polygon the interior of which would be filled with a uniform colour, whilst PIXEL ARRAY was a rectangular area specified in World Coordinates (see Chapter 6) and transformable. "The mapping from transformed cells to the pixels of a raster display is implementation dependent." This quote from the description of the function highlights the contrasting attitude between the GSPC interest in accessing and controlling the physical pixels of the display and the GKS view of a virtual world. The rendering of GSPC's PIXEL ARRAY was described as being "done with regard to the view surface's native coordinate system and as such is device dependent." The GKS definition had been changed to something very close to the eventual standard, by the time that GKS 6.6 [10] appeared.

It is interesting to note that the perceptions in this area are still very divided with current arguments in SC24/WG3 over the inclusion or non-inclusion of a PIXEL ARRAY function (addressed at physical pixels) in Addendum 1 of CGM [86]. In that particular case the arguments also include the temporal one that a metafile is intended to be stored for later interpretation. In the general case the dimensions of physical pixels on the device eventually used to render a metafile cannot be determined and nothing can be guaranteed about the relationship of any physical pixels to the other output primitives, which all exist in the world of virtual coordinate systems and are therefore subject to transformation at the time of interpreting the metafile. The arguments continue.

It is probably in the area of output primitives and attributes that the recommendations of the 1979 Editorial Board were least effectual. It is interesting to note some of the recommendations that didn't get reflected in the revised documents. The major issues discussed related to:

- the use of Current Position;
- whether or not to include 3D primitives;
- the appropriateness of DRAW (GKS) and ESCAPE (GSPC) for inclusion in the lowest level definition.

On the first two topics the two systems continued to differ, whilst for DRAW and ESCAPE variants of both are now in GKS ISO 7942. Also interesting is the lack of reported discussion of the need for support of raster graphics, but there were obviously more fundamental differences at that time to worry about! Raster graphics was discussed at the Bologna meeting, but the discussion was not taken forward at that time.

The attribute model in GKS was refined considerably in the Review Meetings following the Editorial Board. The first major advance was made at the Melbourne meeting in 1981, when it was recognized that different attributes were appropriate for different primitives and hence it was not sensible that there should be one pen for all primitives. Instead separate pens were defined for each class of primitive. The terminology was changed also. Pen numbers became *primitive indices* and the term *bundle* was introduced to describe the collection of attributes controlled by a primitive index. The term *bundle table* was introduced to describe the table which gave the correspondence between primitive indices and the bundle values.

It was recognized that some attributes of primitives are concerned with the geometry of the primitive, for example character height, whilst others, for example colour, are concerned with non-geometrical appearance. By the end of the Abingdon meeting in 1981 (GKS Version 7.0), agreement had been reached on which properties, or *aspects*, were geometrical and which were non-geometrical. The view was taken that geometrical aspects should have the same value on all workstations on which a primitive was displayed, whereas non-geometrical aspects could potentially have different values on different workstations. The non-geometrical aspects were controlled by primitive indices and bundle tables. Each workstation had its own set of bundle tables and so different representations for a particular primitive index value could be defined on different workstations. The aspects of primitives that were controlled by each mechanism are listed in Table 5.1 in Section 5.4 below. For some primitives, most notably TEXT, it took some time to agree on which aspects should be workstation independent and which should be workstation dependent.

Strong input was received from the USA prior to the Steensel meeting in 1982 that the more direct approach of workstation independent specification of bundled aspects was still needed by some applications. This was finally resolved by introducing a mechanism for the application to specify whether the value of a particular aspect for a particular primitive should be taken from a bundle table or a workstation independent attribute. This is described in Section 5.4.1.

Further reflection and experience have clarified thinking in this area. Aspects such as linetype are commonly used in two ways by applications. First to achieve differentiation between instances of primitives and second to prescribe a precise appearance, meaningful to the application, which is to be reproduced exactly on all workstations. An example of the second type is the use of particular linestyles in cartography to represent particular terrain features such as railway tracks of different kinds. Differentiation is handled quite well by existing standards, but precise appearance control is not and this is an area that is being considered by the GKS Review (see Chapter 14).

5.4 GKS output primitives and attributes

5.4.1 Attribute binding in GKS

The appearance of primitives on the display surface of a workstation is controlled by their *aspects*. Two types of aspects are distinguished, *workstation independent aspects* which have the same value on all workstations on which the primitive is displayed, and *workstation dependent aspects* which may have different values on different workstations.

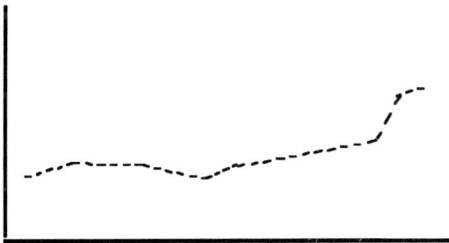

Figure 5.1(a) Simple use of bundles attributes

The values of aspects are controlled by *attributes*. For workstation independent aspects, there is one attribute per aspect. For workstation dependent aspects, two methods of specification are possible, *bundled specification* and *individual specification*. Bundled specification uses a lookup table approach. A single attribute for each primitive, the *primitive index*, controls the values of all the workstation dependent aspects of the primitive. The primitive index is an index into a table, the *primitive bundle table*, which specifies values of all the workstation dependent aspects for that type of primitive. Each workstation has its own set of bundle tables and each type of primitive has its own bundle table.

A set of *Aspect Source Flags* (ASFs) controls the mode of specification of each aspect. Some aspects may be specified individually, whilst others are specified by a bundle.

Attributes are bound to primitives when they are created and cannot subsequently be changed.

Figure 5.1(a) shows the simplest use of the bundle mechanism when the ASFs all select bundled specification. Figure 5.1(b) illustrates an example of mixed mode working.

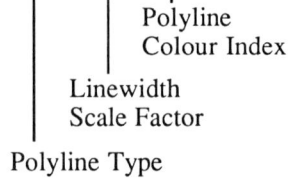

Figure 5.1(b) An example of mixed mode working

This technique for distinguishing the source of aspect values was only introduced at the GKS DIS stage as a result of realizing that some applications needed to treat certain aspects as workstation independent in an environment of multiple active workstations. This treatment essentially views these aspects as belonging to the virtual picture.

5.4.2 GKS output primitives

There are six primitives in ISO 7942 GKS [13]:

- POLYLINE, which draws a sequence of connected lines through successive points given in a point list (figure 5.2).
- POLYMARKER, which takes a list of points and displays a marker at each point.

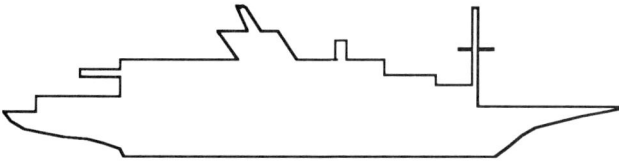

Figure 5.2 An example of a polyline

- TEXT, taking a character string and reference point and using the text attributes to define the shape and its placement relative to the point.
- FILL AREA, which generates an area defined by a set of bounding edges derived from a list of points (figure 5.3).
- CELL ARRAY, which the application defines to GKS as a rectangle parallel to the axes, divided into a number of identically shaped cells. These can be used to generate a colour raster image.
- GENERALIZED DRAWING PRIMITIVE (often called GDP), which is a standardized way of using non-standardized primitives.

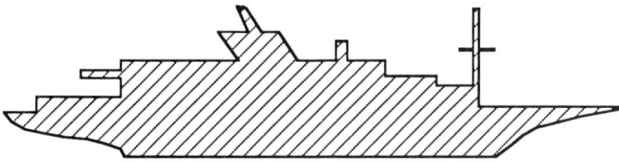

Hatched Fill Style

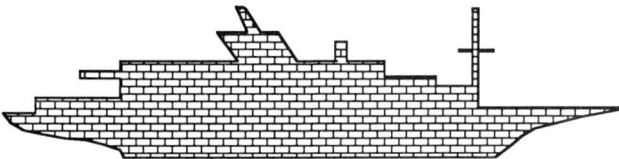

Pattern Fill Style

Figure 5.3 Examples of the use of Fill Area with hatch and pattern fill

Due to limitations on space it is impossible to describe the detail of these primitives and the control available over their appearance in the GKS standard. Table 5.1 gives a list of the various aspects for each primitive.

There are in addition a number of other attributes of primitives (for example ASPECT SOURCE FLAGS and PICK IDENTIFIER which are used in connection with PICK input, see Section 7.3.1 and Chapter 8). Note that the CELL ARRAY has no aspects, but its definition includes Colour

Indices for each cell within the primitive invocation itself, rather than as aspects applied to the definition as it progresses down the pipeline.

Table 5.1 Aspects of GKS Primitives

Primitive	WS Independent Aspect	Potentially WS Dependent Aspects
POLYLINE	None	Linetype Linewidth Scale Factor Colour Index
POLYMARKER	None	Marker Type Marker Size Scale Factor Colour Index
FILL AREA	Pattern Reference Point Pattern Size	Fill Area Interior Style Fill Area Style Index Colour Index
TEXT	Character Height Character Up Vector Text Path Text Alignment	Text Font and Precision Character Expansion Factor Character Spacing Colour Index
CELL ARRAY	None	None
GDP	May include aspects of other primitives	

The basic primitives of GKS (ISO 7942) have been extended in three ways as the family of graphic standards has grown. Firstly the CGM and CGI have extended the range of 2D primitives provided, addressing the requirements for longer term storage initially and the consequent needs to define protocols to devices capable of interpreting the stored pictures. In another direction the definitions of GKS-3D and PHIGS have necessitated the review of the GKS set of primitives for the implications of moving to a 3D environment. Finally since the basic set of GKS primitives was defined some 5 years before the next proposal in the family was finalized, in both the CGI/CGM group and in the 3D API group, new ideas and a review of GKS primitives for convenience and completeness have been continually taking place. This review has led to some additional features in all the newer standards which are not explicitly required to meet the needs of a device level standard (CGI/CGM) or of the 3D environment (GKS-3D/PHIGS) in a pure GKS environment.

5.5 CGM/CGI extensions to GKS output primitives

5.5.1 Common extensions

The major changes introduced by the CGM [85] initially and subsequently adopted by the CGI [103] have been designed to broaden the range of predefined primitives to better accommodate the requirements of applications likely to use the metafile for storage of pictures, where pictures archived now may well have a useful life of several years. For example a drafting package might be used to produce a picture now, which is then archived and used as part of a database of part designs, which is still in use in the mid 1990's. Thus when the picture is interpreted editing packages are likely to have been developed which will use the more complete definition of a primitive as, say, a circular arc to allow appropriate manipulation of the picture's components and subsequently display the amended picture on devices which may well be more capable of hardware display of a wider range of primitives than are current devices.

Rather than simply expand the range of individual primitives, each with an independent and complete list of aspects, the GKS aspect groupings described above have been applied to a group of primitives in CGM and CGI. Thus the POLYLINE primitive of GKS has been replaced by a class of primitives in CGM. Table 5.2 lists the classes of primitives in CGM and the GKS primitive from which the aspect set has been derived.

Table 5.2 CGM Primitive Classes and their GKS Equivalents

GKS Primitive	CGM Primitives
POLYLINE	POLYLINE
	DISJOINT POLYLINE
	CIRCULAR ARC 3 POINT
	CIRCULAR ARC CENTRE
	ELLIPTICAL ARC
POLYMARKER	POLYMARKER
TEXT	TEXT
	RESTRICTED TEXT
	APPEND TEXT
FILL AREA	POLYGON
	POLYGON SET
	RECTANGLE
	CIRCLE
	ELLIPSE
	CIRCULAR ARC 3 POINT CLOSE
	CIRCULAR ARC CENTRE CLOSE
	ELLIPTICAL ARC CLOSE
CELL ARRAY	CELL ARRAY
GDP	GDP

Note that even where the names of the primitives are identical, there may have been a need to define a different parameterization to reflect the different part of the pipeline at which the DI/DD interface exists (see Chapter 2). For example the CELL ARRAY element in CGM uses a three point definition, which describes a parallelogram, rather than the two point definition in GKS used to describe a rectangle. This parameterization is required in order to describe the GKS CELL ARRAY, which by the time it is stored in the metafile may well have been transformed by the segment transformation (see Section 6.3.3) from the initial rectangle into a parallelogram.

As another example the TEXT primitives in CGM all include a flag which is used to indicate whether the string in the primitive is complete or whether it will be continued with additional characters added using the APPEND TEXT primitive. The APPEND TEXT primitive is included to allow a text string to be assembled from several pieces, in between which some of the text attributes (e.g. font) may have been changed. This change was incorporated since in the case of remote interpretation of a metafile, in either time or space, it is not possible to inquire the end point of the previous text string and thereby arrange for subsequent parts to be properly concatenated. In fact the INQUIRE TEXT EXTENT facility in GKS is also difficult to use to guarantee proper concatenation of mixed font strings and the CGM feature is therefore in this case, partly an extension of the GKS functions to provide a more complete functionality.

There have also been extensions to the range of primitives in the CGM, which are purely to provide enhanced functionality. RESTRICTED TEXT is a case in point, which is provided to allow the guarantee of producing text which does not go outside a particular part of the display surface.

5.5.2   Extensions due to DI/DD requirements

Two other CGM primitives, the DISJOINT POLYLINE and the POLYGON, are provided in part in order to accommodate the differing requirements of the device level standard. Both are introduced so that clipped primitives may be efficiently handled, but have the effect of providing wider functionality. For example a cross-hatched FILL AREA may be coded as a POLYLINE primitive for the boundary and DISJOINT POLYLINE for the cross-hatched interior, which could also be used to describe a dashed line at the device level.

The POLYGON primitive appears very close to the GKS FILL AREA, but in fact is parameterized differently in order to allow a device level standard to handle the encoding of a FILL AREA, which may have been clipped before transmission to a display. This therefore includes the extra parameterization of edge visibility flags which are used to control the visibility of each edge of the polygon, but of course may also be used in their own right.

5.5.3   Additional primitives in the CGI

A major difference in the way the CGI is defined is that CGI output primitives are described as functions which produce graphic objects in the CGI pipeline. A CGI function (e.g. POLYLINE) creates a graphic object consisting of geometry and attributes. The standard then describes the progression of the object from the client interface to the device in terms of the state of the object and the manipulations on it. This description is required since the CGI is describing much more of the internal structure of the graphics pipeline in order to address a wide range of device architectures.

As noted in Chapter 3 the CGI [103] is some way behind the other members of the family of graphics standards, and as such is being developed incorporating some additional features which had not been considered appropriate for earlier standards. Most notable amongst these is the CLOSED FIGURE facility which allows the CGI client to define a complex shape and use the filled area attributes to render the final boundary. The shape is assembled from a combination of line class primitives and filled area primitives, which between them define a number of closed loops. As part of allowing the complete definition of the boundary, it also became necessary to introduce the CIRCULAR ARC CENTRE BACKWARDS primitive, which also has no direct equivalent in the CGM.

As the CGI project has evolved there has been recognition of the implications of an underlying difference between the original primitive set and the compound objects (closed region and compound text). This distinction is being highlighted progressively more in successive revisions of the document and allows more precise definition of which aspects the client is allowed to change during the construction of a compound graphical object and what values will be used in rendering.

The CGM Addendum 1 [86] project is doing much to bring the two standards back into line, and is expected to include the CLOSED FIGURE facility and the CIRCULAR ARC CENTRE BACKWARDS primitive mentioned above.

5.5.4 Additional aspect specification modes

In GKS, the linewidth and marker size aspects are specified as a fraction of the nominal linewidth or marker size that the workstation on which the primitive is to be displayed is capable of. The value computed in this way is mapped by the workstation to the nearest value supported. A similar mechanism is also used in GKS-3D [15] and PHIGS [16].

CGM provides this mechanism, but also allows linewidth, marker size and edge width to be specified as an absolute size in Virtual Device Coordinates (see Chapter 6 for an explanation of coordinate systems in CGM and CGI). The specification modes of linewidth, marker size and edge width may be specified independently in CGM. They are specified by elements within picture descriptors, which means that the modes may be changed between pictures but cannot be changed within a picture.

CGI provides the same specification modes as CGM. The mode may be changed freely.

As part of the discussions on the nature of these modes, the additional CGI clipping modes (see Section 6.5) and the inheritance filter (see Section

7.3) successive versions of the CGI are introducing progressively better definitions of the terms "attribute" and "control". The DIS text is expected to distinguish between them on the basis that attributes are static and associated with the graphic objects at creation time, whereas controls, if changed by the client, may be retrospective. A clipping mode in this context becomes an attribute, whereas colour table settings are controls.

5.6   3D extensions

The main problems in determining the primitives required to define a 3D system related more to the purpose of the extension and the relationship to the original 2D system. This was clarified when it was decided that an objective should be that a GKS 2D program should run on a GKS-3D implementation and produce the same results (with the considerable limitation that GKS already contained a large number of implementation dependencies).

In addition it was decided that GKS-3D should be an entirely 3D system, rather than a mixture of 2D and 3D. This has the simplifying effect that all 2D functions used in the 3D environment are interpreted as a shorthand notation for something which is really a 3D primitive on the z=0 plane. The GKS 2D effect is therefore only intended to be maintained for those programs which do not use any of the 3D functionality. In that case the 2D calls would be interpreted correctly as defining the underlying 3D primitive.

For each of the six functions in GKS which create primitives the effect of calling it in a 3D environment is specified in the document, in a section which lists the equivalent 3D function call. Thus a POLYLINE 2 function is equivalent to a POLYLINE 3 function, with z coordinates set to zero.

The only primitive in GKS-3D which is genuinely additional to the 2D system is the FILL AREA SET, which allows a number of polygons to define a complex boundary of the filled area, with islands and lakes. In addition there is an entry in the EDGE bundle, which allows the application to select whether the edges of the filled area are visible or invisible.

There are a number of other new attributes introduced in GKS-3D, only some of which are specifically to meet the needs of 3D. The system includes a VIEW INDEX, as an attribute of each primitive, which could have been included in similar form in GKS 2D. It is however more significant in 3D since the views being indexed may be different on different workstations, allowing multiple views (with for example, different projections) to be generated in parallel.

A second attribute added for all primitives is the HLHSR IDENITIFER (Hidden Line/Hidden Surface Removal Identifier), which is interpreted in a workstation specific manner. Such a parameter would not have had much application in GKS 2D.

Finally where GKS included only an RGB model of specifying colour, GKS-3D allows the application to select between four alternatives (RGB, CIE, HSV and HLS).

The interesting feature of GKS-3D is, in some sense, the way in which it has not actually added any genuine 3D primitives (for example sculpted surfaces or simple volumetric shapes). In fact, of the 2D GKS primitives only POLYLINE and POLYMARKER are potentially non-planar – all the others are defined as appearing on a flat surface and specifically will be rendered in an implementation dependent way if the parameters do not define the required planar object to within a small tolerance.

The PHIGS standard includes all those previously defined in GKS–3D, and adds one more primitive, ANNOTATION TEXT RELATIVE. This primitive is designed to remain within a plane defined effectively in image space such that if the view of an object is altered the text nevertheless can be made to remain in the image plane without distortion.

6
Coordinate Systems

6.1 Introduction

It is generally accepted that the user of a graphics system should be able to define graphics in a coordinate system relevant to the application. It is also accepted that this coordinate system is unlikely to be the one specified for the device by the manufacturer. As a result there is a need to transform user coordinates to device coordinates. The problem that arises is what kinds of user coordinate system should be supported, and how should the mapping to device coordinates be specified.

The Seillac I Workshop [45] in 1976 recognized that transformations in graphics systems are used for two different purposes, (a) for constructing a picture out of smaller items (referred to as *modelling transformations*), and (b) for viewing a picture (referred to as *viewing transformations*). It was recognized that one of the problems with existing packages was that they did not distinguish between these two types of transformations. Seillac I resolved that there should be a clear distinction between these two types of transformations and that a kernel graphics system should be designed which would only use transformations for viewing a previously constructed picture. Modelling was seen as an activity that belonged above the level of a kernel graphics system. GKS was designed with this separation in mind.

This chapter looks at the development of coordinate systems in GKS and in the related 2D standards, CGM and CGI. Later sections look at coordinate systems in the 3D application program interface standards, GKS-3D and PHIGS.

6.2 Development of coordinate systems in GKS

6.2.1 Background

The purpose of coordinate transformations in GKS is to enable pictures constructed from output primitives described in coordinate systems convenient for the user to be displayed on multiple workstations each operating with potentially a different coordinate system. Given the design goal of device independence in GKS, it has also to be possible to move an application from one device environment to another without changing the overall program structure.

From the application program standpoint, there will be a preferred coordinate system or systems in which it is convenient for the application program to work. This might be a cartesian coordinate system, or it might be polar coordinates or logarithmically scaled coordinates.

Device coordinate systems also exhibit great diversity. There is no commonly accepted direction for the axes or location of the origin. A raster device typically has the origin at the bottom left hand corner with x coordinate values increasing from left to right and y values from bottom to top. However, vector refresh devices exist where the x and y axes are oriented in the normal mathematical senses, but the origin is located at the centre of the screen rather than at the bottom left. For pen plotter devices or film recorders, it is not uncommon for the origin to be at the top left hand corner with x increasing across the paper and y in the direction of motion of the paper (downwards). All these variations had to be accommodated in the standard. A further problem is presented by the metric in device coordinate space and the need to be able to produce pictures to a precise scale on the output device. This is very important, for example, in application areas such as engineering drawing and cartography.

Some devices do not have a meaningful metric in device coordinate space, for example it is not meaningful to ask for a line to be drawn precisely 2 cms long on a raster refresh device. The display surface itself is curved and the size of the image will depend on the alignment of the device and will vary from device to device. For other devices such as precision pen plotters or photo plotters, there is a meaningful metric and it does make sense to ask for a line 2 cms long to be drawn.

A further complication arises since graphics standards support both graphical input and graphical output. Frequently graphical input containing positional information is generated by the operator by reference to some part of a picture that the application has displayed. In such cases it may be convenient for the application if the positional information is returned in the same coordinate system as was used to generate the picture. In other cases there may well not be such a relationship, for example, when a digitizer is being used to digitize a picture; however even here, the application program will want to have some control over the coordinate system to ensure that the information is stored in an appropriate form for subsequent reuse.

6.2.2 GKS version 3

GKS version 3 [6] recognized two coordinate systems: *user coordinates*, *normalized device coordinates* (NDC). User coordinates were a cartesian coordinate system in which the coordinate data of output primitives were expressed. Normalized device coordinate space is an intermediate coordinate system which provided a common coordinate system for all workstations. The maximum visible region of NDC space is the unit square.

The transformation from user coordinates to device coordinates was defined as two stages, first a *window to viewport transformation* mapped user coordinates onto normalized device coordinates. The transformation was defined by two rectangular regions, a window and a viewport. The transformation between the two coordinate systems was a combination of scaling and translations, which mapped the window region in one coordinate space to the viewport region in the other. NDC space was then mapped onto the maximum display space of the workstation. The application could select a smaller display region with the function SET REQUESTED DISPLAY SPACE SIZE. The size was specified as a fraction of the maximum.

The simplest model would have been to insist that all devices viewed the whole of the NDC space within the unit square. However allowing some control over what part of NDC space is seen on a particular device allows different parts of the picture to be viewed on different devices, which is important in many applications.

In GKS version 3, a single transformation from user coordinates to NDC could be defined at any time. This meant that if the normalization transformation was changed, knowledge of the previous transformation was lost. Positional information in graphical input was returned in user coordinates by transforming device coordinate positions by the inverse of the window to viewport transformation and the inverse of the display space to NDC transformation.

The chief limitation with this system was that more than one user coordinate system might be used in the creation of the picture, yet positional information could only be returned in the one, current, user coordinate system.

6.2.3 Subsequent developments

The major change to coordinate systems that occurred during the development of GKS was the addition of multiple normalization transformations at the Melbourne, Florida, meeting in 1981. The term *world coordinate system* replaced the term 'user coordinate system'. The latter was used to describe the coordinate systems which the application program uses. The term *normalization transformation* refers to the window to viewport transformation which maps world coordinates to NDC. Multiple normalization transformations were introduced chiefly to assist in returning positional information in graphical input in a sensible coordinate system. Input is not the subject of this chapter, but the topic is covered fully in Chapter 8.

An explicit *workstation transformation*, also a window to viewport transformation, was introduced to define the mapping from NDC to *device coordinates* (DC). Each workstation had a single workstation transformation.

This replaced the SET REQUESTED DISPLAY SPACE SIZE function of version 3.

Clipping is often considered along with coordinate systems in a graphics system. The clipping operation restricts graphical output to some region of interest in some coordinate space. The main issues with clipping include: what shape regions should be allowed, what coordinate space should clipping be defined in, how should the region be specified, should there be more than one clip? As will be explained in more detail shortly, two clips are allowed in GKS, one to the viewport of the normalization transformation (*normalization clip*), the second to the boundary of the workstation window (*workstation clip*). The first can be enabled or disabled by the application program. The second is compulsory and cannot be disabled.

There was considerable discussion during the development of GKS about whether the normalization clip region should be specified independently of normalization transformations; in other words should it be a rectangular region that was not necessarily the viewport of a transformation. The arguments were always resolved in favour of the normalization transformation viewport, largely on the basis of a minimality argument.

The coordinate systems and transformations in GKS ISO 7942 are described in the next section.

6.3 Coordinate systems and transformations in GKS

6.3.1 Normalization transformation

Coordinate data in the parameters of an output primitive in GKS are specified in *world coordinates* (WC), a cartesian coordinate system. If the application program does not find a cartesian coordinate system a natural system to work in, then the application must handle the transformation from the natural user coordinate system to WC.

World coordinates are transformed to an intermediate coordinate system called *normalized device coordinates* (NDC) by a window to viewport mapping termed a *normalization transformation*. The normalization transformation serves two purposes, first to scale parts of a picture defined in different world coordinate systems to a common NDC coordinate system, second to control the placement of those parts in the NDC space. These ideas are illustrated in figure 6.1.

The aspect ratios of window and viewport may differ in the normalization transformation, leading to differential or anisotropic scaling of the picture part in x and y coordinates. The boat in figure 6.1 is transformed isotropically, whilst the house is transformed anisotropically.

GKS allows multiple normalization transformations to be defined at the same time. In figure 6.1 separate normalization transformations for the house and boat can be defined and the appropriate one selected for the output of the house and boat using the SELECT NORMALIZATION TRANSFORMATION function.

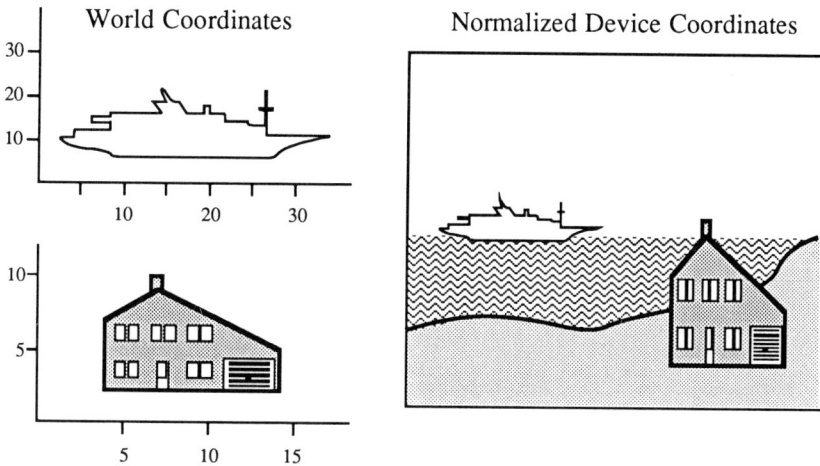

Figure 6.1 Assembling the Normalized Device Coordinate picture

This tends to lead to a different style of programming with the normalization transformations, rather like declarations, being defined at the head of the program and not changed. Systems which only allow a single transformation give rise to a programming style which mixes calls to primitives with changes in coordinate system making the program more difficult to understand and maintain [30].

A GKS implementation provides a finite number of normalization transformations (at least 2 at output level 0 and at least 11 at levels 1 and 2), all of which are initialized to the identity transformation which maps the unit square in WC space to the unit square in NDC space. Normalization transformation 0 is special in that it cannot be redefined ever. This provides a mechanism for the application to define output directly in NDC and also ensures that a world coordinate equivalent position exists for all graphical input containing positional information (see Chapter 8).

6.3.2 Workstation transformation

The workstation transformation allows different regions of NDC space to be displayed at different positions on different workstations. The workstation can be thought of as a camera focused on the NDC space. Each workstation can focus on a specific part and can zoom in or out. The method of defining which part of NDC space is to appear on the workstation is through a workstation window to viewport mapping. The function SET

WORKSTATION WINDOW specifies the rectangular region of NDC space within the unit square which will be displayed on the workstation. The SET WORKSTATION VIEWPORT function defines where on the display screen the view of NDC space will appear. The workstation viewport is a rectangular region specified in the appropriate device coordinates.

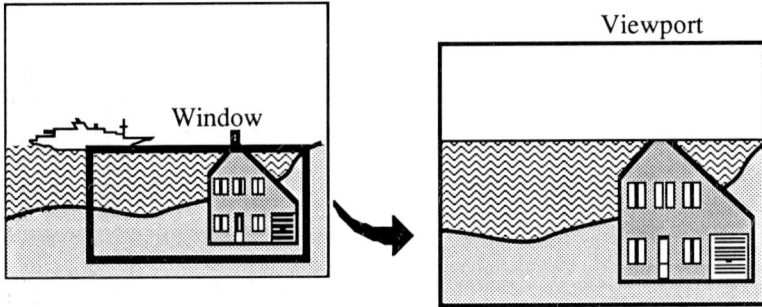

Figure 6.2(a) Window to viewport mapping example

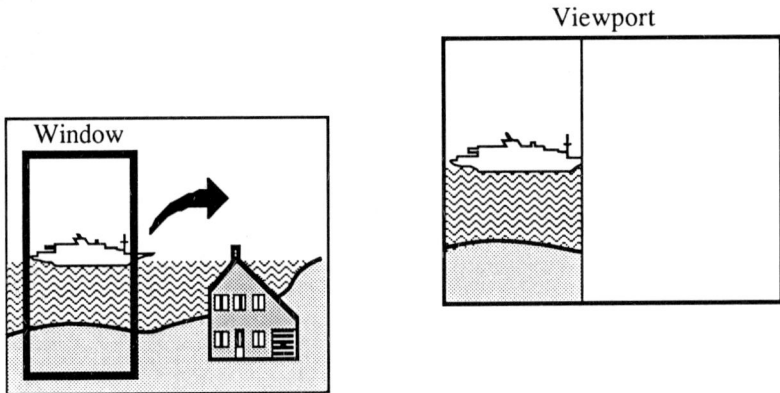

Figure 6.2(b) Window to viewport mapping example

The normalization transformation allows the aspect ratios of the window and viewport to differ, the workstation transformation, on the other hand, maps the workstation window to the largest possible region of the workstation viewport with the same aspect ratio. The philosophy is that the normalization transformation provides picture composition while the workstation transformation views the already composed picture.

If the workstation window and viewport have different aspect ratios, the complete window is displayed on the device in the correct aspect ratio, using a rectangle with its bottom left hand corner coincident with the bottom left hand corner of the specified viewport and with the largest size possible. Figure 6.2 shows some examples of the viewport used when the window and viewport have different aspect ratios.

Figure 6.3 illustrates the combination of normalization transformations and workstation transformations.

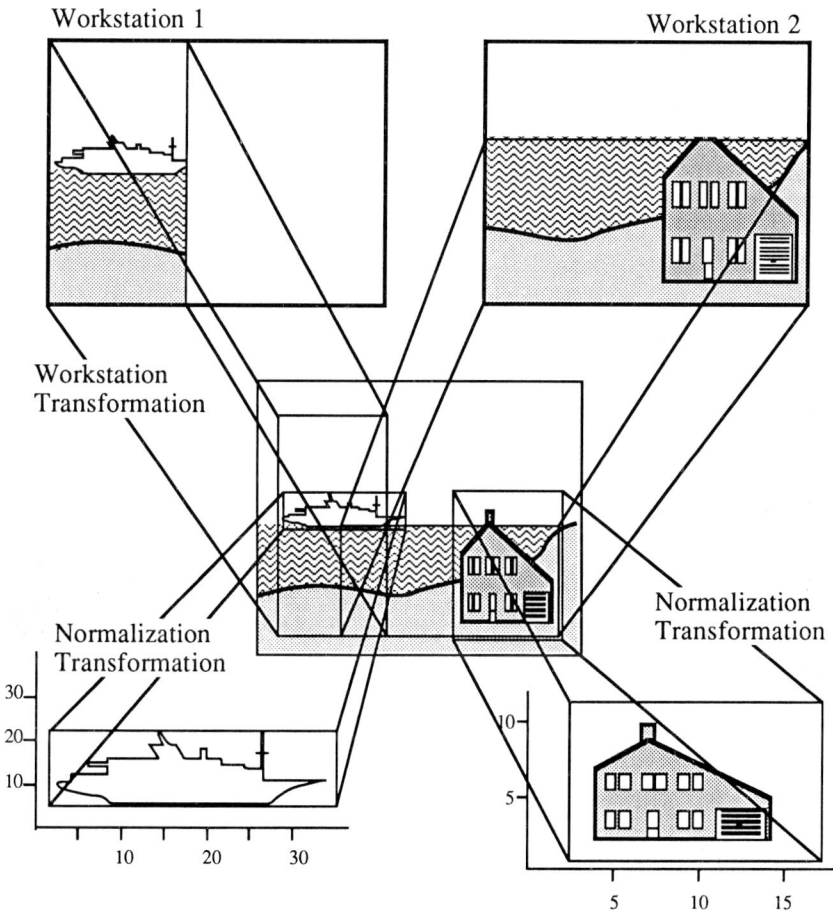

Figure 6.3 Combining normalization and workstation transformations

The handling of device coordinates in GKS requires some additional comment. To accommodate the variations in device coordinate systems found in real devices and typified by the examples given in Section 6.1, device coordinates in GKS are in fact an abstraction from real device coordinates and would be better thought of as workstation coordinates. The GKS device coordinate system assumes that the origin of device coordinates is at the bottom left hand corner of the display space, that x coordinates increase from left to right and y coordinates from bottom to top. This is the coordinate system in which GKS entities specified in device coordinates are given. There is an internal transformation from this coordinate system to the real device coordinate system; the details of this transformation are completely hidden from the user of GKS.

The workstation description table of each workstation records the type of coordinate system employed by the device and the limits of the display space. GKS provides an inquiry function to enable the application program to obtain this information. The inquiry function:

INQUIRE DISPLAY SPACE SIZE(WSTYP, IND, UNITS, RX, RY, IX, IY)

returns the characteristics of a workstation of type WSTYP. IND is an error indicator. UNITS indicates whether the device is addressed in metres or not. RX and RY give the maximum size of the display either in metres, if precise scaling is possible, or the device coordinates used if not. IX and IY give the display size in terms of addressable positions. With this information it is possible to set normalization and workstation transformations so that pictures can be drawn at a precise scale on devices capable of precise scaling.

6.3.3 Segment transformation

There is an additional transformation which applies only to primitives stored in segments, the *segment transformation*. Segment transformation is an attribute of a segment and the same transformation applies to all the coordinates in the segment definition. This transformation provides a convenient way to move objects, or parts of objects, around on a display surface in response either to some computation or to some operator direction.

The segment transformation is defined by a 2×3 transformation matrix which in its most general form allows a transformation involving translation, rotation, scaling and shearing to be defined. This considerably complicates the output pipeline of GKS, especially for the TEXT and CELL ARRAY primitives. The shape of the primitive is transformed, rather than just the positional parameters defining the primitive.

The complete GKS viewing pipeline is shown in figure 6.4. It will be seen that the segment transformation is applied in NDC space and is a mapping from NDC space onto itself.

Two utility functions, EVALUATE TRANSFORMATION MATRIX and ACCUMULATE TRANSFORMATION MATRIX are provided to help the applications programmer to construct transformation matrices. The first calculates a transformation matrix for a transformation consisting of translation, rotation and scaling components. The second calculates a matrix which is the composition of a matrix representing a transformation with translation, rotation and scaling components, with another transformation matrix. The order of the transformations is fixed: input matrix, scale, rotate and translate.

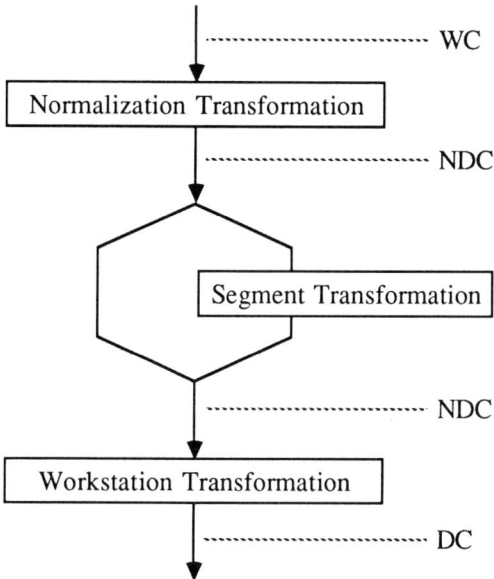

Figure 6.4 GKS viewing pipeline

6.3.4 Clipping

Two clips are defined in GKS, the *normalization clip* which occurs after the segment transformation and before the workstation transformation and the *workstation clip* which follows the normalization clip. Interestingly, none of the standards includes shielding - the ability to remove that part of a primitive that falls within rather than outside a specified region. Shielding has often been discussed, but has not as yet been incorporated.

The normalization clip is an optional clip, which clips output to the boundary of the viewport of the currently selected normalization transformation. By default, this clip is enabled. It can be disabled and enabled by the SET CLIPPING INDICATOR function.

There is only a single global clipping indicator, rather than one per normalization transformation.The selection of a different normalization transformation leaves the setting of the clipping indicator unchanged.

For primitives stored inside segments, clipping is rather more involved. When a primitive is stored in a segment, if the clipping indicator is set to CLIP, a clipping rectangle (which is the viewport of the currently selected normalization transformation) is stored with the primitive. When the primitive is subsequently displayed, it is clipped against this clipping rectangle. If the clipping indicator is set to NOCLIP when a primitive is stored in a segment, a clipping rectangle which is the unit square is stored with the primitive.

One rather odd feature is that clipping rectangles are not transformed by the segment transformation. Thus if a segment is shifted by changing its segment transformation, transformed primitives will continue to be clipped against the original clipping rectangles.

The workstation clip is a clip to the workstation window of each workstation and cannot be disabled. GKS is defined in such a way that an implementation can combine the two clips into a single clip which may lead to more efficient implementations.

6.4 The Computer Graphics Metafile (CGM)

CGM [85,89,100] has a certain compatibility with GKS but also allows a wider range of functionality so that it can be used for the interchange of graphical information in a wider context than just GKS. This is reflected in the coordinate systems in the standard. Some relevant Addendum 1 [86] facilities are described later in this section as they extend the functionality of CGM in the area of coordinate systems.

CGM pictures are at the level of NDC coordinate space in GKS. Primitives in CGM are described in a coordinate space called *Virtual Device Coordinates* (VDC). The metafile description element, VDC TYPE, declares whether the VDC coordinates in the whole of a metafile are specified as integer or real values. VDC space is a 2D cartesian space of infinite precision and infinite range, however, only a finite range and precision will be representable in an actual metafile. The elements VDC INTEGER PRECISION and VDC REAL PRECISION specify the precision with which VDC integer and real values, respectively, are represented in the metafile. The range of the VDC space comprises the coordinates representable in the format specified by the VDC type and appropriate VDC precision. This range has a distinct granularity which is determined by the precision. Irrespective of the aspect ratio of the range and the granularity within the range, it is implicit that one VDC unit in the x direction represents the same distance as one VDC unit in the y direction in VDC space.

VDC extent ((0,0),(500,400))

VDC extent ((0,400),(500,0))   VDC extent ((500,0),(0,400))

VDC extent ((500,400),(0,0))

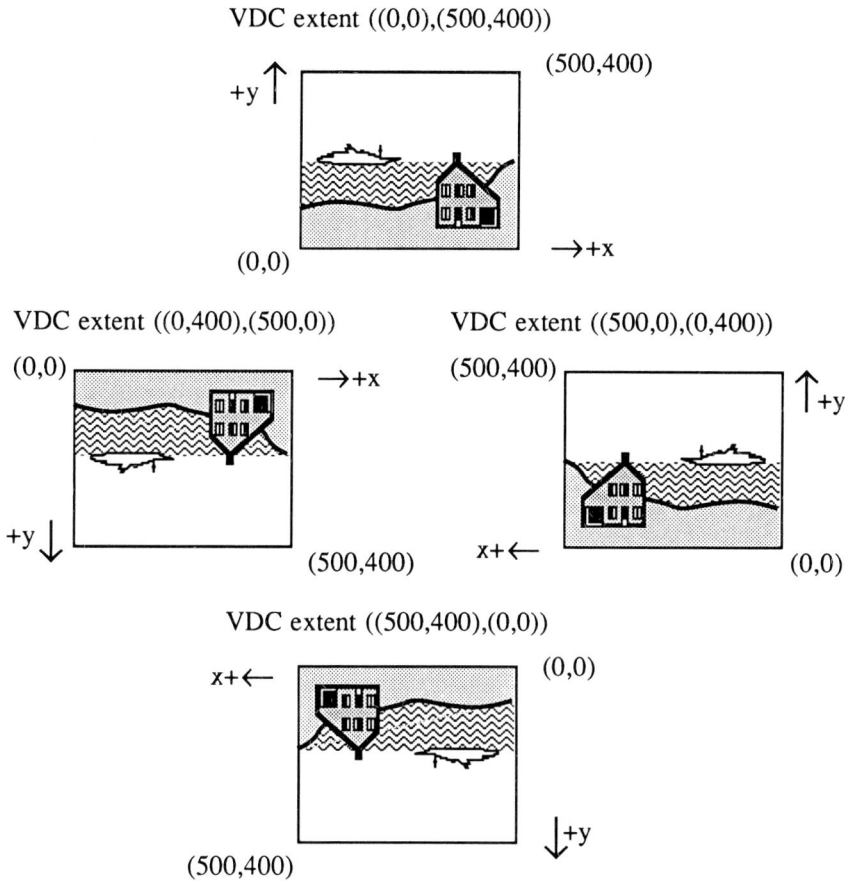

Figure 6.5 Coordinate systems arising from different VDC Extent specifications

VDC extent defines the region of interest for a picture. Whilst it is intended that the visible portion of the image should be contained within the VDC extent, the specification of values outside the range of VDC extent is permitted in CGM elements, providing of course that the values fall within the VDC range.

VDC extent is specified by the VDC EXTENT picture description element. This element has two parameters, *first-corner* and *second-corner*. As well as defining the rectangular VDC extent region, these parameters are also used to establish the sense and orientation of the VDC space in which a particular picture is embedded. For each axis, positive is defined from the first specifying point towards the second. Positive angles go from the positive x axis toward the positive y axis. Figure 6.5 illustrates the coordinate systems arising from different VDC extent specifications.

The ability to specify range, extent, sense and orientation of the VDC space provides a CGM generator with a great deal of flexibility to configure a metafile to suit particular requirements. For example, if a metafile is targeted to a specific device with a certain addressability and orientation of axes, then the metafile can in general be generated to take advantage of the characteristics of that device and so as to eliminate the need for transformation of the coordinate information when the metafile is interpreted. At first sight this might seem like a loss of device independence, however, only regular CGM elements have been used to tailor the metafile in this way and so to another CGM interpreter the picture appears just like any other picture, defined in a particular VDC coordinate space, which can be rendered on any other device, albeit after coordinate transformation.

There is one other important property of VDC space which has not yet been mentioned. VDC space may be either an *abstract space*, to be mapped to an arbitrary size on a physical device, or it may be a *metric space*, to be mapped to a particular size. The mode can be selected on a picture-by-picture basis, using the SCALING MODE element. The element has two parameters, the first indicates the mode, the second is a scale factor which specifies the number of millimetres per VDC unit when metric mode is selected.

CGM supports clipping to a single rectangular region in VDC space, specified by the CLIP RECTANGLE element. Clipping is controlled by a clipping indicator which is set to *on* or *off* by the CLIP INDICATOR element. When clipping is off, a CGM interpreter might clip the graphical output to some limit such as VDC extent or the display surface boundaries if this is needed by the devices supported by the implementation.

CGM Addendum 1 [86] provides support for picture segmentation which includes an element to specify segment transformation matrices. This is described in Section 7.3.2.

CGM provides no control (other than in metric mode) over the size and position at which a picture is displayed on a device. Elements are proposed for Addendum 1 which would provide such control:

DEVICE VIEWPORT SPECIFICATION MODE VSU-specifier, scale-factor
DEVICE VIEWPORT first-corner, second-corner
DEVICE VIEWPORT MAPPING isotropy-flag, horizontal-alignment-flag, vertical-alignment-flag

The first element determines the manner and units in which the device viewport is defined; the second specifies the device viewport. The third provides control information for the mapping of VDC to the device viewport. The VDC extent is mapped to the device viewport. The functionality contained in these elements is taken from the computer graphics interface (CGI) and is described in the next section.

6.5 The Computer Graphics Interface (CGI)

Primitives and most other coordinate data in CGI [103] are expressed in Virtual Device Coordinates (VDC), which is the same concept as VDC in CGM. CGI provides functions to control the type and precision of VDC coordinates. The sense and orientation of the axes in VDC space are controlled by a VDC EXTENT in exactly the same way as in CGM.

CGI is concerned with displaying pictures on real devices. A device viewport is defined, to which the VDC extent is mapped. This is similar to the workstation transformation though some additional control and generality is provided in CGI.

There are three ways of specifying the device viewport: as a percentage of the display surface, in millimetres with a scale factor or in physical display address units. The DEVICE VIEWPORT SPECIFICATION MODE function controls the mode setting.

In GKS, the workstation transformation is isotropic (see Section 6.3.2) and the workstation window is mapped to the largest rectangle with the same aspect ratio in the workstation viewport, in the case where the aspect ratios of workstation window and viewport differ. It is expected that the VDC extent to device viewport mapping will also be isotropic, but CGI does not mandate this. The mapping is controlled by the DEVICE VIEWPORT MAPPING function. The first parameter specifies whether an isotropic mapping is required or not. If an isotropic mapping is not specified, the mapping will map the x and y extents independently; the mapping will be linear in x and y but not necessarily the same.

In GKS, the isotropic mapping from workstation window to workstation viewport is chosen so that the bottom left hand corners of the window and viewport are co-incident. CGI allows more control than this. The largest rectangle of the correct aspect ratio is aligned in the device viewport according to independent horizontal and vertical alignment parameters. The possible values are: LEFT, CENTRE, RIGHT; BOTTOM, CENTRE, TOP. Figure 6.6 illustrates some of the effects that can be obtained. GKS corresponds to horizontal alignment LEFT and vertical alignment BOTTOM, with the isotropy flag set to FORCED.

Clipping in CGI is similar to clipping in CGM. A single CLIP RECTANGLE in VDC space can be specified: by default it is the VDC extent. CGI however specifies three modes of clipping. The mode is selected by the value of CLIP INDICATOR. The possibilities are:

(1) Clip to clip rectangle. In CGI this means to the intersection of the clip rectangle with the viewport and the physical display bounds. This ensures that no output can go beyond the physical display bounds of the view surface. This is illustrated in figure 6.7(a).

(2) Clip to *view surface*. This is illustrated in figure 6.7(b).

(3) Clipping off, which means "really-off". Devices which would be damaged by an attempt to produce output outside the device limits are unlikely to be operated in this mode.

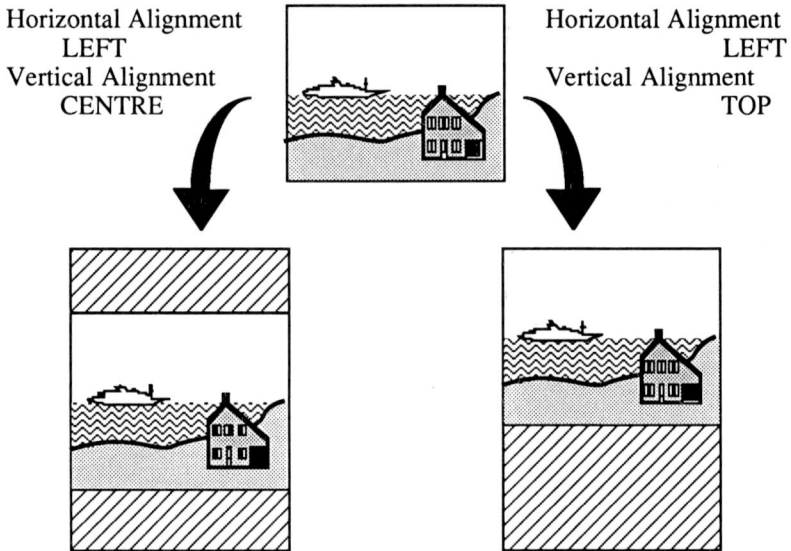

Figure 6.6 Mapping VDC picture to the display surface

The result of using the clip indicator is a definition of an effective clipping boundary. The CGI 2nd DP text [103] also includes a means to control the interaction of this with the rendering process, which calculates the area covered by a primitive from its parameterization. The control allows definition of whether clipping will be done before (LOCUS), after (SHAPE) or both before and after rendering (LOCUS THEN RENDERING). The control applies specifically to lines, markers and edges and the clipping modes for each are independent. These modes have been introduced partly to accommodate the GKS definitions of clipping actions required, which are differently specified for polyline and polymarker primitives.

6.6 3D Coordinate systems and transformations

6.6.1 Introduction

3D coordinate systems and transformations are considerably more complex than their 2D counterparts. The major addition to GKS-3D and PHIGS compared to GKS, is the *viewing pipeline* which permits different views and projections of a 3D scene to be generated.

The paper by Carlbom and Paciorek [33] is a very readable discussion of the methods of representing three-dimensional objects on a two-dimensional display surface. Such methods may attempt either to convey the general appearance of an object as in a photograph or to depict the object so that metric properties such as distances and angles can be derived. The paper describes *planar geometric projections* which are obtained by passing lines called projectors one through each point of the object and determining the image formed by the intersections of these projectors with a *projection plane*. The projectors emanate from a single point called the *centre of projection*. When this point is located at infinity, the projectors are all parallel and a *parallel projection* is obtained. A *perspective projection* results when the point is not at infinity. Perspective projections illustrate the general appearance of an object; parallel projections primarily attempt to represent metric properties.

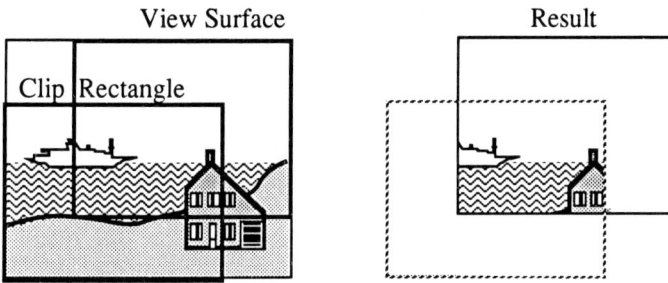

Figure 6.7(a) Clipping to Clip Rectangle

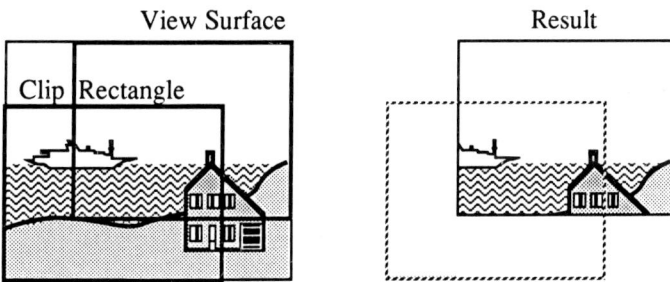

Figure 6.7(b) Clipping to View Surface

The history of the viewing transformations in GKS-3D and PHIGS is long and complicated, and will not be discussed in detail here. The major issues as always in the development of standards are what functionality is appropriate to the field of application of the standard, and how can this be provided in a manner that is both concise and convenient for users of the standard.

The starting point for viewing in GKS-3D and PHIGS was the viewing model developed in GSPC Core. This is described in [18,19,25,33].

A projection plane was defined by a point called the *view reference point* and a vector defining a normal of the plane, *the view plane normal*. The projection plane is positioned at a specified distance, the *view plane distance*, from the view reference point, perpendicular to the normal.

The "up" direction in the projection plane is specified by the *view up vector*. This direction will be vertical in the resulting projection. The view up vector and the view plane normal determine a coordinate system referred to as the UVN system.

A parallel projection is specified by a vector indicating the direction of the projectors and a perspective projection by the centre of projection which is defined relative to the view reference point.

In the first version of GKS-3D [5] the viewing pipeline was an extension of the GKS pipeline in which a viewing transformation was inserted between the normalization and workstation transformations. First a 3D normalization transformation was applied, followed by a 3D segment transformation for primitives stored in segments, and then a 3D normalization clip. A projection was then introduced after which a 3D workstation transformation was applied. Viewing was allowed to be workstation dependent. This was achieved by binding a view index to primitives as they were created. The view index was an index into a workstation dependent view bundle table which contained representations of the view indices.

The view was defined by a view reference point, view up vector and view plane normal, from which a view matrix was computed and stored in the view bundle table.

The projection mapping was defined by a projection type (parallel or perspective), a projection point or direction, view volume and view plane. The view volume was defined by six clipping planes, two parallel to the view plane at near and far distances, and four passing through the sides of the view window and projection point (for perspective transformation) or parallel to the projection direction (for parallel projection).

There was an optional clip to the view volume, which was controlled by three clipping indicators, the window clipping indicator, far clipping indicator and near clipping indicator.

It was traditional to use a right-handed coordinate system to describe the object to be viewed and a left-handed system to describe the view. After lengthy arguments it was finally agreed that in GKS-3D and PHIGS all coordinate systems would be right-handed.

From that model, the viewing pipeline contained in GKS-3D [15] and PHIGS [16] evolved.

6.6.2 GKS-3D viewing pipeline

The GKS-3D viewing pipeline is shown in figure 6.8.

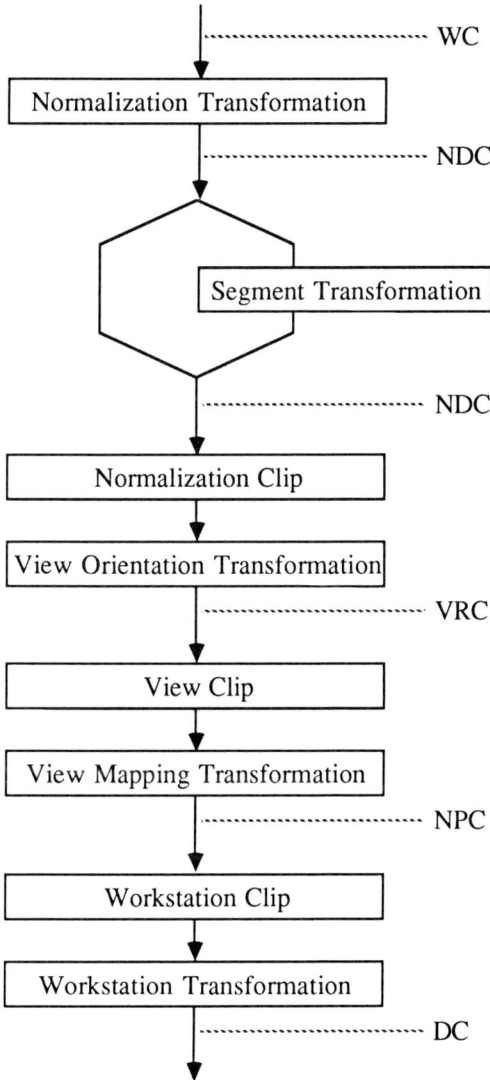

```
                                     ········· WC
        ┌──────────────────────────┐
        │ Normalization Transformation │
        └──────────────────────────┘
                                     ········· NDC

              ┌─────────────────────────┐
              │  Segment Transformation │
              └─────────────────────────┘

                                     ········· NDC
        ┌──────────────────────────┐
        │     Normalization Clip     │
        └──────────────────────────┘
        ┌──────────────────────────┐
        │ View Orientation Transformation │
        └──────────────────────────┘
                                     ········· VRC
        ┌──────────────────────────┐
        │        View Clip          │
        └──────────────────────────┘
        ┌──────────────────────────┐
        │ View Mapping Transformation │
        └──────────────────────────┘
                                     ········· NPC
        ┌──────────────────────────┐
        │     Workstation Clip       │
        └──────────────────────────┘
        ┌──────────────────────────┐
        │ Workstation Transformation │
        └──────────────────────────┘
                                     ········· DC
```

Figure 6.8 The GKS-3D viewing pipeline

Functions are provided to assist with the definition of the viewing operation. These are shown in figure 6.9. The initial NDC coordinates are changed to Viewing Coordinates by defining a View Reference Point and a set of axes associated with it. The intention is that this point has some relationship to the object to be viewed and makes the setting up of the projection transformation that much easier.

Once the Viewing Coordinates are established, Front and Back Planes are defined which specify the limits of the object to be viewed. A Projection Reference Point can be specified and a Projection Plane which allows the object to be viewed by projecting it onto the projection plane. The view window specifies that part of the projection plane to be output to the workstation. Both parallel and perspective projections are provided.

The view orientation transformation rotates the NDC coordinate system to orient the picture to correspond to the viewing direction. The view mapping transformation projects this rotated view onto the view plane. The View Reference Coordinate System (VRC) is a rotated version of NDC; the xy plane of VRC is parallel to the view plane. The view mapping converts VRC into Normalized Projection Coordinates (NPC).

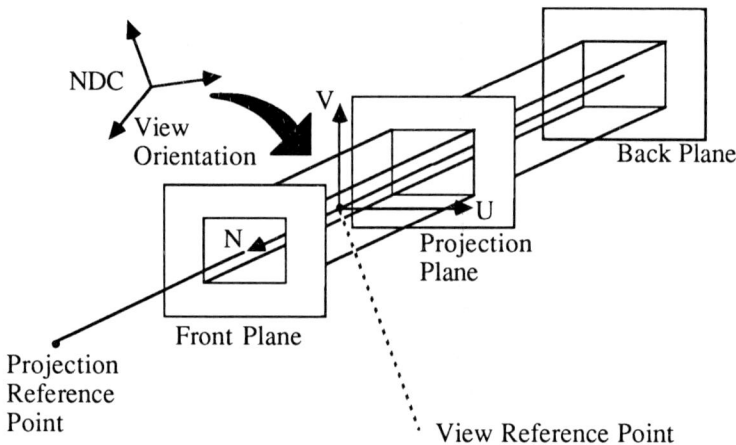

Figure 6.9(a) Parallel projection view volume

The workstation transformation converts NDC to device coordinates (DC). All the coordinate systems in GKS-3D, including DC, are 3D coordinate systems. To make this clear, some authors refer to the coordinate systems as WC3, NDC3 and DC3, but the Standard itself uses the designations WC, NDC and DC to emphasize the relationship to GKS.

The mathematics behind 3D transformations is explained in the excellent book by Penna and Patterson [66] and the tutorial by Herman [47]. The paper by Singleton [75] gives valuable guidance on implementing the pipeline and the paper by Herman *et al* [50] gives a very effective method of improving the efficiency of the pipeline based on insights from projective geometry. Some case studies in the use of GKS-3D are contained in [60].

The viewing transformation to be applied to each primitive is determined by a view index bound to the primitive when the primitive is created. Each workstation has a view bundle table which contains the viewing transformations defined on that workstation. Different views of the primitive may therefore be obtained on different workstations.

6.6.3 PHIGS viewing pipeline

Coordinates in structure elements are expressed in *modelling coordinates*. These are transformed to *world coordinates* (the PHIGS equivalent of GKS-3D's NDC3 coordinate space), by a *modelling transformation*. Thereafter the PHIGS pipeline for viewing is identical to that in GKS-3D.

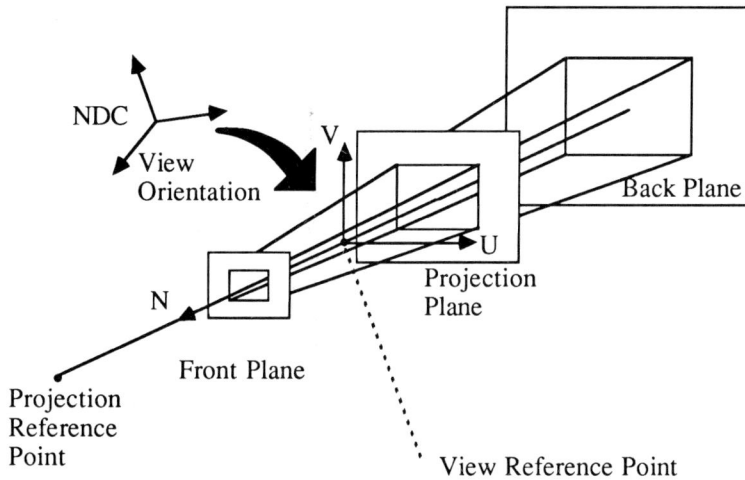

Figure 6.9(b) Perspective projection view volume

When a structure is invoked during structure traversal, it inherits a current transformation matrix from its parent, which becomes the *global modelling transformation* of the structure. This matrix can be modified by the SET GLOBAL MODELLING TRANSFORMATION function, but when the traversal returns to the parent structure its value is reset to the value initially inherited by the child.

Local modelling transformations do not affect the global transformation but are concatenated with it in the order $G.L$ to produce a composite *current transformation matrix, CTM* . Local transformation matrices, L , can be pre-concatenated ($CTM := CTM . L$), post-concatenated ($CTM := L . CTM$), or replaced ($CTM := L$). These permit local sets of axes to be used to define pictures.

PHIGS also has a very powerful modelling clip facility. An arbitrary number of half-spaces may be specified and intersected to create a convex volume to be used as a clipping volume. These half-spaces are specified in structure elements in modelling coordinates and are subject to the composite modelling transformation, and can be changed during structure traversal.

Modelling clipping is useful for selecting a portion of a complex object that is available for viewing. Because the clipping half-spaces are transformed, the same portion of, for example, a robot arm, is always visible, even when the whole object is transformed.

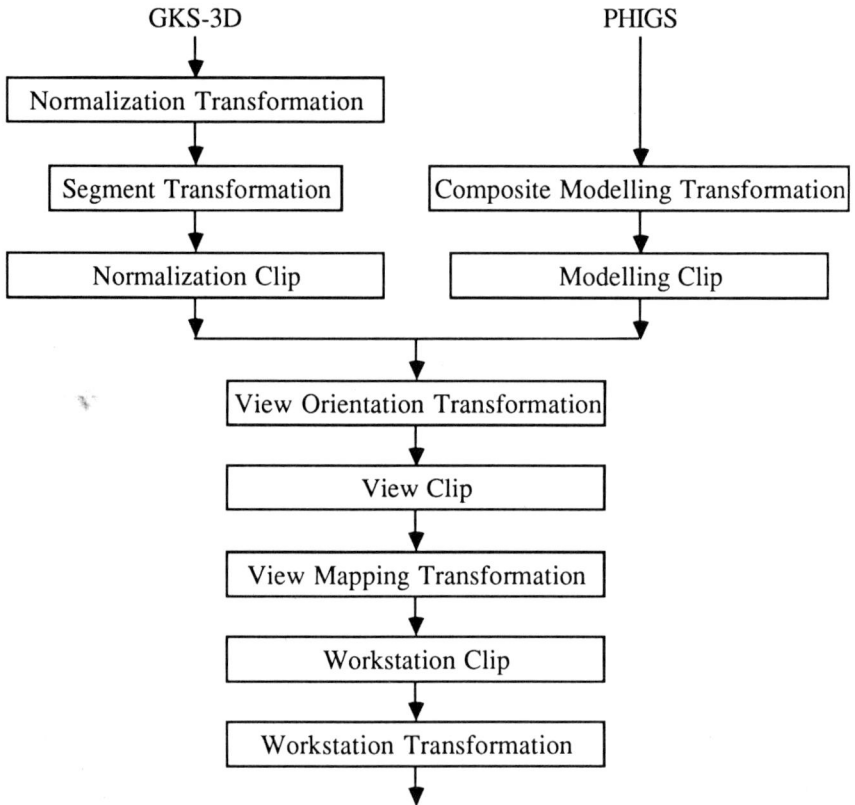

```
        GKS-3D                              PHIGS
          │                                   │
          ▼                                   │
┌─────────────────────────────┐               │
│ Normalization Transformation │              │
└─────────────────────────────┘               │
          │                                   ▼
          ▼                    ┌─────────────────────────────────────┐
┌─────────────────────────┐    │ Composite Modelling Transformation  │
│ Segment Transformation  │    └─────────────────────────────────────┘
└─────────────────────────┘               │
          │                                   ▼
┌─────────────────────────────┐    ┌─────────────────────────┐
│     Normalization Clip      │    │     Modelling Clip      │
└─────────────────────────────┘    └─────────────────────────┘
          │                                   │
          └───────────────┬───────────────────┘
                          ▼
        ┌─────────────────────────────────┐
        │ View Orientation Transformation │
        └─────────────────────────────────┘
                          │
                          ▼
        ┌─────────────────────────────────┐
        │            View Clip            │
        └─────────────────────────────────┘
                          │
                          ▼
        ┌─────────────────────────────────┐
        │    View Mapping Transformation  │
        └─────────────────────────────────┘
                          │
                          ▼
        ┌─────────────────────────────────┐
        │         Workstation Clip        │
        └─────────────────────────────────┘
                          │
                          ▼
        ┌─────────────────────────────────┐
        │   Workstation Transformation    │
        └─────────────────────────────────┘
                          │
                          ▼
```

Figure 6.10 The complete GKS-3D and PHIGS output pipelines

Although modelling clip sounds like a straightforward generalization of more restricted forms of clipping, it turns out to be very complicated. The reason is that the modelling clip is related to the modelling transformation, which is in general a projective transformation (specified by a 4×4 matrix) rather than an affine transformation (describable by a 3×4 matrix). Such transformations can give rise to singularities which require very careful treatment. In practice most modelling transformations will be affine, but PHIGS implementations have to handle the general case. Herman and Reviczky give an excellent statement of the problem in [51,84] and a solution.

The complete GKS-3D and PHIGS output pipelines are shown in figure 6.10.

7
Storage Mechanisms

7.1 Introduction

This chapter examines the storage mechanisms incorporated in the various standards. There are really three fundamental questions concerning storage mechanisms:

(1) What is being stored?
(2) What operations can be performed on storage?
(3) Why is it being stored?

The last question is in many ways the most important. A standard should have a clear reason for storing information; when this is the case, the answers to the other two questions are generally immediately apparent. When the reasons for storage have not been properly thought through, the resulting design often results in storage of information in seemingly strange states, coupled with equally strange sets of operations on the data. The major reason for storage is information re-use and the form this re-use will take needs to be carefully considered.

Two kinds of storage in graphics devices have had an influence on the design of graphics standards, not least because if information has to be stored there is an obvious argument that storage should be efficient; if information is stored in the device anyway, then it is wise to make as much use of this as possible, and not duplicate equivalent information elsewhere in the system. The kinds of storage in question are display lists in vector refresh displays and frame buffers in raster graphics devices.

7.2 Early days

GKS Version 3 [6] had an interesting structure. Graphical information could only be defined whilst a segment was open. Segments could be stored in either or both of two places, on a workstation or in a global storage called the *GKS-file*. Segments stored on a workstation could only be reused subsequently on that workstation. Segments stored in the GKS-file could be reused on other workstations. Operations were provided to transfer graphical information from the GKS-file to the application program for long-term storage and from the application program back into the GKS-file.

Graphical information could be sent to a workstation in one of two ways, either concurrently with the definition of each output primitive, or in a batched way such that all the graphical information stored in a segment was sent to the workstation for display when the segment was closed.

Segments could be made visible/invisible, detectable or highlighted. Segment transformation was also possible. There was a DELETE SEGMENT function and a function to delete the entire contents of the GKS-file.

GKS Version 3 did not have a well developed attribute binding model and it is difficult at this distance to be precise about the state in which graphical information was meant to be stored in the workstation segment storage and GKS-file. It appears that information was essentially stored in normalized device coordinates. Interestingly, the window to viewport transformation which was the equivalent of the normalization transformation in ISO GKS could not be changed whilst a segment was open.

Once a segment had been closed, it was not possible to modify the information in the segment or add more primitives to the segment.

Segmentation is also linked with pick input, again influenced by the combination of lightpen and refresh display hardware, the common basis for the more highly interactive applications of the time. Such devices would typically return a segment name as the result of pick input and this is what GKS Version 3 returned as the result.

Segmentation in Version 3 provided a single level of storage in that segments could not refer to other segments. The more advanced (and costly!) vector refresh displays of the time allowed some form of subpicturing or picture subroutine mechanism, but this idea was not adopted in GKS.

Core '77 [18] took a rather different approach. Core described the purpose of segmentation and naming (the two are linked) as "to permit application programs to modify the picture displayed on a view surface and to facilitate application program/operator interaction". Core provided a single level of segmentation (for picture modification) and an additional level of naming within segments (through a pick identifier associated with primitives) for use with the PICK input device.

Core '77 supported multiple devices through the concept of multiple view surfaces. Each device had a single view surface. Multiple view surfaces could be selected and all selected view surfaces would display the images of segments as defined by a viewing transformation. View surfaces could be neither selected nor deselected whilst there was an open segment.

Segments defined *images* which were part of the picture displayed on a view surface. The synthetic camera analogy was an important concept in Core and a segment corresponded to a snapshot of an object. Opening a segment corresponded to opening the shutter on a camera and closing a segment to closing the shutter. Application programs could specify that a segment be visible during creation, in other words, that output primitives were displayed as they were added.

Core '77 had two fundamentally different types of segments, *retained* and *non-retained*. Retained segments remained in existence until explicitly deleted; non-retained segments essentially disappeared as soon as they were closed. Non-retained segments were useful in the description of pictures, but could not be subsequently reused in any way.

Segments in Core '77 had dynamic attributes whose values could be changed anytime after the segment had been created. Segment attributes allowed the segment's image to be made invisible or visible, highlighted or non-highlighted, detectable or non-detectable. The position, orientation and size of the image could also be altered by an image transformation. Four types of retained segment were defined; retained with no image translation, retained with 2D translation, retained with arbitrary 2D transformation and retained with arbitrary 3D transformation. These types were defined in order that an implementation could choose an efficient storage format for segments.

Output primitives in segments appear to have been stored in normalized device coordinates after application of the viewing transformation. Whilst a segment was open, the viewing transformation could not be altered.

If this discussion of storage in GKS Version 3 and Core '77 seems rather vague, it is at least in part because the documents themselves are vague and do not give clear answers to two of the questions posed in Section 7.1, namely what was being stored and to a lesser extent, why it was being stored.

At this distance in time, the Editorial Board Report [46] on Core '77 and GKS Version 3 makes interesting reading. The DIN representatives argued that the concept of a Core segment was the same as the concept of a segment on a workstation. The GKS-file was seen by them as a form of storage not supported by the Core. It effectively allowed the user to manage the flow of traffic around the system because segments in the GKS-file could be copied onto workstations and transferred to the application for long-term storage. A number of recommendations of the Editorial Board effectively suggested that there should be a filing system for graphical objects at a high level in the system which should be independent of the segment structure. GKS Version 3 effectively used the GKS-file as a means of supporting multiple devices; the Editorial Board took the view that multiple devices should be supported at levels below the GKS-file.

In the terminology of the reference model in Chapter 3 of this book, the Editorial Board were effectively saying that they saw the need for storage at the application level in a graphics system as well as at the virtual level.

There was also a discussion around segment storage *per se* also. Segment storage was understood to be storage for pictures rather than storage for objects, in other words, storage at a lower level in the system than the application level. By the time of the Editorial Board meeting, GSPC's philosophy on non-retained data had altered somewhat from Core

'77. The idea of non-retained segments had been dropped in favour of allowing output primitives to be created and viewed outside segments, though it was noted that this decision might change again in the future. Recommendations on segments included:

(1)   GKS should have a 'rename segment' function.

(2)   It should be possible to output primitives to more than one view surface with different pen representations (bundle representations in later terminology) without using the GKS-file system.

(3)   GKS should consider a second level of naming in segments.

(4)   There should be a mechanism for creating invisible segments and subsequently making them visible. Version 3 did not allow the attributes of the open segment to be changed, whereas Core '77 did.

The Editorial Board recommendations were incorporated in Version 5.2 of GKS [8]. This version included the multiple workstation concept which addressed (2) above. The GKS-file concept *per se* disappeared. A special workstation, called *workstation independent segment store* was introduced. The contents of segments stored on this workstation could be inserted into the open segment.

Segment storage was a major area of discussion at the Abingdon WG2 meeting in October 1981 which led to the production of the GKS DP text. Discussion centred around the three questions posed at the start of this chapter. The resulting model is described in the next section. The model went a long way in clarifying what is stored in segments, by clearly relating segments to the output pipeline. The issue of application level storage distinct from other levels of storage was lost, but is one of the central design concepts in PHIGS. CGI later took up the issue of physical layer storage in its provision of raster functionality.

The following sections look at storage in the current standards under the headings of:

•   Virtual level storage
•   Application level storage
•   Physical level storage

This seemingly illogical order has been adopted because it is easier to explain PHIGS after GKS.

7.3 Virtual level storage

7.3.1 GKS and GKS-3D

ISO 7942 GKS [13] allows output to be sent to multiple workstations. Workstations may be in one of three states — OPEN, ACTIVE or CLOSED.

The functions OPEN WORKSTATION and CLOSE WORKSTATION set workstations into the OPEN and CLOSED states respectively. The

functions   ACTIVATE   WORKSTATION   and   DEACTIVATE
WORKSTATION set an OPEN workstation into state ACTIVE and an
ACTIVE workstation into state OPEN respectively.

Leaving aside segment storage for the moment, output primitives are
displayed on all the ACTIVE workstations. Distribution of primitives to
workstations occurs at a point in the pipeline after the normalization
transformation has been applied and attributes have been bound from the
current values held in a data structure called the *GKS State List*. The
geometry of the primitive is in NDC space. If the bundled mode of
specification of aspects is being used, the aspect values are obtained from the
workstation dependent bundle tables held in a data structure called the
Workstation State List. The primitive is transformed by the workstation
transformation and rendered on the workstation's display surface. This is
illustrated in figure 7.1.

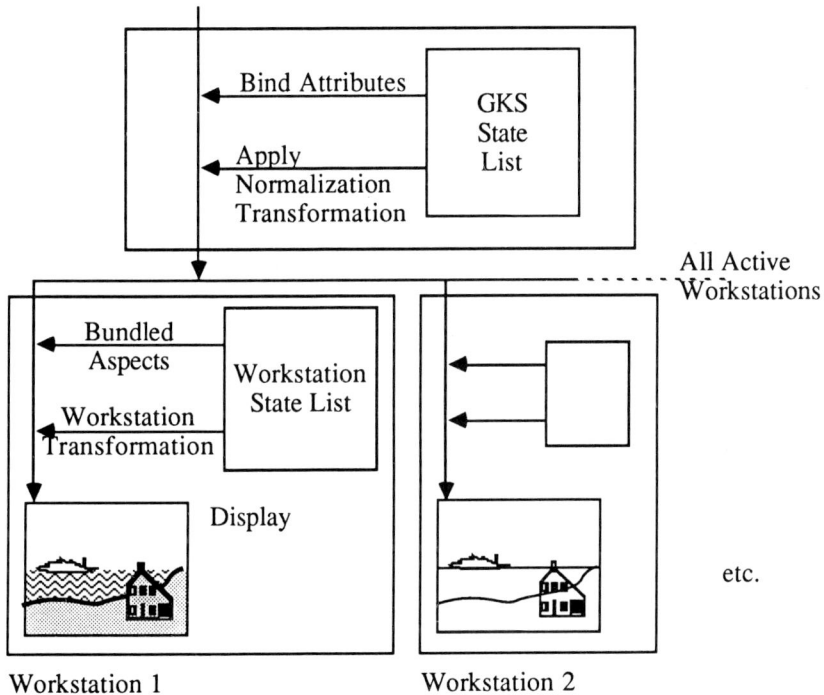

Figure 7.1 Association of bundled attributes on multiple workstations

This is the basic structure in GKS which allows primitives to be output to
multiple display surfaces and for the application to tailor their appearance
taking into account the capabilities of each particular workstation (through
setting different bundle table entries on each workstation). It is in this
framework that segment storage is added.

There are two kinds of segment storage, *workstation dependent segment storage* (WDSS) and *workstation independent segment storage* (WISS). WDSS is considered first.

Segments in GKS are collections of primitives in NDC space with attributes bound to them. Workstations (optionally) have an associated WDSS. The function CREATE SEGMENT creates a new empty segment with a specified name in the WDSSs of all the ACTIVE workstations. Subsequently created output primitives are stored in the segment in all the WDSSs whilst the segment remains open. The function CLOSE SEGMENT closes the open segment. Only one segment may be open at a time and the activation state of a workstation may not be changed whilst a segment is open. This latter condition ensures that a segment with a given name has the same contents in each of the WDSSs in which it is held. Once closed, a segment cannot be re-opened.

Operations on WDSS include RENAME, DELETE SEGMENT FROM WORKSTATION and DELETE SEGMENT (which deletes a segment from all the WDSSs in which it is stored).

A second level of naming is provided, following the Core approach. Primitives have an associated PICK IDENTIFIER attribute which is returned to the application program by the PICK logical input device together with the name of the segment in which the primitive picked is stored. This allows an application to set up a structured name space for primitives, allowing a fine degree of control over the information returned when the operator picks something on the display surface.

So far, segments have been presented as a mechanism for structuring NDC pictures, and their utility in connection with pick input has been hinted at. This is not the only use of segments however. Other uses arise from the attributes associated with segments. Segments have five attributes:

(1)   segment transformation;

(2)   visibility;

(3)   highlighting;

(4)   segment priority;

(5)   detectability.

Segment transformation is a general 2-dimensional transformation that is applied to the segment before it is subjected to the workstation transformation. This transformation applies to all the primitives in the segment and may specify a combination of rotation, scaling, shearing and shifting. *Visibility* allows segments on a workstation to be either invisible or visible. An invisible segment is not displayed and its primitives cannot be selected by PICK input. *Highlighting* causes a segment to stand out on a workstation to attract the operator's attention. The precise method of highlighting (blinking etc.) is left to the implementor to decide. Segment priority indicates which of several segments should appear in the foreground if they overlap in NDC space. *Segment priority* is also used to decide which primitive should be identified in pick input if primitives in segments with differing priorities overlap. *Detectability* defines whether or not the contents of a segment are sensitive to pick input.

Segment attributes are global in the sense that the values of the attributes of a segment are the same for each workstation in whose WDSS the segment is stored. The framework is illustrated in figure 7.2.

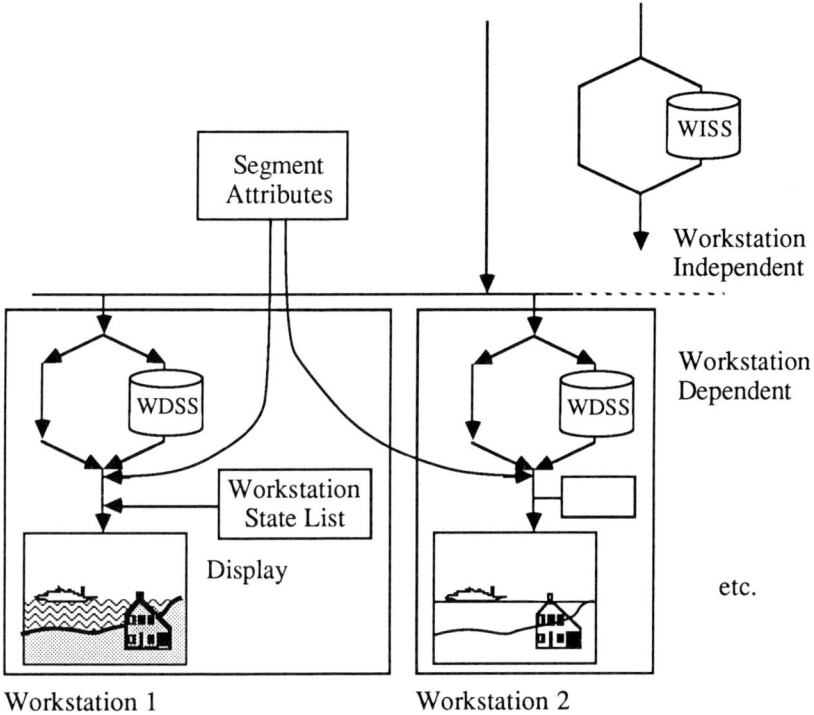

Figure 7.2 Segment attributes apply globally

Segment attributes give added power to the segment mechanism in that parts of pictures can now be moved around in NDC space, made selectively visible or invisible, highlighted, and made sensitive to pick input. These facilities are genuinely useful in constructing interactive application programs.

There is one limitation which is worth a brief mention. As will be seen in Chapter 8, LOCATOR input is returned to the application program in world coordinates. Segment transformations are not taken into account in this. There are strong arguments that segment transformations in the output pipeline have nothing to do with the relationship between device coordinates and world coordinates in the input pipeline. However, it does mean that the application has to be careful in giving positional hints to the operator using output involving segments, otherwise the position returned may not be quite what the application expected!

WDSS as presented enables primitives to be structured and manipulated in certain ways. There are, however, some "obvious" manipulations that are missing, for example, it is not possible to move or copy a segment defined on one workstation to another; nor is it possible to use segment storage as a symbol facility. One cannot define a resistor as a segment and then display multiple instances of the resistor in different places in NDC. Equally it is not possible to define a red resistor in one place and a blue one in another. Given the place segment storage occupies in the pipeline, there is considerable argument as to what facilities are appropriate at that level and what belongs to higher or lower levels. There can be a fine distinction between structuring mechanisms which are basically modelling, and structuring mechanisms used to achieve picture compression (typically so that it will fit into a display file!) at lower levels. The argument is not developed here, however it is an argument that continues to occupy the minds of those involved in standardization activities.

Some of the functionality mentioned in the previous paragraph is provided by the second type of segment storage in GKS, Workstation Independent Segment Storage, WISS.

WISS is treated as a special kind of workstation, which has a segment store, but no display surface. An implementation has at most one WISS. If WISS is OPEN and ACTIVE when a segment is created, then the segment will be stored in WISS. Segment attributes apply to segments in WISS, just as to segments in WDSS. What makes WISS different is the operations that are available for segments stored in WISS that are not available for segments stored in WDSS. There are three such operations provided by the functions ASSOCIATE SEGMENT WITH WORKSTATION, COPY SEGMENT TO WORKSTATION and INSERT SEGMENT.

ASSOCIATE SEGMENT WITH WORKSTATION copies a specified segment from WISS into the WDSS of a specified workstation. The effect is as if the workstation were active when the segment was created. COPY SEGMENT TO WORKSTATION applies the segment transformation to the primitives in a specified segment and sends the results to the specified workstation as a collection of primitives outside segments. The primitives are not stored in a segment on the specified workstation.

INSERT SEGMENT applies the segment transformation to the primitives in a specified segment. Another general 2D transformation specified as a parameter to INSERT SEGMENT is then applied. The resulting primitives are sent to all ACTIVE workstations. If there is no open segment, the primitives will be displayed on each ACTIVE workstation as primitives outside segments. If there is an open segment, the primitives will be stored in the open segment. Attributes of the inserted segment other than the segment transformation are ignored.

WISS functionality does give some useful capabilities, though INSERT SEGMENT is often criticized for offering inadequate modelling capability at an inappropriate level in the system.

Some of the issues in implementing segment storage are discussed in the paper by Duce and Hopgood [39].

GKS-3D has the same model of segment storage as GKS; the segment and insert transformations are generalized to 3D affine transformations, and 3D primitives are stored in segments.

7.3.2 CGM

CGM ISO 8632 does not provide any capabilities for structuring pictures in terms of segments. However a segment capability is proposed for incorporation in Addendum 1 to CGM [86].

Graphical primitive elements, attribute setting elements and certain control elements can be grouped together, between BEGIN SEGMENT and END SEGMENT, into segments. Two types of segments are defined, *local* and *global*. Local segments are defined in picture bodies and can only be referenced from the picture body which contains the definitions. Global segments on the other hand, are defined in the metafile descriptor part of the metafile and can be referenced by any of the pictures in the metafile. These scope rules have been chosen to minimize the amount of a particular metafile that has to be interpreted in order to interpret individual pictures. If segments could appear anywhere, the worst case would require interpretation of the entire metafile in order to find the definition of any particular segment.

Local segments are a part of the picture in which they are defined, in other words when the picture description is interpreted the primitives stored in the segments will be displayed. The contents of global segments are only displayed if explicitly copied into a picture by the COPY SEGMENT element, which is equivalent to inserting the primitives of the referenced segment into the picture description at the point at which the element occurs.

The parameters of COPY SEGMENT are the segment identifier of the segment to be copied (which may be either a global or a local segment), a copy transformation matrix and a segment transformation application flag. The copy transformation is applied to all primitive elements before they are copied. The segment transformation application flag determines whether or not the transformation specified by the segment's segment transformation attribute is also applied to primitives in the segment during the copy operation. Normally the attributes associated with primitives in segments are copied with the primitives. However there is an INHERITANCE FILTER element that allows the current values of specified attributes to be associated with primitives, rather than the values set in the segment.

CGM segments have four segment attributes:

(1) transformation;
(2) highlighting;
(3) display priority;
(4) pick priority.

The attributes of a segment can only be set whilst the segment is open and only before the first primitive is inserted into the segment. Segment attributes cannot be changed thereafter.

These facilities and restrictions are entirely in accord with the purpose of CGM which is static picture capture. It will be seen that these capabilities are not adequate for the dynamic audit-trail type metafile capability provided by Annex E of GKS, for example in GKS segment transformation can be changed after primitives have been inserted into a segment. An Addendum to GKS is being processed [14] which further extends CGM to allow dynamic picture capture. This is based on CGM Addendum 1 with the addition of a small number of new elements (for example SEGMENT VISIBILITY) and with some of the above mentioned restrictions on the order of occurrence of elements removed. Some elements, for example the segment attribute elements, are given the GKS meanings rather than the CGM Addendum 1 meanings.

The purist is likely to object to the perversion of the clean concept of static picture capture in this way, but this is just one example of what happens when ideas and understanding develop at different rates, and there is no overall reference model to guide the development. The unifying threads that run through these extensions to CGM are the encoding schemes. The extensions have all been incorporated within the framework provided by the three standardized encoding schemes (see Chapter 10).

7.3.3 CGI

Segment store in the CGI 2nd DP [103] allows groups of graphic objects to be stored and manipulated. Segment store is located at a similar place in the pipeline to segment store in GKS, that is after primitive attributes and clipping rectangles have been bound to primitives, but before bundled aspects are bound and before rendering and the VDC to device mapping are applied.

The segment manipulation functions are similar to the functions in GKS: creation, deletion, renaming and copying. Unlike GKS, segments may be reopened after being closed and additional objects may be appended to the end of the segment, but objects already in the segment cannot be modified or deleted.

Segments have six attributes:

(1) highlighting;

(2) visibility;

(3) detectability;

(4) display priority;

(5) pick priority;

(6) transformation.

Segment attributes can be modified as in GKS.

CGI provides a COPY SEGMENT operation. The COPY SEGMENT element in CGM Addendum 1 derived from this operation. If there is a segment open at the time of a COPY SEGMENT then the contents of the specified segment are copied into the open segment. If there is no segment open, the copied objects are rendered immediately as non-retained data. The copy operation has an associated copy transformation and segment transformation application flag, which behave in a similar way to the corresponding parameters of the CGM COPY SEGMENT element described in the previous section.

There is also an inheritance filter mechanism which determines which properties of primitives (clipping rectangle, attributes etc.) are copied unchanged by the copy operation and which are replaced by the appropriate current values from the corresponding CGI current state. In terms of the attribute/control distinction made in Section 5.5.4 the copy operation creates new graphic objects with fixed attributes. These attributes are either copied from the original segment with the definition of the graphic objects geometry, or taken from the current settings with the choice determined by the inheritance filter. The DIS text is expected to include a switch to determine how the clip rectangles from the old segment definition are combined with the currently set values, allowing either replacement (as required for GKS support) or composition.

CGI caters for a wider variety of needs than just a GKS driver and allows a more complex control structure governing when segment redrawing takes place, for example. It is inappropriate to enter into the details of that here. As noted above there are also richer facilities in the area of clipping control and the behaviour of clipping rectangles under copy transformations, but again this is beyond the scope of this book, and the exact details will in any case be changed in the DIS text. There is a general philosophy in CGI that emerges here, namely that if some behaviour might be required in some circumstances, then provide that behaviour, but allow it to be turned on or off under the control of a mode flag.

7.4 Application level storage

The comments of the Editorial Board on the need for a file structure or object storage above the level of picture or virtual storage were taken up in the PHIGS standard, ISO 9592, and this is a key concept in this standard. PHIGS is aimed at applications with requirements for rapid modification of graphical data that describe geometrically related objects.

In PHIGS, the creation and display of a picture are very explicitly independent phases. At the heart of PHIGS is a *centralized structure store* (CSS) which is available to all workstations. Graphics is generated from the CSS by a process called *traversal*.

A *structure* consists of a sequence of *structure elements* (the order is important; two structures containing identical elements but in a different order will not necessarily generate the same graphical output). Structure elements are the fundamental units of data in structures and represent entities such as output primitives, attributes and transformations.

Structures may contain invocations of other structures stored in CSS. This is achieved by using the 'execute structure' element, which during traversal causes processing of the current structure to be interrupted whilst the named structure (and its descendants) is traversed. Structures may thus be organized as networks, though structure networks may not be recursive as there is no control mechanism in PHIGS that would allow the recursion to be terminated.

To represent the wheels on a car only one wheel structure is needed which is instanced four times. The robot arm is a favourite example of a hierarchical structure. A representation as a PHIGS hierarchy is given in [60]. The arm can be moved about the elbow joint, say, and the lower arm, wrist and grippers will move accordingly. This is achieved using modelling transformations. The modelling transformation which controls movement about the elbow joint is set in the structure which represents the elbow joint and then propagates down the hierarchy to affect the lower arm, wrist and grippers. The design of hierarchies and transformation systems which behave in the correct manner turns out to be a rather difficult task.

PHIGS does not have the concept of workstation activation and deactivation. Instead, a structure network is viewed on a particular workstation by explicitly *posting* the root of the structure network to the workstation. Posting a structure to a workstation causes the structure network to be traversed.

Traversal can be thought of in several ways and implemented in more [20,58]. One way to *think* of traversal is to think of it as a process associated with each posted structure network. The traversal process extracts structures from the CSS and interprets the structure elements, generating graphical output on the workstations to which the structure network is posted.

To explain traversal, a traversal state list is introduced. This state list is similar in concept to the GKS state list of GKS, but unlike that state list, the values of entries in the traversal state list cannot be inquired. Interpretation of attribute setting structure elements such as set polyline index and transformation structure elements set corresponding entries in the traversal state list. Interpretation of an output primitive structure element such as polyline is accomplished as follows. The data in the structure element are transformed by the composite modelling transformation to WC and the polyline is clipped by the modelling clip. The appropriate polyline attributes are bound from the traversal state list and the resulting primitive is sent to all workstations to which the structure is posted. On each workstation the view and workstation transformations and clipping are applied and aspect values from the bundle representations are bound as necessary. The resulting object is displayed.

When an execute structure element is interpreted, the current traversal state list is saved and the executed structure, or child structure, is then traversed. The child structure inherits the traversal state list from the structure by which it was called. Subsequent attribute and transformation setting structure elements only affect the traversal state list associated with the child. When traversal of the child structure is completed, the traversal state list of the parent is restored to the values in force before traversal of the child structure began. Changing attributes and transformations within the child thus has no effect on the parent. The overall system structure is illustrated in figure 7.3.

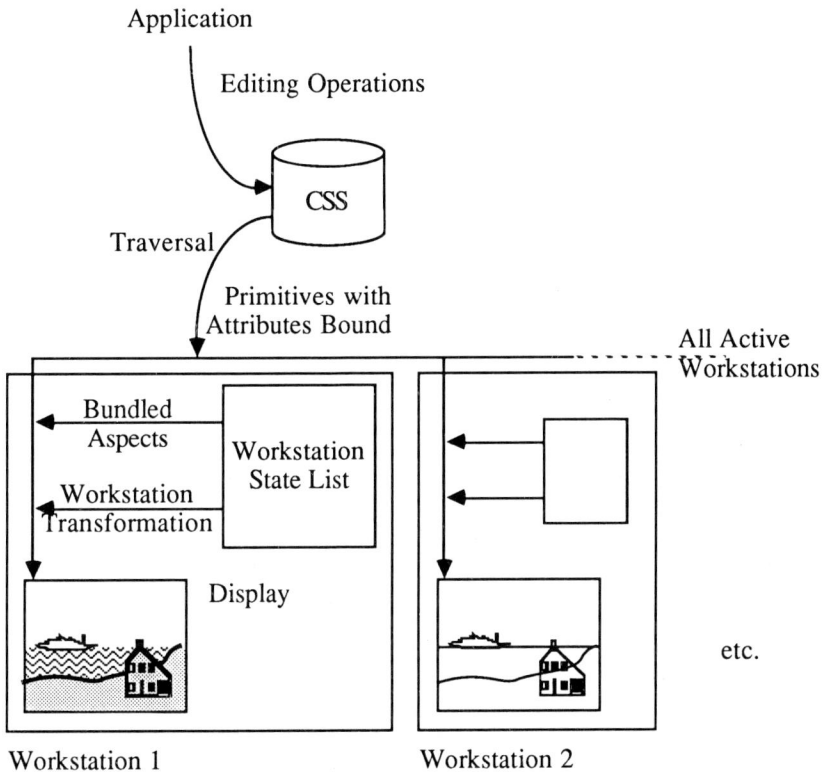

Figure 7.3 Traversal time binding of attributes

PHIGS structures do not have attributes. The entities visibility, highlighting and detectability are handled in a more flexible way through the ideas of *name sets* and *filters*. All primitives in PHIGS have a NAME SET attribute, which as the name suggests consists of a set of application supplied names. Each workstation has an invisibility filter and highlighting filter and each PICK input device has an associated pick filter. A filter consists of a pair of sets of names, called the *inclusion set* and *exclusion set*.

A primitive possesses the property controlled by a filter if the primitive's NAME SET attribute has at least one name in common with the inclusion set of the filter and no names in common with the exclusion set. This is a very flexible control scheme.

Editing operations manipulate the CSS. One structure may be opened for editing at a time. There is an element pointer associated with the open structure. New structure elements are inserted at the position pointed to by the element pointer or replace the structure element pointed to by the element pointer. Structure elements can be deleted. Labels can be placed in structures and used in editing operations. The application program therefore manipulates CSS, effectively building a model in the CSS to be viewed by the workstations.

Traversal is conceptually a continuous process which keeps the display of each workstation up-to-date with the contents of the CSS. Thus if the CSS is changed by editing its contents, the changes are immediately reflected on the open workstations. In some architectures this could be inefficient and difficult to achieve and PHIGS therefore defines a complex mechanism to allow the application some degree of control over when and how updating takes place. These mechanisms are beyond the scope of this introduction.

7.5 Physical level storage

7.5.1   Introduction

The incorporation of raster functionality into standards proposals really begins with the Core '79 report [19] which includes a report from the Raster and Color Sub-group of GSPC. The suggestions incorporated there were never actually published in an integrated fashion with the main body of the Core proposal. The '79 report acknowledges that "some future work of the two subcommittees will address these issues," but the results of any discussion that took place have never received wide circulation. However although these were the first suggestions for raster functionality, in the context of this section the most interesting parts are the decisions reported on issues related to storage and manipulation of raster images.

For example it was decided that operations on a raster refresh buffer should not be supported on the grounds that devices with buffers available to the programmer were not universally available and that incorporation of features which relied on the availability of raster storage would therefore render the standard device-dependent. An issue related to the mixing of colours was also resolved such that Core should not support such operations – the closest there appears to have been to consideration of drawing modes (see Section 7.5.3), or logical and/or arithmetic operations, on pixel contents. Thus although the Core report did begin to address the needs for support of raster graphics the only standards project to address the needs of storage and manipulation of raster images began in 1981 with the ANSI X3H3 project on the Virtual Device Interface/Virtual Device Metafile (VDI/VDM). Subsequently this project split into the CGM and CGI projects, the later being brought into the ISO arena in 1985, bringing with it the Raster Part.

The Raster functionality of the CGI [103] provides the facilities to allow the client to create, store, manipulate, and display images defined as sets of pixels. Bitmaps provide a second point in the CGI pipeline (below segmentation – see Section 7.3.3) at which a snapshot of the graphics data, at a particular level of refinement, can be kept and manipulated. It represents a level of storage in the physical level in terms of the reference model outlined in Chapter 3. At this stage many more of the indirect references implied in the functions used in the CGI's client interface have been resolved to define the visible aspects of the primitives. For example, by the time the definition of a polyline is stored in a bitmap, the information available at the CGI/client interface about the current settings of linewidth, etc., have been turned into instructions to set particular pixels in the bitmap.

7.5.2 Representation of storage of bitmaps

The basic units of the raster part are the *pixel* and rectangular arrangements of pixels known as *bitmaps*. The client may define both *full-depth* bitmaps and *mapped* bitmaps. A full-depth bitmap matches the physical characteristics of the physical device in use, in terms of number of bits per pixel and physical dimensions of each pixel. A CGI implementation supporting raster functionality contains one or more displayable bitmaps, which are full depth. There is currently debate as to whether or not clients should be allowed to create displayable bitmaps, although the current text does not allow it (figure 7.4).

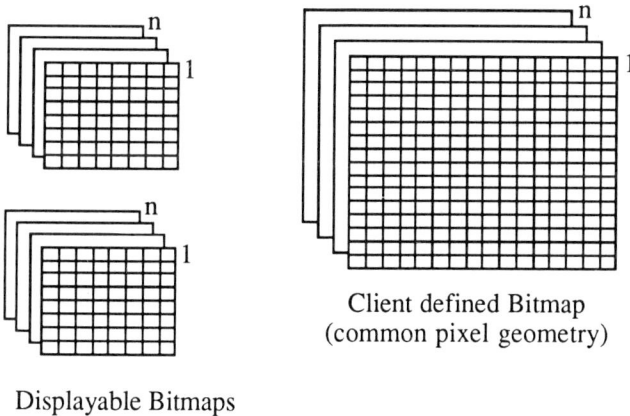

Client defined Bitmap
(common pixel geometry)

Displayable Bitmaps

Figure 7.4 Types of bitmap

The mapped bitmap has only one bit per pixel and any pixel can therefore represent only two colours. When drawing into a mapped bitmap any pixels which would have been set as the currently defined AUXILIARY COLOUR are stored as zeros (background pixels) and all other colours as ones (foreground pixels). The MAPPED BITMAP FOREGROUND COLOUR is then used as the colour in which the foreground pixels are defined when the mapped bitmaps contents are read (figure 7.5).

Bitmaps are defined (using the CREATE BITMAP function) by the CGI client requesting a bitmap suitable for representing a particular portion of VDC space, under the current drawing bitmap's VDC to DC mapping. This defines the position in DC and the number of pixels in x and y required to hold the contents of the region requested. The VDC to DC mapping is stored with the bitmap and may be altered at any time when the bitmap has been selected as the current drawing bitmap. This does not alter the number of pixels in the bitmap but does affect the placement in the bitmap of subsequently drawn primitives. No two bitmaps share common physical memory. Client defined bitmaps may also be deleted.

7.5.3 Drawing and display using bitmaps

A bitmap can be selected as the destination for graphics primitives, by using the SELECT DRAWING BITMAP function. Drawing then follows the same rules as for a display surface but treating the bitmap as the display surface, although there will be no visible effect unless the bitmap in question is also the currently selected displayable bitmap. Each primitive is combined with the pixels of the drawing bitmap according to a pixel-by-pixel logical, arithmetic or comparative combination operation, specified by the setting of the DRAWING MODE.

In a system supporting the raster part of the CGI, a displayable bitmap is a full-depth bitmap, which can be directly tied to the display mechanism. There is at least one displayable bitmap and there may be more. The client can choose which of the displayable bitmaps is actually being shown on the display using the DISPLAY BITMAP function. There is no provision in the current CGI model for the client of a CGI system which supports the raster part to route graphics data directly to the display, by-passing the bitmap storage. This is however assumed to be possible (conceptually) for echos of input actions, which are not stored in any bitmap.

7.5.4 Bitmap manipulations

These functions are of two types: functions which move blocks of the image data around, and functions which control the pixel combinations performed during these moves.

There are three functions of the first type:

- SOURCE DESTINATION BITBLT (figure 7.6)
- TILE THREE OPERAND BITBLT (figure 7.7)
- PIXEL ARRAY

Mapped Bitmaps are one bit deep and mapped:-

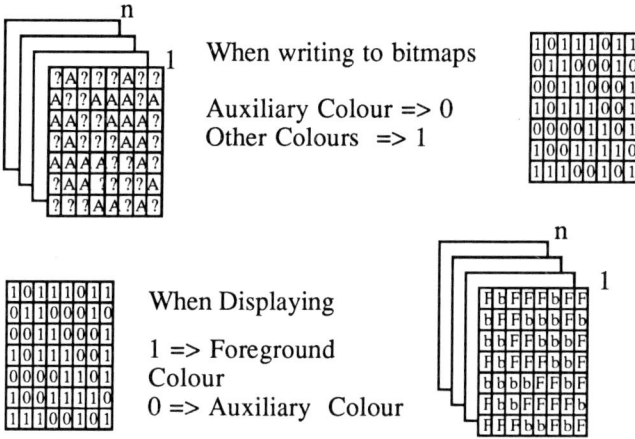

When writing to bitmaps

Auxiliary Colour => 0
Other Colours => 1

When Displaying

1 => Foreground
Colour
0 => Auxiliary Colour

Figure 7.5 Writing to, and displaying from, mapped bitmaps

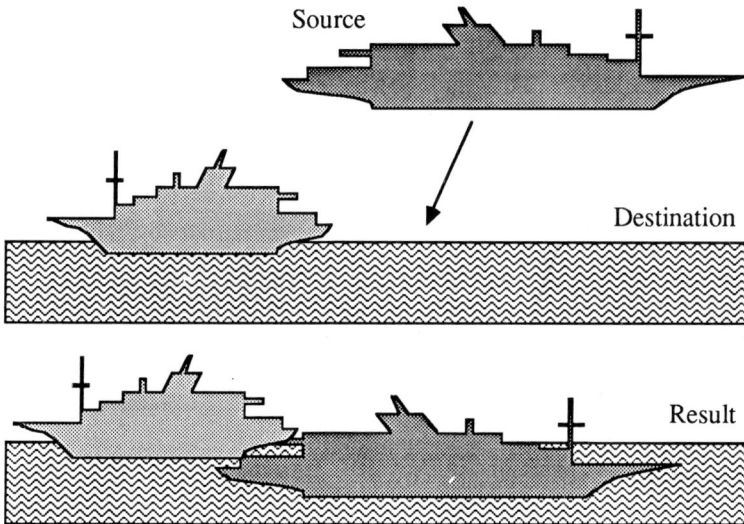

Source

Destination

Result

Figure 7.6 Typical two operand bitblt (source destination bitblt)

All of the above functions support the movement and combination of rectangular pieces of bitmaps in memory. For the source destination BitBlt a rectangular source array of pixels is combined with a region of the same dimensions in the currently selected drawing bitmap, according to a logical, arithmetic or comparative operation specified as a parameter to the function.

The PIXEL ARRAY function is regarded as a source destination BitBlt where the source is a data structure in the client's address space and the pixel-by-pixel combination operation is specified by the currently selected DRAWING MODE.

For the three operand BitBlt there are two source pixel arrays, which play different roles. The first operand is called the pattern and is repeated as required to cover the whole of the destination region. The second operand matches the destination area in size (number of pixels). Any pixel values of AUXILIARY COLOUR in this second source are used in controlling transparency. If transparency is set to TRANSPARENT those pixels in the destination bitmap where the equivalent source pixel has the value of AUXILIARY COLOUR are not affected by the BitBlt operation. There are 256 potential logical combinations of the bits in the three pixels.

Source

Pattern

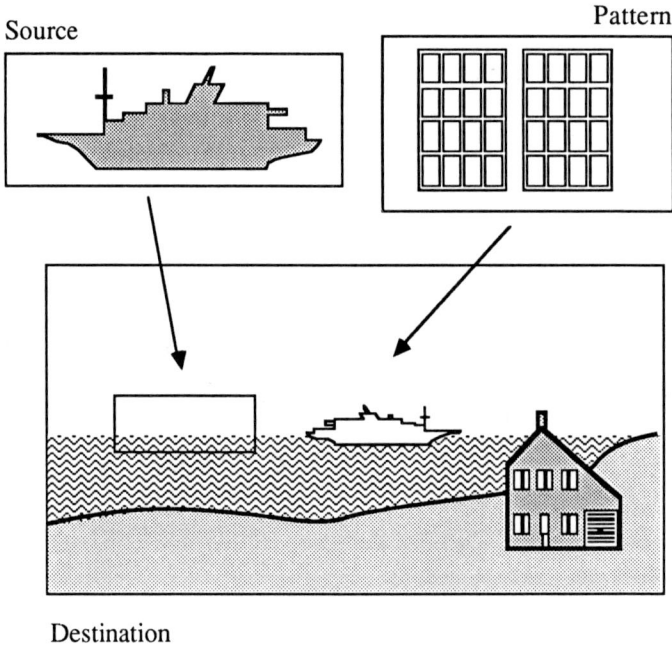

Destination

Figure 7.7(a) Typical set of operands to a three operand bitblt

Figure 7.7(b) Possible result of the three operand bitblt

TRANSPARENCY is specified in Part 3 of the CGI. Its effect is that, where the source in the two operand BitBlt, or the second source in the three operand BitBlt, have the value of the background colour, then, if *transparent* is set, the destination pixel is unaffected. If the setting is *opaque*, all pixels are treated identically.

7.5.5 BITMAP interior style

The Raster part includes a further interior style (BITMAP) for use with filled area primitives. This interior style involves filling the interior of the filled area with a repeated pattern from a bitmap. The contents of this bitmap may well have been previously defined by the CGI client. To use this facility a function has to be provided by the CGI to allow the client to specify the FILL BITMAP's identifier.

8
Input Primitives and Modes

8.1 Introduction

This chapter considers the approaches taken to graphical input in GKS, GKS-3D, PHIGS and CGI. One of the unifying features of this collection of standards is the common input model that they share. Before describing the model it is useful to look at some of the background to its development. The chapter concludes with a short discussion of some of the limitations of this model and points to some of the directions currently being considered for its extension in future revisions of the standards.

It was a design criterion of GKS that application programs should be portable from one device environment to another without requiring major changes to the program's structure. This criterion leaves open the possibility of supplying, say, different parameter values to initialization functions, in order to tailor the application to a new environment. Satisfying this criterion is made difficult by the wide variety of kinds of input devices available. These include keyboards, dials, touch panels, lightpens, tablets, joysticks, tracker balls, mice and gloves.

Some kind of abstraction away from the peculiarities of physical device hardware has to be found in order to achieve device independence. In the case of graphical input, the key to abstraction lies in the types of input values returned by the different types of physical input devices. Such thinking led to the idea of *virtual* or *logical input devices*. The essence of the idea appeared in a paper in 1968 by Newman [64]; the concept was elaborated in a series of articles by Cotton [35], Wallace and Foley [43] and Wallace [79]. The idea is that the application program has available a range of virtual input devices, the only visible aspect of which is the type of value returned. Five basic classes were identified: *locator* to indicate a position, *pick* to select a displayed entity, *valuator* to input a single real number, *keyboard* to input a character string and *button* to select from a set of possible alternative actions and choices.

For each class of logical input device, there is a natural physical device, for example the natural pick device is a lightpen, for a valuator it is a potentiometer, for locator a tablet. However, any of the logical input device types can be simulated by (almost) any physical device, for example a keyboard could be used to type in the value of the coordinates to be returned by a locator device, or a tablet with keyboard overlay could be used to emulate a keyboard device.

The next section looks at how this idea has evolved and been incorporated in the present graphics standards.

8.2 History

8.2.1 GKS version 3

The earliest version of GKS which exists in English translation is GKS Version 3 [6], produced by the DIN editors in November 1978. Five types of logical input device were provided corresponding to five classes of input primitives:

(1) LOCATOR: providing positions in user coordinates. User coordinates in version 3 were roughly equivalent to world coordinates in GKS ISO 7942, but only a single normalization transformation could exist at any time (see Section 6.2.2).

(2) VALUATOR: providing real numbers in the range (0,1).

(3) CHOICE: providing integer numbers specifying alternatives.

(4) PICK: providing names of segments.

(5) TEXT: providing a character string.

Input devices were associated with workstations. Different workstations could provide input devices of different classes. A fully equipped workstation had one input device for each class of input primitives. There was no requirement that all five classes had to be available at a particular workstation. Each workstation description table contained a list of the primitives available on that workstation.

Low level prompting and echoing were regarded as device and implementation dependent facilities of the workstation. High level prompting and echoing were considered to be the responsibility of the application program. No control over low level prompting and echoing was given to the application program.

Input could only be obtained from active workstations and in GKS version 3, only one workstation could be active at any one time.

Only one input mode, REQUEST mode, was provided. The application could request input from the operator, but the initiative lay totally with the application.

Interestingly, the input functions all returned a series of input primitives, rather than just one. The input function for locator input devices, for example, was:

REQUEST SET OF LOCATORS

Parameters: maximum number of input items
number of input items entered
positions in user coordinates

The function returned the number of items entered; the end of input was indicated by the operator activating an implementation dependent "end of input" switch.

The description of REQUEST SET OF LOCATORS states that a complex interaction sequence might be performed to enter one input primitive, for example:

(1) prompting of the operator by the system;

(2) activation of the input primitive by the operator;

(3) echoing of the input value by the system;

(4) confirmation of the input value by the operator.

However, as noted earlier, the application was given no control over prompting and echoing and it was not mandatory for an implementation to recognize these phases.

There was no standardized mechanism for defining the choices to be provided to the operator by a choice device.

8.2.2 GSPC Core

This section describes the input facilities in the draft of Core '79 considered by the Editorial Board [46].

The Core system provided 3 levels of input capability: Level 1, none; Level 2, synchronous; Level 3, complete. The facilities of each level are summarized in Table 8.1.

Table 8.1 Core Input Functionality Levels

	Level 1	Level 2	Level 3
Functional Capabilities	None	Synchronous	Complete
Device initialization	N	Y	Y
Synchronous interactive functions	N	Y	Y
Echo control	N	Y	Y
Explicit enable/disable	N	N	Y
Event queue management	N	N	Y
Sampled device read functions	N	N	Y
Associations	N	N	Y

The Core input facilities were also based on the concept of logical input devices, but in a richer form than the facilities of GKS Version 3. Core recognized six classes of logical input device, which were divided into two disjoint sets: those that could only cause *events* and those that could only be *sampled*. Event devices could be used by the operator to signify events to the application. Whenever an event was caused by an event device, an event report was created which contained data related to the state of the device when the event occurred. Event reports were placed in a first-in/ first-out event queue, from which they could be removed by the application program. Four of the six classes of logical input device were event devices:

(1)   PICK - identifies a segment and a primitive within a segment through a two-level naming structure consisting of segment name and pick identifier.

(2)   KEYBOARD - provides a character string.

(3)   BUTTON - provides logical "buttons" (the ability to choose amongst alternatives).

(4)   STROKE - provides a series of positions in normalized device coordinates. Both 2 and 3 dimensional strokes were supported.

Two of the six classes were sampled devices:

(5)   LOCATOR - provides a position in normalized device coordinates. Both 2 and 3 dimensional locators were supported.

(6)   VALUATOR - provides a scalar value within an application defined range.

Unlike GKS, the LOCATOR device returned positional information in normalized device coordinates rather than user or world coordinates. It was the responsibility of the application program to relate such values to the application's coordinate systems; the graphics system made no attempt to do this. To even start to do this in a sensible manner requires the graphics system to have knowledge of multiple world coordinate systems; Core did not have this facility (neither in fact did GKS Version 3) and so leaving it to the application was not an unreasonable design decision.

An implementation of the Core had to provide a well-defined minimum set of logical input devices at level 2 or 3. These had to be provided either through physical devices or simulation. The required logical input devices were as given in Table 8.2.

Devices were referenced by their device class (PICK, KEYBOARD etc) and a number within the class, called the *device number*.

Core also provided a mechanism for associating sampled devices with event devices. When an event occurred, the values of the associated, enabled, sampled devices were put into the event report for that event. The event report could thus be a complex structured object. Associations could be many to many, so that, for example, one particular sampled device could be associated with several event devices.

Logical input devices had to be initialized and enabled before asynchronous input could be obtained from event or sampled devices.

Initialization ensured that the device was available to the application program, enabling the device permitted input from the device. For associated devices, only data from enabled associated devices would be included in the event reports. Once an event report had been added to the input queue, it was unaffected by enabling, disabling, initializing or termination of devices.

Table 8.2 Logical input devices required in Core

No of Devices	Device Type
1	PICK device
1	KEYBOARD device
1	STROKE device
1	LOCATOR device
4	VALUATOR devices
8	BUTTON devices

Two functions were provided to initialize devices. The first, INITIALIZE DEVICE, initialized a specified device in a specified class. The second, INITIALIZE GROUP, initialized a specified set of devices in a specified device class.

Seven functions were provided for enabling, disabling and termination. ENABLE-DEVICE, ENABLE-GROUP, DISABLE-DEVICE, DISABLE-GROUP, enabled or disabled single devices or multiple devices within a class. Similarly, TERMINATE-DEVICE and TERMINATE-GROUP, terminated single or multiple devices respectively. Before a terminated device could be used again, it had to be initialized. There was also a DISABLE-ALL function which disabled all enabled devices.

Limited control was provided over the way in which logical input devices were echoed to the operator. A small number of predefined echo types were defined, which could be selected by the application program. For all device classes, echo type 0 meant no echoing, and echo type 1 was an implementation dependent technique which would be appropriate to the way a particular logical input device was realized in a particular implementation. Other echo types were input device dependent, for example, echo type 3 for a stroke device was "connect successive positions by solid lines". Functions were provided to set the echo type for a single device or group of devices.

It was also possible to associate a segment with locator or valuator logical input devices. In the case of the locator device, echo type 7 was segment dragging. For the valuator device, a number of echo types were defined which enabled a particular valuator device to control the value of a particular parameter in the segment's transformation matrix.

There were also functions to specify the view surface and a reference echo position for use by certain echo types.

There were other device characteristics which could be altered by the application program independently of the enabled/disabled status of the device. The characteristics that could be set included the following:

- Pick aperture for software simulation of a pick device. The aperture is the closeness criterion for picking and was defined in NDC space.

- The input buffer size, initial string and initial cursor position for a keyboard device. The initial string was displayed at the echo reference position. The cursor position specified the position in the string at which the next character typed by the operator would appear.

- The coordinate position used to initialize the locator position every time a locator device was enabled.

A number of inquiry functions were provided to determine device characteristics and capabilities, for example the number of devices of a particular class available, the echo type of a device, the devices with which a particular device is associated, the other devices implemented by the same physical device as a specified logical input device, and the devices associated with a specified device.

Three functions were provided to obtain input from sampled devices: READ-LOCATOR-2, READ-LOCATOR-3 and READ-VALUATOR.

Event handling was rather more complicated. Event reports were entered into the event queue by logical input devices; the application program polled the event queue with the function AWAIT-EVENT. The function parameters included a timeout parameter and the effect was to wait until the timeout period expired or there was at least one event in the queue (whichever occurred first) and then to remove the top event report from the event queue and return to the application program the identity of the logical input device that generated the event report.

If the timeout period expired without any events arriving, a null device class and identifier were returned. The top event report in the queue was moved to the current event report (a 1-place buffer). GET functions, one per device class (except BUTTON which had no associated data) were provided to return the data held in the current event report. These included functions to access data from sampled devices associated with the device generating the event report.There were also functions to flush all events, or events from specified devices or classes, from the event queue.

As mentioned earlier, Core also included synchronous input. The functions provided were:

```
AWAIT-ANY-BUTTON
AWAIT-PICK
AWAIT-KEYBOARD
AWAIT-STROKE-2
AWAIT-STROKE-3
AWAIT-ANY-BUTTON-GET-LOCATOR-2
AWAIT-ANY-BUTTON-GET-LOCATOR-3
AWAIT-ANY-BUTTON-GET-VALUATOR
```

Synchronous input could only be obtained from initialized devices; however the devices did not have to be enabled.

There are two interesting points to note about the functions listed above. First, every function had a timeout parameter. The system would wait for an event to occur from the specified device, or the timeout to expire. If an event occurred, the data associated with the event were returned. At level 3 of input, the event queue was flushed when the function was invoked.

The second point of interest is that it was possible to obtain input from a locator or valuator associated with a button device, but more complex device associations were not supported for synchronous input.

8.2.3 Editorial Board recommendations

The recommendations of the Editorial Board [46] had a deep influence on the development of the input facilities in GKS and subsequent standards. They make interesting reading today!

The minimality of GKS compared to Core was noted. It was pointed out by DIN that GKS had initially included sampled and event input, but this had been abandoned in favour of a very simple input module, which could be interfaced to Fortran READ. A high level module containing sample and event input was envisaged as a later addition.

The Editorial Board felt that the GKS facilities were too restrictive and strongly urged DIN to incorporate event and sample input. There was also a recommendation to GSPC that sample and event should be considered as operating modes for all classes of logical input devices. The mode would be specified when a device was enabled.

There was also discussion of the decision in GKS to return locator input in user (world) coordinates, whilst GSPC Core returned positions in normalized device coordinates. Core was a 3D system and the difficulties caused by singular viewing transformations were recognized. However, it was felt to be important to relate locator input to the picture on the screen and there was encouragement to provide input in user coordinates, possibly as an option.

8.2.4 Development of the GKS input model

Version 5 of GKS [7] incorporated the recommendations of the Editorial Board. Five classes of logical input device were provided:

(1) LOCATOR providing a position in world coordinates;

(2) VALUATOR providing a real number;

(3) CHOICE selects an alternative;

(4) PICK provides a segment name and a pick identifier;

(5) STRING provides a character string.

Three types of mechanism were provided for obtaining input from a workstation:

(1) REQUEST: a tuple of input primitives of one input class was read from the workstation. The application was suspended until the input was entered or an end-of-input action was performed.

(2) SAMPLE: the current setting of an input device was inspected and the current value was delivered back without waiting for an operator action.

(3) EVENT: one input queue was built up into which input primitives from various sources were stored in order of time of generation. The application program could inspect the queue to determine if it contained any input primitives, and if so the source from which they came.

For REQUEST type input, five functions were provided, one per input class, each of which returned a sequence of values, rather than a single value. An example is REQUEST TUPLE OF LOCATORS. The application could specify the maximum number of inputs allowed. GKS waited until the requested number of inputs had been entered or an end-of-input action was performed by the operator. REQUEST TUPLE OF LOCATORS effectively eliminated the need for a STROKE input primitive (see Section 8.3).

For SAMPLE input, the input devices had first to be enabled. Separate ENABLE and DISABLE functions were specified for each device class. A SAMPLE function was provided for each device class, for example, SAMPLE LOCATOR. These functions returned the current value of the specified input device to the application program.

For EVENT type input, there was one input queue. The operator was able to enter input primitives into the queue from any enabled input device. Two functions were provided to interrogate the queue: READ EVENT and AWAIT EVENT. If the queue was not empty both functions behaved in the same way, returning the input class and input device identification of the oldest event in the queue. The input data could be obtained by use of the GET function corresponding to the appropriate input class. In the case that the input queue was empty, READ EVENT would return to the calling program immediately reporting that the queue was empty, whereas AWAIT EVENT would wait until an input was entered. There was no concept of timeout as in Core.

Two other functions were provided for handling EVENT input, READ WORKSTATION EVENT and AWAIT WORKSTATION EVENT. These behaved like READ EVENT and AWAIT EVENT, but only looked at the events in the queue arising from a specified workstation. FLUSH functions were provided to delete all the primitives from the queue and to delete all primitives from a specified device.

REQUEST type input could only be obtained from disabled devices. An input device could be in one of 3 states: disabled, enabled for SAMPLE type input or enabled for EVENT input. Every device could operate in each of the three types, thus accommodating the Editorial Board's recommendations.

Echoing of input could be switched on and off by the SET ECHO function. The positioning of the echo could be controlled by SET ECHO POSITION. It was not possible to control the type of echoing provided as could be done in Core, but the initial values of LOCATOR and VALUATOR input devices could be controlled.

The function SET CHOICE STRINGS allowed a text string to be associated with each alternative of a CHOICE device; these strings could be used in a variety of ways by an implementation to prompt or give help to the operator of the device. The function ASSIGN SEGMENT TO CHOICE allowed the application program to define a previously created segment as a menu for CHOICE input. This segment would be used in conjunction with a pick input device to return the pick identifier of the item selected as the CHOICE value.

LOCATOR input positions were returned in world coordinates (GKS Version 5.2 only had a single normalization transformation). NDC positions could be obtained by specifying an identity normalization transformation.

From this brief description, it will be seen that the input facilities in GKS Version 5.2 were, as requested, modelled fairly closely on the Core facilities, though there were some interesting differences.

Core allowed sampled devices to be associated with event devices. There was no equivalent of this in GKS Version 5.2, though as will be seen shortly, this facility is provided in a weaker form in ISO 7942. Core provided a range of echo types which could be selected by the application program. GKS Version 5.2 did not provide any control over echo type. The only control was to turn echoing on or off.

Like Core, GKS Version 5.2 provided a number of inquiry functions to inquire device status and characteristics.

Input received considerable attention during the review of GKS Version 6.6 at the WG2 meeting held in Abingdon, U.K., in October 1981. The major criticisms [68] of the input facilities in Version 6.6 centred around:

(1) The precise datatypes to be returned by the different classes.

(2) The different levels of detail at which different kinds of input behaviour were specified.

(3) The lack of uniformity among the different logical device classes as to the details of their behaviour.

(4) The lack of a clear distinction between the concepts of:
    Simulating a logical device using particular types of hardware;
    Prompting an operator for input;
    Echoing an operator's actions;
    Acknowledging an operator's generation of events.

(5) The difficulty of relating any of these "output" concepts to logical input devices.

The origins of these deficiencies and criticisms lay in the lack of a clear underlying model of input. The outcome of the meeting was a refined and generalized model of logical input devices which now forms the basis for the input facilities in GKS, GKS-3D and PHIGS.

The input model is described in Section 8.3. In terms of facilities, the Draft Proposal [11] provided five classes of logical input devices, LOCATOR, VALUATOR, CHOICE, PICK and STRING, each of which could operate in three modes, REQUEST, SAMPLE and EVENT. A level structure was introduced into GKS. Input level *a* had no input facilities, level *b* provided REQUEST mode only and level *c* provided full input. REQUEST input functions returned a single value of the input class. There was a single event queue, but simultaneous events could be recorded in the queue, providing a Core-like association capability in limited form as is explained in Section 8.3.

A range of prompt and echo types was provided for each device class and control over echo position and device initialization were also provided. Every GKS implementation providing input was required to provide at least one device of each class. PICK input only exists with output levels 1 and 2 (the GKS level structure is described in Section 3.3.6).

The main change at the DIS stage in the development of GKS was to add a sixth class of logical input device, STROKE, which was felt to be necessary in order to provide a sensible data type onto which to map physical devices such as tablets which can return a stream of positional information rather than just a single value.

8.3 The GKS input model

The GKS input model is described in more detail in [70].

The data that can be input to an application program by the operator are divided into different types and a class of logical input device is defined corresponding to each. GKS defines six different types, but the model is not limited to any particular number of types. The types in GKS are:

(1) *LOCATOR*: a position in world coordinates and the associated number of the normalization transformation used to convert back from device coordinates via normalized device coordinates to world coordinates.

(2) *STROKE*: similar to LOCATOR except it represents a sequence of world coordinate positions rather than a single position.

(3) *VALUATOR*: a real number in some range.

(4) *CHOICE*: an integer representing a selection from a set of choices.

(5) *PICK*: the name of a selected segment and a PICK IDENTIFIER indicating which collection of primitives in the segment has been picked.

(6) *STRING*: a character string.

Logical input devices are characterized by a *measure* and a *trigger*. The measure describes the type and value of the input to be returned to the application. The trigger is an event, which for certain styles of input, determines when the measure value is returned to the application program. The measure essentially determines how the operator controls the logical data value, and the trigger determines how the operator indicates that the current value is important.

The LOCATOR and STROKE measures call for some additional comment. Both return positions in world coordinate space (see Chapter 6). One of the difficulties in returning LOCATOR and STROKE positions in world coordinates is that different parts of a picture are typically defined in different world coordinate systems. If the graphics system is to return sensible world coordinate values, it needs knowledge of all the world coordinate systems from which the picture is composed, and some mechanism for resolving ambiguities caused by overlapping coordinate systems. GKS allows multiple normalization transformations to be defined. For input, the locator position in device coordinates is transformed by the inverse of the workstation transformation to give a position in normalized device coordinates. The normalization transformations are then scanned to determine the normalization transformations within whose viewports the position lies. A priority mechanism is used to select a unique normalization transformation in the event that the locator position lies within the viewport of more than one normalization transformation.

Normalization transformations are ordered by *viewport input priority* such that no two transformations have the same priority. If the LOCATOR position lies within the viewport of more than one normalization transformation, the normalization transformation with highest priority is selected. The LOCATOR position is transformed from normalized device coordinates to world coordinates by the inverse of the selected normalization transformation. The number of the normalization transformation used is a part of the LOCATOR measure value. Normalization transformation 0 is defined as the identity transformation from a unit square in world coordinates to the unit square in normalized device coordinate space (the maximum visible region of NDC space), so every LOCATOR position lies at least in the viewport of normalization transformation 0.

STROKE input is handled in a similar manner. All the points in the STROKE lie within the viewport of the normalization transformation which is used in the transformation from normalized device coordinates to world coordinates. This means that if a STROKE device is used in SAMPLE mode, the normalization transformation number which is a component of the device's measure, may change as more points are added to the STROKE.

Logical input devices may operate in three modes:

(1) *REQUEST*: Logical input devices in REQUEST mode behave rather like Fortran READ. A request is made by the application program for a measure to be returned from a specified device. GKS waits until the operator has set the measure to the desired value and has activated the trigger.

(2) *SAMPLE*: In SAMPLE mode the current measure is returned whenever requested by the application program. No triggering is involved when a logical input device is sampled.

(3) *EVENT*: A number of logical input devices may be active together. Each time the trigger for a particular device is activated, the current measure value and data identifying the device are added to a single queue of input events for all the devices used in event mode. The application program can interrogate the queue to retrieve input events. It is possible to couple more than one logical input device to the same trigger so that multiple events, known as *simultaneous events*, can be generated from a single trigger event.

Logical input devices also have associated attributes, some of which are under application program control, whilst others are fixed by the implementation, but may vary from implementation to implementation. Attributes include:

(1) The current operating mode (REQUEST, SAMPLE or EVENT).

(2) The particular simulation of the logical device using physical devices.

(3) The method of informing the operator that a measure process has come into existence, and thus that the associated physical devices can be manipulated. This is called the *prompt*.

(4) The method for informing the operator of the current measure value of a logical input device. This is called the *echo*.

(5) The way in which the operator is informed of a significant firing of the device's trigger. This is called *acknowledgement*. A significant trigger firing is one satisfying a REQUEST function invocation or one which adds events to the input queue.

(6) An initial value, for use by the measure process when it comes into existence for the device.

(7) A switch to turn echoing on and off.

The attributes may also include additional information for use by a particular simulation of a logical input device.

An interaction involves an operator and a logical input device. While an interaction is underway, the operator controls the measure. While no interaction is underway, the operator has no control over the measure and the application program has no means of finding out its value. In REQUEST mode, a single call to a REQUEST function controls the entire interaction. In SAMPLE and EVENT mode, the interaction starts when either operating mode is selected and continues until the mode setting function is invoked again for that device. This invocation might start a new interaction with the device in the same operating mode. The stages in an interaction are:

(1) A measure process is created for the device, and its value is set to the initial value in the device's state.

(2) If the trigger process for the device is not in existence, it is created.

(3) The operator is prompted for input, using the specified technique.

(4) If the echo switch in the device's state is ECHO, the current measure value is echoed using the specified echoing technique.

(5) As the operator manipulates the device, the trigger may fire. In REQUEST mode, the current measure value is delivered to the application program and the interaction ceases. In EVENT mode, an event report is added to the event queue; the interaction continues. The trigger has no effect in SAMPLE mode.

(6) If the trigger firing is significant, it is acknowledged.

(7) Eventually the measure process dies, either because in REQUEST mode the trigger fires, or in SAMPLE and EVENT modes the device's operating mode is reselected.

(8) When a trigger process has no associated measure process, it also dies.

8.4 Realization of the model in GKS

Input devices in GKS are associated with workstations. GKS recognizes six categories of workstation, two of which have input capabilities: OUTIN and INPUT. A workstation of category OUTIN has a display surface and associated input devices. A workstation of category INPUT has no display surface (output capabilities), but does have input capabilities. A digitizer, for example, could be packaged in GKS as an INPUT workstation, a vector refresh display with keyboard, button box, dials and lightpen, as an OUTIN workstation.

A GKS implementation supporting input must provide the operator with at least one logical input device of each appropriate class.

The PICK input class only applies to GKS implementations supporting output level 1 or 2. The logical input devices may be associated with different workstations.

GKS has 3 input levels (Table 8.3).

Table 8.3 GKS Input Levels

Input Level	Facilities
a	no input facilities
b	REQUEST input only
c	REQUEST, SAMPLE and EVENT input

At level c, every logical input device must be capable of operating in all three modes.

For REQUEST input, six functions are provided, REQUEST <class>, one for each class of logical input devices. Each REQUEST function has a

STATUS parameter, which can return with the value OK or NONE. The value OK means that the operator completed the input in the normal manner. The value NONE means that the input data are invalid because a break has been indicated. How a break is indicated depends on the input device and is implementation dependent. For a LOCATOR device, an invalid locator position could be interpreted as a break. Alternatively, the device might have 2 buttons, one to signal normal completion, the other a break.

The function REQUEST CHOICE can return an additional status value, NOCHOICE, to indicate that no choice item has been selected. REQUEST PICK can return a status value, NOPICK, to indicate that no item has been picked.

For SAMPLE input there are six functions; one for each logical input device class. SAMPLE CHOICE and SAMPLE PICK have an associated status parameter which can return values OK or NOCHOICE and OK or NOPICK respectively.

For EVENT input the input queue is interrogated by the function

AWAIT EVENT(TIMEOUT, WS, DVCLASS, DV)

If the queue is empty, the application program is suspended until an event is generated, or a maximum of TIMEOUT seconds has elapsed. The timeout parameter can have value 0, in which case the function returns without suspending the application program. If the queue is not empty, the parameters WS, DVCLASS and DV return the identity of the device which generated the first event in the queue and the event report is removed from the queue and transferred to the *current event report.*

Six GET <class> functions are provided to retrieve input data from the current event report. GET CHOICE and GET PICK have status parameters as for SAMPLE CHOICE and SAMPLE PICK.

For EVENT mode input, it is possible for one trigger firing to generate multiple event reports on the input queue. The event reports are marked as belonging to a group of simultaneous events. The AWAIT EVENT function and current event report mechanisms return input events one at a time, rather than returning a whole group of simultaneous events at once. There is an inquiry function, INQUIRE MORE SIMULTANEOUS EVENTS, which can be used to determine which events resulted from the same operator action. Having removed the first event of the group from the queue, invocation of this function will return a parameter value MORE if there are further events on the queue from the same trigger firing as the event report just removed, and the value NOMORE otherwise.

Six functions SET <class> MODE are provided to select the operating mode of a logical input device. A parameter to these functions also controls whether echoing for this device is turned on or off. The default state of a logical input device is REQUEST mode and echoing on.

Logical input devices are initialized by the INITIALIZE <class> functions. Again there is one per device class. These functions have the form:

INITIALISE <class>(WS, DV, initial values, PE,
    XMIN, XMAX, YMIN, YMAX, LDR, DR)

The first two parameters are the workstation identifier and device identifier for the device to be initialized. Next follow one or more parameters defining the initial value for the device. The parameter, PE, defines the prompt and echo type for the device. The next four parameters define the area of the display space in which echoing is to take place and the remaining two parameters constitute the input data record (see below). GKS standardizes a small number of prompt and echo types for each device class. Other types can be standardized through the procedures for the Registration of Graphical Items (see Chapter 13). Prompt and echo type 1 for each device class is defined to be a device dependent technique for each device class. A flavour of the prompt and echo types in the standard is given by the prompt and echo types for LOCATOR and CHOICE, shown in Table 8.4

Table 8.4 Examples of GKS prompt and echo types

Class	Type	Description
LOCATOR	1	device dependent technique which must be available
	2	crosshair cursor intersecting at the current measure
	3	tracking cross with its centre at the current measure
	4	rubberband line from initial value to current measure
	5	rectangle with one corner at the initial value and the opposite corner at the current measure
	6	a digital representation of current measure coordinates
CHOICE	1	device dependent technique which must be available
	2	prompt using built-in prompting mechanism, for example lights associated with buttons
	3	the prompt is a display of character strings, representing a menu: the operator selects a string
	4	similar to 3, but the operator types in the character string
	5	prompt using a segment: the choice number corresponds to the pick identifiers in the segment

Every GKS implementation has to provide prompt and echo type 1 for each device class. It is implementation dependent whether more prompt and echo types are provided. Prompt and echo types with negative values are device and implementation dependent. Positive values are either standardized in GKS or are reserved for registration. Where positive values are provided by an implementation they have to conform to the specification in the standard or in the Register of Graphical Items.

GKS also provides a mechanism for supplying additional information to logical input devices, for use where further control is provided over the way in which they interact with the operator. An example is control over the size of a tracking cross for a LOCATOR device. Such information is provided through *input data record* parameters (LDR - length of data record and DR - data record) to the INITIALISE <class> functions. The format and contents of the input data record vary from device to device. For some classes of logical input devices, certain entries in the data records have specific meanings, for example:

VALUATOR: two values, occupying the first two positions in the data record are compulsory for all prompt and echo types; lowest value and highest value. These define the endpoints of the range within which data from the valuator lie.

CHOICE: For prompt and echo type 2: an array of logical values specifying for which elements of the CHOICE the built-in prompting capability of the device is to be turned on. For prompt and echo types 3 and 4: an array of character strings to be displayed. For prompt and echo type 5: a segment name.

8.5 GKS-3D

GKS-3D [15] has the same input model as GKS. The LOCATOR and STROKE logical input device classes are generalized to accommodate 3D input and the more complex viewing pipeline in GKS-3D.

In GKS-3D all the coordinate systems are 3D (see Section 6.6.2). A viewing transformation is inserted between the normalization transformation and the workstation transformation. As explained earlier, a view index is bound to each output primitive. This index is an index into workstation dependent view bundle tables, which define the view transformations corresponding to each view index. Normalization transformations and viewing transformations are separately ordered by input priority using identical mechanisms to GKS.

The LOCATOR measure is generalized to consist of a position in (3D) world coordinates, a normalization transformation number and a view index. The computation of the measure value from a position in device coordinates is more complex than in GKS, in part because the pipeline is more complicated, but also because the transformations in GKS-3D do not necessarily have inverses. The measure value is computed in the following way:

(1) The device coordinate position is transformed to normalized projection coordinates by the inverse of the workstation transformation. If the workstation transformation has no inverse, the z component of the position in NPC space is set to the minimum z value of the workstation window.

(2) Of the view representations whose view clipping limits contain the position, the one with the highest view transformation input priority is selected. View representations whose viewing transformations have no inverses are not considered. The inverse of the selected transformation is applied to obtain a position in normalized device coordinate (NDC) space.

(3) Of the normalization transformations whose viewports contain the position in NDC space, the one with the highest viewport input priority

is selected. The inverse of the selected transformation is applied to obtain a position in world coordinate space.

A STROKE measure consists of a sequence of positions in world coordinates, a normalization transformation number and a view index. Computation of STROKE measures proceeds in a similar way to the computation of LOCATOR measures and STROKE measures in GKS. All positions in the stroke lie within the view clipping limits associated with the selected view index and within the viewport of the selected normalization transformation number.

The LOCATOR and STROKE devices are conceptually 3D devices. When 2D input devices are used, a z value is appended either internally (from the workstation state tables) or externally (by, for example, requesting the operator to type in a value).

For compatibility with GKS, the 2D functions REQUEST LOCATOR, SAMPLE LOCATOR, GET LOCATOR and the corresponding STROKE functions are also provided. These discard information from 3D devices and it is implementation dependent whether the operator is required to provide a z coordinate first.

8.6 PHIGS

PHIGS provides the same classes of logical input devices as GKS-3D.

PICK input in PHIGS has been extended to give more information about the object that has been picked. In GKS and GKS-3D, the PICK device returns the name of the segment and the pick identifier within the segment. As a structure element in PHIGS could be executed as part of one or more parent structures, some applications will need to know more than just the local structure name. Consequently, in PHIGS it is possible to recover the path through the hierarchy that led to the invocation of the structure element that has been picked. This is expressed as a sequence of structure name and element positions, the latter indicating the element position in each structure which contains the execute structure element by which the next structure in the sequence is invoked.

8.7 Computer Graphics Interface (CGI)

8.7.1 Classes, modes and control

The CGI defines an abstract graphics device which is capable of accepting input and generating, storing and manipulating pictures. CGI currently only caters for 2D input and output and controls only a single output device.

Three device classes are defined, OUTPUT, INPUT and OUTIN. The first has no input capabilities, the second no output and the third provides both input and output capabilities. Whilst a CGI device only supports a single output device, several input devices may be associated with one CGI device.

CGI essentially supports the GKS input model, but being at a lower level, additional control capability is also provided. The scope of CGI is not limited to providing an abstract or virtual device interface for GKS and so some generalization has also been incorporated. CGI support includes the device classes and operating modes of GKS.

CGI supports eight device classes, which include the six classes of GKS. The input classes are:

(1) *LOCATOR*: a position in Virtual Device Coordinates (VDC).

(2) *STROKE*: a sequence of positions in VDC.

(3) *VALUATOR*: a numeric value in a device dependent range.

(4) *CHOICE*: an integer representing a selection from a set of choices.

(5) *PICK*: a segment identifier and the pick identifier of the primitive picked.

(6) *STRING*: a character string up to a device dependent maximum length.

(7) *RASTER*: an array of pixels.

(8) *GENERAL*: the input equivalent of a GENERALIZED DRAWING PRIMITIVE on output.

The two new classes are RASTER and GENERAL. The former is an abstraction of pixel capture devices; the latter provides an extension capability for input which is analogous to that provided by GENERALIZED DRAWING PRIMITIVE for output.

The LOCATOR and STROKE datatypes differ from the GKS LOCATOR and STROKE types because CGI is at a lower level. The GKS normalization transformation is considered to take place above the level of CGI. The positional information is expressed in VDC. VDC coordinate systems may be specified for input devices that are independent of that used for graphical output. The mapping is defined by an input extent rectangle in VDC space which maps onto an input viewport in the coordinate space of the input device. Different mappings can be specified for each class of devices.

Each logical input device measure value has an associated flag, which indicates whether the value is valid or not. A locator position outside the input extent, for example, is an INVALID measure.

CGI supports the three operating modes of GKS logical input devices, REQUEST, SAMPLE and EVENT. A fourth mode is also defined in CGI, called ECHO REQUEST. This mode is designed to cater for situations where an input device supporting CGI INPUT category only, is to be echoed on a separate CGI device. The overall effect to be achieved is a CGI OUTIN device, but two CGI devices are involved which have to be synchronized in some way. This topic is addressed further below.

In GKS the composition of logical input devices in terms of associating measures with triggers is fixed by the implementation and is not under application program control. CGI gives some control to its clients to determine the association of measures and triggers; clearly this functionality is appropriate in a device level standard regardless of its desirability at higher levels. Each CGI implementation providing input capability provides a fixed number (which may be zero) in each of the eight classes. Each logical input device has an associated list of triggers. Any input device may have more than one associated trigger and any trigger may be associated with more than one device. A function ASSOCIATE TRIGGERS is provided to define the triggers associated with a particular device. CGI also provides for some triggers to be non-dissociable from each device, meaning that these triggers will always be associated with the device, regardless of the changes made by the ASSOCIATE TRIGGERS function.

8.7.2 Initialization

More control over prompting, echoing and acknowledging is provided than in the application program interface standards. The function SET ECHO CONTROLS enables echoing, prompting and acknowledging to be each either enabled or disabled for a particular device. There is a predefined set of echo types for each device class. The echo types broadly correspond to the GKS prompt and echo types, for example, for the CHOICE device:

(1) Implementation dependent.

(2) Invoke built-in device prompting capability. The echo data record contains a prompt array which indicates, for each device prompting alternative, whether that alternative is to be prompted.

(3) Display CHOICE strings. The choice strings are contained in the echo data record and are displayed within the echo area, when selected by the operator "using an appropriate technique" (for example light pen). This is a mixture of prompt and echo, when the choice is made by typing alternatives on a keyboard.

(4) Variant of CHOICE strings display.

(5) Display segment and CHOICE pick identifiers. The echo data record contains a segment identifier for a segment to be displayed within the echo area. The pick identifiers in the echo data record are mapped to the CHOICE numbers.

The SET ECHO DATA function also sets the prompt type for a particular device. The selection is again made from a predefined set, which is the same for each input class. The types are:

(1) Implementation dependent.

(2) Prompt by sounding a tone. For devices capable of multiple tones, a tone identifier is given in the echo data record.

(3) Prompt by displaying one from a set of device prompt outputs, such as icons.

(4) Display a prompt message from the echo data record.

Acknowledgement type is also controlled by the SET ECHO DATA function. The predefined types are:

(1)   Implementation dependent.

(2)   Acknowledge by sounding a tone. For devices capable of multiple tones, a tone identifier is given in the echo data record.

(3)   Display an acknowledgement message from the echo data record.

The client is able to initialize the measure of a logical input device using the PUT CURRENT <class> MEASURE functions. The client can set an INVALID value in the measure process. This is useful because it enables the client to detect if the operator has changed the measure value.

The SET <class> DEVICE DATA function is provided to control other aspects of the device's behaviour, for example the maximum number of positions in a stroke.

8.7.3 REQUEST and SAMPLE modes

CGI provides REQUEST mode functions which are very similar to the GKS functions but with the addition of a timeout parameter. A timer is started when the function is invoked and serves to prevent hangups. Control reverts to the client either when the operator causes a trigger to fire or the timeout period expires. The function also returns to the client the identity of the trigger which fired.

For SAMPLE mode input, SAMPLE <class> functions are provided. These return the current measure value of a logical input device.

8.7.4 EVENT mode

For EVENT mode input each CGI device has its own input queue. The ENABLE EVENTS function sets a logical input device into EVENT mode and DISABLE EVENTS returns a logical input device to the quiescent state.

The AWAIT EVENT function interrogates the queue and, as in GKS, initiates a timer if there are no events in the queue. If there is an event in the queue before the timeout expires, the identity of the device from which the event originated is returned to the client. Event reports are removed from the queue with DEQUEUE <class> EVENT functions. Unlike GKS, a timestamp return parameter is used to indicate multiple simultaneously triggered events. There is also an AWAIT EVENT QUEUE TRANSFER function to transfer the whole queue to the client. The function may return only part of the queue, reflected in a NOMORE, MORE return flag.

Several functions are provided for event queue management. INITIALIZE and RELEASE EVENT QUEUE allow the client to set the queue to an initial empty state and to release the resources allocated to the queue, respectively. There are also functions to temporarily suspend the event queue: BLOCK EVENT QUEUE and UNBLOCK EVENT QUEUE. Blocking prevents the addition of more events to the queue, but does not destroy events already in the queue. Unblocking restores the normal operation of the queue. These functions can be of use in coordinating multiple devices. There are also FLUSH <device> EVENTS and FLUSH EVENTS functions which allow selective or complete removal of events from the queue.

8.7.5 ECHO REQUEST mode

ECHO REQUEST mode is a variation on REQUEST mode which is designed to allow an INPUT CGI to provide the client with enough information to support the echoing of the input on a separate OUTPUT or OUTIN CGI. The problem to be solved is how to indicate changes in the measure value to the client prior to completion of the interaction. The approach adopted is the following.

The INITIALIZE ECHO REQUEST function initializes the device and returns control to the client. The client can then invoke the ECHO REQUEST function. In ECHO REQUEST mode a special trigger is associated with the logical input device, called the *measure monitor*. This trigger fires when the device's measure value changes. When the ECHO REQUEST function is invoked, the measure monitor trigger is initiated. Control is returned to the client whenever a trigger fires. This will be either the measure monitor trigger indicating that the measure value has changed, or one of the other triggers associated with the device signifying termination of the interaction. When control is returned to the client, the trigger's identity and current measure value are also returned.

Echo output functionality is defined for OUTPUT and OUTIN devices, through the functions:

INITIALIZE <class> ECHO OUTPUT
UPDATE <class> ECHO OUTPUT
RELEASE ECHO OUTPUT
SET ECHO OUTPUT CONTROLS
PERFORM ACKNOWLEDGEMENT

Echo output facilities also include functions to set the echo, prompt and acknowledgement states associated with the device. These are analogous to the functions provided for OUTPUT and OUTIN devices.

8.8 Shortcomings and future directions

Some authors have criticized the notion of logical input devices, arguing that smooth interaction can only be achieved when the characteristics of the physical output devices are taken into account. Moving one application from one device environment to another may require the whole structure of the interaction to be redesigned and this cannot be achieved merely by changing a few parameters on an initialization function. This view does not so much attack the notion that input devices can be characterized at a high degree of abstraction by classes of datatypes, as launch an attack on the degree of control over the device afforded to the application program. It is in the area of control that most criticism has been directed toward the GKS input model.

The GKS input model *per se* is readily extensible in terms of adding new classes of logical input values and devices, and in allowing many to many trigger/ measure mappings and logical input devices whose values are tuples of the basic types. The realization of the model in GKS gives no control over such measure/trigger associations to the application program; the device configuration is implementation dependent and cannot be varied by the application program. The association of multiple measures with a single trigger can only be taken advantage of in EVENT mode input; this facility is not available in REQUEST mode.

An example of the usefulness of this facility is provided by the Tektronix crosshair cursor input device. An input value is triggered by pressing a key on the keyboard. Typically applications wish to make use of the position and key. The clean way to represent such a device in GKS is as a combination of LOCATOR and CHOICE devices, the LOCATOR indicating the positional information, and the CHOICE device which of the possible keys was depressed. The trigger is then the action of depressing any key and this trigger is associated with both LOCATOR and CHOICE devices. Proposals have been made for incorporating such functionality in GKS-3D and PHIGS in REQUEST mode [79], but these have not as yet gained acceptance. The view is that such functionality should be considered as part of the GKS Review process (see Chapter 14).

The functionality of the Core system which allowed input devices to control the parameters of segment transformation matrices has not been found in later proposals, though the need for closer coupling between input and output in graphics standards has been recognized. The lack of close linking between input and output in PHIGS has been commented upon but no firm proposals have emerged for providing enhanced functionality in a clean and general way.

The predefined prompt and echo and acknowledgement types have also been seen as too restrictive, and there is a desire to see much greater application program control over these attributes. In the context of window management systems, the neatest solution to this problem currently is provided by SUN Microsystem's NeWS [208,211]. Here the clients of the system can download PostScript code into the server to handle prompting, echoing and acknowledgement. Whilst there is a desire to see equivalent functionality in the graphics standards, there are currently no proposals on the table for how to achieve this.

In spite of the criticisms mentioned here, it remains true that the GKS input model gives a clean conceptual basis to the input functionality in the standard, and considerably richer functionality could be achieved without changing the underlying model, but by realizing it with much more flexible control. A Study Group is currently looking at the Input Model (see Chapter 14).

Part 3
The Rules

9
Language Bindings

9.1 Introduction

Computer graphics systems are written in, and used from, a wide range of programming languages. One approach to this would be to define a separate standard computer graphics system for each programming language. This would make it very difficult to ensure any degree of commonality across the family of standards resulting, but has been adopted in at least one case (see below).

The approach adopted in the computer graphics standards is to define the functionality of the computer graphics system using abstract functions and datatypes and then, in a separate standard, provide bindings of these functions and datatypes to particular programming languages. A similar approach is followed in the Computer Graphics Metafile, when the functionality of the metafile is presented as an abstract syntax, and subsequent parts of the standard define concrete representations of this syntax. These representations are called encodings and are described further in Chapter 10.

There are currently four language binding standards under development: ISO 8651 Graphical Kernel System (GKS) language bindings; ISO 8806 Graphical Kernel System for three dimensions (GKS-3D) language bindings; ISO 9593 Programmer's Hierarchical Interactive Graphics System (PHIGS) language bindings; and language bindings for the CGI project ISO 9636 are currently beginning to be developed at the working draft stage. Each standard is a multi-part standard, with each part corresponding to a different programming language. A consistent numbering scheme for parts is used across all the standards as shown in Table 9.1.

Table 9.1 Standard part assignments for multi-part language bindings

Part Number	Language
Part 1	Fortran
Part 2	Pascal
Part 3	Ada
Part 4	C

The different parts of the multi-part standard have been allowed to progress independently through the standardization process, in terms of voting. The GKS Fortran binding, for example, is a full International Standard, yet the C binding is now (November 1989) a Draft Proposal. Whilst this is allowed for all ISO multi-part standards it obviously requires careful management to keep the parts in step and the approach has not been used in other areas of graphics standardization. The language binding Working Group have taken very considerable care to ensure that this independent processing of documents does not lead to needlessly dissimilar standards.

Language bindings can only be standardized for programming languages which have themselves some status as standards. Language bindings to C lag behind those for Fortran, Pascal and Ada, because the standardization of C itself lags behind these other languages in the ISO process. Language bindings to other programming languages, for example, Algol 68, LISP, Modula 2, Occam and Prolog have been reported in the literature [27,122], but they cannot enter the standardization arena in advance of the respective programming languages.

The other possibility (thankfully rare) is that graphics facilities may been standardized within the standard definition of the programming language in a way which provides different facilities from those in the graphics standards themselves. The only case of which we are aware of this happening is the Basic Standard, which includes a chapter on graphics facilities.

9.2 GKS language bindings

9.2.1 Background

Each of the abstract functional standards (excluding CGM, which defines a file format) defines a set of functions for computer graphics programming. The standards make use of a collection of abstract data types in describing these functions. A typical function interface description (from GKS) is the following:

POLYLINE

Parameters

In number of points	(2..n)	I
In points WC		n x P

This definition states that the POLYLINE function has two input parameters, the first is an integer of at least 2 (range 2..n), the second an array of points in world coordinates. A language binding for the POLYLINE function has to define how the function and its parameters are to be represented in the programming language.

GKS is defined in terms of the following datatypes: integer, real, string, point, name (used for example, for workstation identification, segment name, GDP identifier, pick identifier), enumeration type (a set of fixed constant values, for example NOCLIP and CLIP). Combinations of simple datatypes are also used, for example, vectors of values, matrices, lists of values, arrays of values, ordered pairs of different types, or data records (compound types whose content and structure are not defined in the Standard; an example is the input data record on the logical input device initialization functions which is used to provide additional implementation dependent information to control the logical input device, see Section 8.4). Other groups have added to this list partly as a consequence of feedback from those defining language bindings.

Coordinate data may be in world, normalized device, or device coordinates. Permitted value ranges are specified in a number of ways: a condition (for example >0), a range of integer values (for example (1..4)), a range of integer values with an implementation dependent upper bound (for example (4..n)), a set of values constituting an enumeration type, or ordered lists of any of these.

There are some conventions used in the GKS document which can cause difficulties for language bindings. There are examples of functions in GKS which are essentially the same function, but applied to different primitives or other entities. Examples are the logical input device initialization functions, and the functions to set bundle table entries. The first is essentially the same for all logical input device classes, the second is essentially the same for all types of bundles. GKS defines separate functions for each of the logical input device classes in the first case, and bundle types in the second.

GKS also defines a very large number of inquiry functions, whose purpose is to return values of entries in the GKS state tables. These entries take various forms, including simple values, lists of values, sets of values, and sparse arrays (in which some entries are undefined). The GKS functional description has adopted particular ways of describing each form.

A typical function to inquire a state list entry which is a single value is:

INQUIRE LEVEL OF GKS

Parameters:

Out	error indicator		I
Out	level of GKS	(0a,0b,0c,1a,1b,1c,2a,2b,2c)	E

The error indicator is used to indicate whether the information is available, and if not, the reason for non-availability.

Where several state list entries logically belong together, they are grouped together in a single function, for example:

INQUIRE CURRENT PRIMITIVE ATTRIBUTE VALUES

Parameters:

Out	error indicator			I
Out	current polyline index		(1..n)	I
Out	current polymarker index		(1..n)	I
Out	current text index		(1..n)	I
Out	current character height	WC	>0	R
Out	current character up vector	WC		2 x R
Out	current character width	WC	>0	R
Out	current character base vector	WC		2 x R
Out	current text path		(RIGHT,LEFT,UP,DOWN)	E
Out	current text alignment		(NORMAL,LEFT,CENTRE, RIGHT, NORMAL,TOP, CAP,HALF,BASE,BOTTOM)	2 x E
Out	current fill area index		(1..n)	I
Out	current pattern width vector	WC		2 x R
Out	current pattern height vector	WC		2 x R
Out	current pattern reference point	WC		P

An example of a list of values is provided by normalization transformations. A GKS implementation can support an implementation dependent number of normalization transformations. These are numbered from 0 to n. Defaults are provided for all transformations. Transformations are held in a list ordered by priority. Two inquiry functions are provided. The first, INQUIRE LIST OF NORMALIZATION TRANSFORMATION NUMBERS returns a list of normalization transformation numbers, which is ordered by viewport input priority. To obtain the window and viewport corresponding to a particular transformation number, the following function is defined:

INQUIRE NORMALIZATION TRANSFORMATION

Parameters:

In	normalization transformation number		(0..n)	I
Out	error indicator			I
Out	window limits	WC		4 x R
Out	viewport limits	NDC		4 x R

An example of a sparse table or array is provided by the polyline bundle table. The size of the bundle table supported by an implementation is implementation dependent. Entries in this table need not be contiguous, for example representations might be defined for polyline index values 1, 3 and 5, but not for 2, 4 and 6. The following pair of inquiry functions is provided to return information about the polyline bundle table.

INQUIRE LIST OF POLYLINE INDICES

Parameters:

In	workstation identifier		N
Out	error indicator		I
Out	number of polyline bundle table entries	(5..n)	I
Out	list of defined polyline indices	(1..n)	n x I

INQUIRE POLYLINE REPRESENTATION

Parameters:

In	workstation identifier		N
In	polyline index	(1..n)	I
In	type of returned values	(SET,REALIZED)	E
Out	error indicator		I
Out	linetype	(-n..-1,1..n)	I
Out	linewidth scale factor	≥0	R
Out	polyline colour index	(0..n)	I

The first indicates which polyline indices have representations defined for them. The second returns the representation for a specified polyline index.

The function INQUIRE SET OF SEGMENT NAMES IN USE returns a set of values.

INQUIRE SET OF SEGMENT NAMES IN USE

Parameters:

Out	error indicator		I
Out	number of segment names	(0..n)	I
Out	set of segment names in use		n x N

The approaches taken to these and other language binding issues in the Fortran, Pascal and Ada GKS bindings are now briefly described.

9.2.2 GKS Fortran binding

ISO 8651-1 [110] defines the GKS language binding interface for ISO Fortran 77 (ISO 1539).

The first difficulty encountered in binding GKS to Fortran concerns naming. It will be clear that GKS uses very long names and Fortran imposes severe restrictions on the lengths of subroutine names and identifiers. There is also the problem of naming conflicts between names used in the GKS binding and names used by the application program and other libraries. The language binding cannot solve the latter problem, but it does give help in containing the problem by mapping all the GKS function names to Fortran subroutine names which start with the letter "G".

A complex algorithm is used to map the GKS function names to a unique acronym consisting of not more than 5 letters. The algorithm first reduces plurals to singulars, compound terms are reduced and each remaining word is either deleted or replaced by an abbreviation. The process is designed to generate unique names consistently. Example names are shown in Table 9.2.

Table 9.2 Example names from Fortran binding

GKS Name	Derivation	Fortran Name
POLYLINE	PL	GPL
INQUIRE LEVEL OF GKS	Q-LV-KS	GQLVKS
INQUIRE NORMALIZATION TRANSFORMATION	Q-N-T	GQNT

In general there is a one-to-one correspondence between the functions of GKS and Fortran subroutines. Some exceptions to this are discussed shortly. In general also, the order of GKS function parameters is preserved in the order of subroutine parameters, though it is sometimes necessary to insert extra parameters, for example the lengths of arrays for output parameters.

The GKS integer and real datatypes are mapped to INTEGER and REAL respectively in Fortran. The string datatype causes a problem. The Fortran standard defines a subset Fortran in addition to the full standard. The full language allows variable length strings, the subset does not. Two bindings are provided for the string datatype, CHARACTER*(*) in the full language, and an INTEGER denoting the number of significant characters in the string and a CHARACTER*80 containing the string for the subset language. As a consequence, two versions are provided for every function which uses strings, for example GTX is the full Fortran 77 version of the GKS TEXT function and GTXS is the subset version. It is mandatory that GKS implementations provide both.

Points in Fortran are represented as pairs of REALs. Lists of points are represented as pairs of arrays for x and y coordinates respectively. The POLYLINE subroutine definition is thus:

POLYLINE

SUBROUTINE GPL (N,PXA,PYA)

Input Parameters:

    INTEGER N   number of points
    REAL PXA(N), PYA(N)   coordinates of points in world coordinates

Names are mapped to INTEGERS. Enumeration types are also mapped to INTEGERS. The standard defines a list of symbolic Fortran constants which may be included in an application program. In full Fortran 77, these constants may be declared using the PARAMETER statement, in the subset language they can only be declared as variables and given values by a DATA statement. Clearly the latter is much less satisfactory and secure. An example is given in Table 9.3.

Table 9.3 PARAMETER v. DATA statements in Fortran 77 Bindings

Clipping indicator	NOCLIP	CLIP
INTEGER	GNCLIP	GCLIP
PARAMETER	GNCLIP=0	GCLIP=1

Lists of values of a simple type are in general represented as an INTEGER indicating the number of elements in the list and an array whose elements are of the appropriate type. Lists of compound types only arise in inquiry functions; the functions are structured so that only one element of the list is actually returned, and that is represented as a collection of parameters of the appropriate types. Ordered pairs are also represented as collections of parameters of the appropriate types.

Data records are represented as arrays of type CHARACTER*80. Special utility functions are provided to pack INTEGER, REAL and CHARACTER data into the data record and to unpack the data record into individual data items.

The convention that GKS functions correspond one to one with Fortran subroutines is not followed for certain inquiry functions, in particular for functions which return large amounts of data of heterogeneous types and functions which return lists or sets of variable size.

An example of the first kind is INQUIRE CURRENT PRIMITIVE ATTRIBUTE VALUES, described above. This function is broken down into one subroutine per primitive attribute. In this case this gives a total of 12 subroutines, pattern width vector and pattern height vector being treated together as pattern size.

An example of the second kind is INQUIRE LIST OF NORMALIZATION TRANSFORMATIONS. The GKS function returns a list of normalization transformations; the corresponding Fortran subroutine returns the length of the list and the element of the list in a specified position. The definition is:

INQUIRE LIST element OF NORMALIZATION TRANSFORMATION NUMBERS

SUBROUTINE GQENTN (N,ERRIND,OL,TNR)
Input Parameters:
    INTEGER N   list element requested
Output Parameters:
    INTEGER ERRIND   error indicator
    INTEGER OL   length of list
    INTEGER TNR   Nth element of list of transformation numbers, ordered by decreasing viewport input priority

The functions INQUIRE LIST OF POLYLINE INDICES and INQUIRE SET OF SEGMENT NAMES IN USE, described above, are bound in an analogous manner.

9.2.3 GKS Pascal binding

ISO 8651-2 [110] defines the GKS language binding interface for ISO Pascal (ISO 7185) .

GKS functions are mapped to Pascal procedures. Naming is easier in the Pascal binding than the Fortran binding because Pascal permits much longer identifiers than Fortran. The GKS names are mapped to Pascal names beginning with the letter "G". A consistent list of abbreviations has been defined for words used in GKS function names. Words are either used in full, abbreviated, or omitted completely. Using the examples given earlier, typical Pascal procedure names are given in Table 9.4.

Table 9.4 Example names from Pascal binding

GKS Name	Pascal Procedure Name
POLYLINE	GPolyline
INQUIRE LEVEL OF GKS	GInqLevelGKS
INQUIRE NORMALIZATION TRANSFORMATION	GInqNormTran

Upper case initial letters at the start of words are used to improve legibility. Pascal has a much richer typing structure than Fortran and so the mapping from GKS datatypes to programming language types is much less constrained.

The GKS types integer and real are mapped to Pascal integer and real. Pascal allows subranges to be defined, and where subranges are specified in GKS, corresponding subranges are used in Pascal.

Pascal imposes some constraints on strings. Where a string is a component of another data structure, fixed length strings are used. The Pascal standard defines two levels for Pascal, 0 and 1. In level 1, it is possible to pass arrays of different lengths on different calls to the same procedure. In level 0, procedures only accept arrays of a declared fixed size. In level 1, strings are represented as a packed conformant array of characters when the string is a parameter to a Pascal procedure. In Pascal level 0, string is mapped to a fixed length type GAString. The size of this string is an implementation defined constant.

Points in Pascal are mapped to records with x, y (:real) fields. Lists of points are represented as arrays of such records, for example in level 1 Pascal, the POLYLINE function is defined as:

POLYLINE

procedure GPolyline(
    NumPoints : GTInt2;
    VAR Points   :   array [min..max:INTEGER] of GRPoint
    );

type GRPoint   =   record x, y : REAL end;

Enumeration types in GKS are mapped to enumeration types in Pascal, for example:

GEClip = (GVClip, GVNoClip);

Values of enumerated types are prefixed with "GV" and the type names themselves with "GE".

    Sets in GKS are represented as arrays in Pascal where the cardinality of the set is potentially infinite. Otherwise Pascal sets are used. Pascal records and arrays are used extensively to represent more complex data structures. Data records are represented as Pascal records, whose structure is implementation dependent.

    The Pascal binding recognizes rather more structure in the GKS functions than does GKS itself. Variant records are used in the representation of several logically related GKS abstract functions by a single Pascal procedure. This is used in the output primitive representation and input functions. An example is the SET primitive REPRESENTATION functions. The Pascal binding defines a single procedure, GSetPrimRep, the first parameter of which is an enumerated type (GEPrim) which has one of the values GVPolyline, GVPolymarker, GVText, GVFillArea; the representation itself is a variant record of type GRPrimRep, with one variant for each value of the type GEPrim, defining parameters for a bundle of the corresponding kind.

    It is possible that problems could arise in using such an interface on small systems and so the Pascal binding also includes mandatory one-to-one procedures for setting primitive representations and input functions.

    Inquiry functions are in general mapped one-to-one. For the INQUIRE CURRENT PRIMITIVE ATTRIBUTES function described earlier, two bindings are mandated. The first is a one-to-one binding. Exploiting Pascal's typing structure to good effect, this procedure has a simple interface definition:

procedure GInqCurPrimAttr(
    VAR ErrorInd   :   INTEGER;
    VAR PrimAttr   :   GRPrimAttr
    );

The second binding is similar to the Fortran binding of this function, a single procedure for each primitive attribute.

For inquiry functions which return variable amounts of information, for example INQUIRE LIST OF NORMALIZATION TRANSFORMATIONS, the corresponding Pascal procedures have additional parameters which allow the calling program to specify a subset of the information to be returned.

INQUIRE LIST OF NORMALIZATION TRANSFORMATION NUMBERS

```
procedure GInqListNormTranNum(
        Start           :  GTInt1;
        Size            :  INTEGER;
VAR     Done            :  Boolean;
VAR     ErrorInd        :  INTEGER;
VAR     NumNormTran     :  INTEGER;
VAR     NormTran        :  array[min..max:INTEGER] of INTEGER
        );
```

The level 1 definition is given here; the level 0 definition is similar except the type of NormTran is a fixed size array.

The parameters Start, Size and Done are defined as follows. Start specifies an index into the list of available values. Size specifies the number of values to be returned. Done is set to TRUE if the last of the values is returned by the call and FALSE if additional values exist beyond the last value returned by the call.

The binding of INQUIRE SET OF SEGMENT NAMES IN USE is an example of a GKS set data type being mapped to an array in Pascal.

```
procedure GInqSegName(
        Start           :  GTInt1;
        Size            :  INTEGER;
VAR     Done            :  Boolean;
VAR     ErrorInd        :  INTEGER;
VAR     NumSegNames     :  GTInt0;
VAR     SegNames        :  array[min..max:INTEGER] of GTSeg
        );
```

Note the use of Start, Size and Done parameters in this procedure.

9.2.4 GKS Ada binding

ISO 8651-3 [110] defines the GKS language binding interface for ISO Ada (ISO 8652).

Ada provides similar typing structures to Pascal. Two features of Ada distinguish it from Pascal as far as binding to GKS is concerned. The first is the Ada packaging construct, the second is the existence of multi-tasking constructs in Ada.

A package is a general structuring mechanism for Ada programs defining a set of facilities which the rest of the program may use. In the case of the GKS Ada binding, packages are used to specify procedure interfaces and datatypes. Packages can be separately compiled as library units.

GKS defines nine levels of functionality; GKS implementations can implement levels individually or as a single system. The Ada binding defines nine Ada packages, corresponding to the nine levels. Each of the packages has the same name, GKS, to allow an application requiring one level to run with an implementation providing a richer level. The package contents differ depending on the level of GKS that they provide. Associated with each of these packages is a datatype package which provides the appropriate type declarations for that level. These packages are named GKS_TYPES.

An Ada graphics application introduces the packages using the appropriate context specification, for example:

```
with GKS;
use GKS_TYPES;
procedure APPLICATION is
begin
    ....
end APPLICATION;
```

The "with" statement introduces the GKS procedure specifications. Procedures are referenced by their name preceded by the package name, for example, GKS.POLYLINE. The "use" statement introduces the datatypes, but allows entities in this package to be referred to without prefixing the package name. The application program has to ensure that this does not lead to naming conflicts.

The program is then compiled and linked with the appropriate program library corresponding to the level of GKS required.

The binding also defines two generic packages, GKS_COORDINATE_SYSTEM and GKS_LIST_UTILITIES. These support the declaration of types in the GKS_TYPES package. The first defines a variety of types used in supporting each of the GKS coordinate systems. The second defines types and operations for manipulating lists of any of the GKS list types.

The functions of GKS are mapped one-to-one to Ada procedures, with some exceptions noted below. Naming follows very similar principles to the Pascal binding, except that the components of names are separated by underscore characters, and there is no initial distinguishing character (like the "G" in Pascal and Fortran) because names are distinguished from other names used in the application by the package name. Typical Ada procedure names are shown in Table 9.5.

GKS integers and reals are mapped to Ada integer and floating point types respectively. Strings map to the Ada STRING type. Points are defined as records with field selectors X and Y, as in the Pascal binding. Lists of points are represented as arrays of points. Enumeration types are mapped to Ada enumeration types, for example:

type CLIPPING_INDICATOR is (CLIP,NOCLIP);

Table 9.5 Example names from Ada binding

GKS Name	Ada Procedure Name
POLYLINE	POLYLINE
INQUIRE LEVEL OF GKS	INQ_LEVEL_OF_GKS
INQUIRE NORMALIZATION TRANSFORMATION	INQ_NORMALIZATION_TRANSFORMATION

There is no equivalent in the Ada binding of GSetPrimRep in the Pascal binding. Each primitive representation function is mapped to a separate Ada procedure. Likewise, the input functions which are combined in the Pascal binding appear only as separate procedures in the Ada binding.

The function INQUIRE CURRENT PRIMITIVE ATTRIBUTES is bound both as a single Ada procedure and as a collection of procedures, one per primitive attribute, in a manner akin to the Pascal binding.

The function INQUIRE LIST OF NORMALIZATION TRANSFORMATION NUMBERS is bound to an Ada procedure which returns a list parameter. The definition is:

```
procedure INQ_LIST_OF_NORMALIZATION_TRANSFORMATION_NUMBERS
      (ERROR_INDICATOR  :out ERROR_NUMBER
      LIST      : out TRANSFORMATION_PRIORITY_LIST);
```

The type TRANSFORMATION_PRIORITY_LIST is defined as:

```
type TRANSFORMATION_NUMBER is new NATURAL;
type TRANSFORMATION_PRIORITY_ARRAY is array (POSITIVE range <>)
      of TRANSFORMATION_NUMBER;
type TRANSFORMATION_PRIORITY_LIST(LENGTH: SMALL_NATURAL:=0) is
      record
         CONTENTS: TRANSFORMATION_PRIORITY_ARRAY(1..LENGTH);
      end record;
```

Sets in GKS are mapped to lists in Ada, for example:

INQUIRE SET OF SEGMENT NAMES IN USE

```
procedure INQ_SET_OF_SEGMENT_NAMES_IN_USE
      (ERROR_INDICATOR  : out ERROR_NUMBER;
      SEGMENTS      : out SEGMENT_NAMES.LIST_OF);
```

SEGMENT_NAMES is a package defined making use of the GKS_LIST_UTILITIES package. The type definitions are:

```
type SEGMENT_NAME is new POSITIVE;
package SEGMENT_NAMES is new GKS_LIST_UTILITIES(SEGMENT_NAME);
```

Effectively this creates a type and operations for lists whose elements are of type SEGMENT_NAME.

As noted earlier, Ada includes multi-tasking. The Ada binding allows an implementation to refuse access from multiple tasks, but also allows the implementation to permit such access so long as concurrent access to GKS functions does not take place.

9.2.5 GKS C binding

This section is based on the GKS C binding existing at the time of writing, which is the 2nd Working Draft [111]. This project has since progressed to DP, but no text was available at the time of finalising this text. One of the reasons for the slower progress of C compared to Fortran, Pascal and Ada is the fact that standardization of C itself lags behind those other languages.

The C binding follows broadly similar lines to the Pascal binding. The C binding does allow an implementation to substitute macros for functions, but these have to be designed carefully so that the same effects as using a function are achieved. Character strings are terminated in C by a null character, which means that the null character cannot be used as a printing character.

The GKS function names are mapped to C functions which begin with the letter "g". Words and abbreviated are separated by underscores as in the Ada binding.

C requires that compilers recognize internal identifiers to be distinct in at least 31 characters, but for external identifiers, the minimum is only 6 characters. The binding defines a set of short names (as in the Fortran binding) for use in such circumstances and a set of #defines for inclusion in a header file which equate the long names to the set of short names.

C provides an "include" mechanism to allow external files in the compilation and it is common programming practice to define datatypes, symbol definitions and other global entities in a header file. The binding defines the datatypes and other entities that should be included in the file gks.h which would be included by any application program making use of the GKS C binding. The binding also defines a set of constants for the GKS error numbers which can help to make programs more readable.

Typical C function names are shown in Table 9.6.

Points in C are mapped to records with x and y fields as in the Pascal and Ada bindings. The POLYLINE function definition is:

```
void
    gpolyline(
        Gint   num_pt
        Gpt    *array_pt
    );
```

Table 9.6 Example names from C binding

GKS Name	C Function Name	Short Name
POLYLINE	gpolyline	gpl
INQUIRE LEVEL OF GKS	ginq_level_gks	gqlvks
INQUIRE NORMALIZATION TRANSFORMATION	ginq_norm_tran	gqnt

C follows the Ada binding in not having an analogue of the Pascal binding function GSetPrimRep. Each primitive representation function is mapped to a separate C function. An earlier experimental binding [124] went much further in making use of structured datatypes and pointers to compress the binding, but the standards have taken a more conservative line, in part because of the integrity issues that can arise from pointer passing.

For inquiry functions returning variable amounts of information, the C binding requires the application to allocate memory, for example:

```
void
    ginq_list_norm_tran_num(
        Gint   length_ap_list,
        Gint   start_pos,
        Gint   *err_ind,
        Gint_list    *list_norm_tran,
        Gint   *length_list
    );
```

The application allocates memory for the list and passes that list to the implementation. The implementation places the results of the inquiry into the list. The parameter length_ap_list is the length of the application's list. This indicates the number of items that will fit into the list. The second parameter, start_pos, indicates the first item in the implementation's list which is to be copied into the application's list. This is similar to the Start parameter on the corresponding procedure in the Pascal binding. The parameter *list_norm_trans is an output parameter which is a pointer to a structure with fields for the number of elements in the list and a pointer to the elements in the list. The final parameter is also an output parameter which is a pointer to an integer. The implementation places in this parameter the number of items in its list.

9.3 GKS-3D and PHIGS language bindings

The work involved in constructing and understanding the language bindings to GKS-3D and PHIGS has been substantially reduced by the decision taken by WG4 that bindings for future standards will be built on top of the GKS bindings [125] in the sense that the philosophy and approaches adopted will be those used in the GKS bindings and solved problems will not be reopened unless the GKS solutions do not work in the new context for some reason.

The GKS-3D Fortran, Pascal, Ada and C bindings [112-115] are natural extensions of the GKS bindings. The latter are included in the GKS-3D binding standards and new functions and datatypes have been added as necessary. The extension of coordinate data to 3D is handled in the Fortran binding by adding an extra parameter for the z coordinates, an array in the case of lists of points. For Pascal, Ada and C, an additional field has been added to the structure representing points.

The PHIGS bindings [118-121] follow very similar lines to the GKS-3D bindings. The PHIGS Pascal binding is to be a binding to Extended Pascal rather than the current Pascal standard. Work on this will again have to lag behind the standardization of Pascal. It is intended that Extended Pascal should eliminate some of the problems that exist currently in Pascal, for example with string handling and should therefore give a cleaner binding.

9.4 CGI

As noted in Section 3.6, two types of binding are envisaged for CGI, procedural and single entry point. The latter is a common approach taken in the implementation of graphics systems such as GINO-F where all accesses to the device driver go through a single routine. The interface consists of a code defining the driver function required and parameter data which are packed into other arguments of the routine in a specified manner. This style of interface can also facilitate the insertion of a network connection between the DI and DD parts of the system, since, in a well-designed system, a normal procedure call can be replaced by a remote procedure call. The implications of distributing GKS functionality, along these lines, are discussed in [24,41,80]. As noted in Section 3.6, there is not yet an initial draft for the CGI single entry point binding.

There are working drafts for the CGI procedural or library language bindings, as they are now known, for Fortran and C [116,117], and working drafts are expected shortly. DP level text will follow shortly after CGI DIS text is available. These documents follow the same general principles as the API standard bindings.

10
Encodings

10.1 Introduction

CGM is described in Part 1 of the standard in terms of a set of elements which are defined in an abstract manner. Part 1 defines for each element the data or parameters that are associated with the element, for example, the parameter of the POLYLINE element is a point list. Parameters are defined using datatypes at a similar level of abstraction to those used in defining the API standards and CGI.

An alternative approach to CGM would have been to define a concrete rather than an abstract syntax, for example that point lists should be represented as real numbers in a certain format, packed in a certain way. This approach was not taken because different applications of the standard are likely to require parameterizations with different characteristics. If a metafile is to be transmitted across a network, then the representation must be such that the network can transmit it transparently. If a metafile is being transmitted between heterogeneous computer systems then issues of number representation become important. For metafiles which are to be stored and used on the same system, the issues of size and compaction may well be important.

Such issues led to the development of three standardized representation schemes, or *encodings*, for CGM. These are defined in Parts 2 to 4 of the standard as follows:

(1) *Character encoding (Part 2).* The aims of this encoding are compactness and transferability across a network.

(2) *Binary encoding (Part 3).* This encoding aims to minimize the processor effort required to generate and/or interpret the metafile. It is perhaps best suited for storage and retrieval of graphical data within one system.

(3) *Clear text encoding (Part 4).* This encoding is aimed at the requirements of having a metafile that can be read and edited by people. It is almost guaranteed that this format can be used for transfers between any pair of heterogeneous systems.

The main features of each are now described. For more details the reader is referred to [89,100] and the standards themselves [85].

10.2 Character encoding

The character encoding provides a representation of a CGM which is intended for use where it is important to minimize the size of the file, or where transmission through character-oriented communications services is required. This encoding does not optimize processing overhead.

Each metafile element is composed of an opcode followed by parameters as required. The opcodes are encoded as either one or two characters from columns 2 and 3 of the ISO 646 7-bit or 8-bit code table. Graphical primitive elements use single byte opcodes, except for some of the elliptic arc elements which use two bytes. Other opcodes use two bytes.

Parameters are coded in columns 4 to 7 of the code table, though coded representations of the string parameter may use bit patterns from other columns.

There are two fundamental formats used to encode parameters, basic format and bitstream format. Basic format is used to encode enumerated types, indices, integers, reals and non-incremental coordinates. Bitstream format is used for incremental mode coordinates, colour direct and colour index lists. In basic format each byte of each operand has bits reserved to indicate whether it is the final byte of data or not. Rather than fixed lengths, only enough bytes are used to hold a given piece of data so compression is obtained. Bitstream format is more efficient, but is not self-delimiting. Additional information, such as a count, is needed to indicate where the bitstream ends. A Differential Chain Code (DCC) method is used to achieve high compression factors for lists of points. A Huffman code is used to further compress the DCC data.

10.3 Binary encoding

The binary encoding aims to minimize the processor effort required to generate and/or interpret the metafile. It is a sequential collection of bits, organized into 8-bit fields (octets) and 16-bit fields (words). Metafile elements are constrained to start on word boundaries, which may necessitate padding an element with bits to a word boundary if the parameter data do not end naturally on a word boundary.

Elements are represented as a variable length data structure, consisting of an opcode (represented as an element class and element id within the class), the length of its parameter data and the parameter data itself (if any).

Metafile elements are represented in one of two forms: short-form commands or long-form commands. A short form command starts with a one word command header divided into three fields: element class, element id and parameter list length. The short form can accommodate up to 30 octets of data. The long form uses two or more words. The first word format is the same as the short form, with a parameter list length of 31 indicating that the header is a long format. The second word contains the parameter list length in the least significant 15 bits. This format allows the parameter list to be partitioned. If the most significant bit is 0, the count is a complete count. If it is 1, the length is the length of the first partition and the word is followed by further command words, for each of which the most significant bit is the partition flag and remaining bits indicate the length of the partition.

Signed integers are represented in 2's complement form in 8, 16, 24 or 32-bit precision. The same precisions are available for unsigned integers. Fixed point reals may be represented in 32 or 64-bit precision. Floating point reals at 32 or 64-bit precisions are represented in the ANSI/IEEE 754 format.

10.4 Clear text encoding

The clear text encoding is a representation that is straightforward to type, edit and read. It allows a metafile to be edited using a normal text editor and the internal character code of the host system. A metafile in this format consists of a stream of characters forming a series of elements, each of which starts with an element name (OPCODE). The basic syntax is:

OPCODE *<sep>* OPERAND *<sep>* OPERAND ... *<term>*

<term> can be either "/" or ";". *<sep>* can be one of several characters including space, tab and comma. OPCODE is a word like TEXT. The opcode names are derived from the element names. Numbers can be represented in any base from 2 to 16. Reals are represented in a format resembling the En.m of Fortran. Enumerated types are keywords such as LEFT, RIGHT, UP, DOWN.

10.5 Encodings for other standards

The encoding schemes defined in CGM are also used by the CGM Addenda, the PHIGS Archive file and will also be used for the CGI data stream encodings. The CGM encoding schemes are intended to be sufficiently flexible that extension to other applications is a relatively straightforward task.

10.6 Private encodings

The CGM also recognizes that in particular circumstances an organization may wish to make use of an encoding scheme not defined in CGM. Such encodings are called *Private Encodings* and the CGM provides some guidance as to the minimum criteria that these encodings should satisfy. Private encodings should allow:

- All CGM elements to be encoded (other than some precision commands which may not be appropriate to the private encoding)
- Encoding of sufficient precision to permit use of all values in the minimum suggested capabilities in the CGM. This includes the ability to encode at least the range of coordinate data precisions allowed for in the standardized binary encoding.
- Translation from the private encoding to a standard encoding and vice-versa should be possible without loss of information

Private encodings are expected to be useful, for example, in in-house single manufacturer systems to allow a binary encoding specifically tuned to the underlying processor architecture. The level of certification which can be achieved by an implementation which uses private encodings is called "functionally conforming".

11
Formal Specification

11.1 Introduction

The functionality of the first generation of computer graphics standards is described using a combination of natural language and programming language style notation. Each of the classes of standards: application program interfaces, language bindings and interface storage standards are different kinds of entities and consequently somewhat different approaches are used in their definition. This chapter looks briefly at the approaches used in the definition of the application program interface standards and then describes work undertaken in various places which aims to lay the foundations for more formal descriptions of these and future generation standards to be given.

The application program interface standards, GKS, GKS-3D and PHIGS are all defined using essentially the same approach. Each standard provides functionality which is described in terms of a number of concepts. In GKS for example, the central concepts are output primitives, coordinate systems, aspects, attributes, segments, graphical input, workstations and environment. The standard itself is a collection of functions which realize this functionality. Clause 4 of each standard describes the functionality of the standard in natural language, and is organized around the key concepts. Clause 4 of GKS for example, includes sub-clauses on output primitives and their attributes, segments and segment attributes, the logical input device model and measures of each input class. Clause 5 of each standard provides a description of each function in the standard. Clause 5 in general does not repeat information from clause 4, but gives a more stylized description of the function, plus parameters that the function uses and error messages that the function can generate. Clause 6 of each standard describes collections of data structures. These data structures serve two purposes, first they characterize the information that an implementation of the standard has to make available to the application program through appropriate inquiry functions and second they are used in clause 5 to explain the action of the functions which set, return or use information in the internal state of the standard.

Some examples of function definitions from GKS follow to illustrate these points.

POLYMARKER   WSAC,SGOP   L0a

Parameters:
  In   number of points   (1..n)   I
  In   points   WC   n×P

Effect:

A sequence of markers is generated to identify all the given positions. The current values of the polymarker attributes, as given by the GKS state list (see 6.4), are bound to the primitive. The polymarker attributes are listed in 4.4.2.

NOTE

- A marker is visible if and only if the marker position is within the clipping rectangle. The clipping of partially visible markers is workstation dependent.

References:

4.4.1, 4.4.2, 4.4.4, 4.5.3

Errors

5   GKS not in proper state: GKS shall be either in the state WSAC or in the state GKOP

100 Number of points is invalid

The first line of the function definition gives the name of the function, the states in which it is valid (WSAC - workstation active, SGOP - segment open) and the lowest level of GKS which requires the function to be implemented.

The 'Parameters' part of the definition states that this function takes two parameters, the first is an input parameter ('In'), the number of points to be marked, the second is also an input parameter, giving the points. The notation to the right of the parameter names defines the types of the parameters. The first is an integer ('I') greater than zero (range '(1..n)'); the second is a list ('n x ') of points ('P') in world coordinates ('WC').

The 'Effect' section describes what the function does. Notice the references to the GKS state list data structure in the function description. This says precisely which attribute values are bound to the primitive. The 'NOTE' qualifies the function description. The 'References' section indicates the places in the narrative part of the document where a detailed description of the polymarker primitive and its attributes can be found. The 'Errors' section lists the errors that can be generated by this function.

SET POLYMARKER INDEX   GKOP,WSOP,WSAC,SGOP   L0a

Parameters:
  In   polymarker index   (1..n)   I

Effect:

> The 'current polymarker index' entry in the GKS state list is set to the value specified by the parameter. This value is used when creating subsequent POLYMARKER output primitives.

References:

> 4.4.2, 4.4.4

Errors:

8   GKS not in proper state: GKS shall be in one of the states GKOP, WSOP, WSAC, SGOP

66   Polymarker index is invalid

This function sets an entry in the GKS state list, used by the POLYMARKER function. The form of words used in describing this function is used consistently in the definitions of the many functions in GKS which set state list entries. Some care was taken in the drafting of GKS to use natural language in a stylized way, when different instances of a common concept are being described. Whilst this makes for uninteresting reading, it enables the reader to readily spot general patterns within the standard.

INQUIRE CURRENT PRIMITIVE ATTRIBUTE VALUES
GKOP,WSOP,WSAC,SGOP   L0a

Parameters:

Out error indicator		I
Out current polyline index	(1..n)	I
Out current polymarker index	(1..n)	I
Out current text index	(1..n)	I
...		

Effect:

> If the inquired information is available, the error indicator is returned as 0 and values are returned in the output parameters.

> If the inquired information is not available, the values returned in the output parameters are implementation dependent and the error indicator is set to the following error number to indicate the reason for non-availability:

8   GKS not in proper state: GKS shall be in one of the states GKOP, WSOP, WSAC or SGOP

References:

> 4.4.2, 4.11.2

Errors:

> None

This function returns the current values of the primitive attributes held in the GKS state list. Only the first 3 are listed above, there are actually 10 more parameters not listed. The same 'Effect' clause is used in describing all the inquiry functions. The inquiry functions of one particular data structure are listed in the same section of the document: the sections are organized by data structure. The following extract from the GKS state list gives a flavour for the way the data structures are described.

current polymarker index	(1..n)	I	1
current marker type	(-n..-1,1..n)	I	3
current marker size scale factor	≥0	R	1.0
current polymarker colour index	(0..n)	I	1

The left hand column is the name of the state list entry. The next two columns define the type of the entry and the valid values for the entry within that type and the final column defines the initial value for the entry when the data structure is initialized, in this case when GKS is opened.

Another example is the definition of the polymarker bundle table in the workstation state list.

number of polymarker bundle table entries	(5..n)	I	w.d.t
table of defined polymarker bundles,			
for every entry:			
polymarker index	(1..n)	I	w.d.t
marker type	(-n..-1,1..n)	I	w.d.t
marker size scale factor	≥0	R	w.d.t
polymarker colour index	(0..n)	I	w.d.t

The polymarker bundle table is a sparse table, in that there may be values of the polymarker index for which no corresponding bundle table entry is defined. The data structure is effectively represented as the number of entries in the table and a collection of records, the first field of each of which is a polymarker index value and subsequent fields define the representation of that index.

There are a number of comments that can be made on this style of definition.

(1) Natural language descriptions are prone to ambiguity and incompleteness. Looking at the example definitions given above, what is the value of the 'current polymarker index' entry in the GKS state list after SET POLYMARKER INDEX has been invoked with a polymarker index parameter which is invalid? The obvious interpretation is that the state list entry is unchanged, but the function definition does not actually state this.

(2) An imprecise definition makes validation of a standard very difficult, if not impossible. To extend the example above; we could argue that the current polyline index must always have a valid value, because the POLYMARKER function does not give an error if the polymarker index is invalid. Suppose an implementation set the current polymarker

index to the value 1 whenever SET POLYMARKER INDEX was invoked with an invalid parameter? Would this be an invalid implementation?

(3) An informal definition also eliminates any possibility of formally verifying that an implementation conforms to the standard, or of performing any kinds of proofs about the consistency of the standard or of its behaviour in given circumstances.

The remainder of this chapter looks at attempts to apply more formal approaches for specifying software to graphics software, and graphics standards in particular.

11.2 Formal description techniques

Spivey [199] writes that "formal specifications use mathematical notation to describe in a precise way the properties which an information system must have, without unduly constraining the way in which these properties are to be achieved." A specification is concerned with *what* a product should do, not *how* it should be done. Specifications must be understandable which is often used as an argument for informality, but they must also be precise which argues in favour of formality. Woodcock remarks in his Foreword to Cohen's book [154] "software systems are becoming increasingly complex, and a major issue in the design and implementation of software is the management of complexity. It is to mathematics that we must turn to find ways to manage this complexity".

There has been a large amount of research over the last 20 years into formal mathematical methods for the specification of both programming languages and software systems in general. The books by Pagan [196] and McGettrick [190] contain very readable accounts of the work in programming language specification and in formal methods for system specification; the books by Cohen *et al* [154] Spivey [199] Jones [183,184] and Woodcock and Lomes [204] together with the collection of papers by Gehani and McGettrick [172] are good starting points.

Cohen *et al* [154] describe *systems* as follows:

(1) *Systems exhibit behaviour.* The statement of a system requirement consists largely of its observable behaviour. A system's behaviour is observable only when the system is an interactive part of some larger system. Use of a system necessarily involves the observation of the system's behaviour by its user.

(2) *Systems have internal structure.* A system's behaviour is the result of the behaviour of its parts, which may themselves be systems, and of the interrelationships among those parts. It is in this sense that a system can be said to be more than the sum of its parts. The engineer has to be able to predict, from his knowledge of the behaviour of the parts and the effects of their interconnection, the emergent behaviour of the systems

he constructs. This prediction is done, in the first instance, using models of the parts and interconnections, rather than the concrete parts themselves.

The key issue is what kind of models should be used. There are a number of desirable properties of such models including expressive and analytical power, ability to manipulate (for example by property preserving transformations or by composition).

The terms *model-oriented* and *property-oriented* have been used to characterize the main approaches to formal specification.

In the model-oriented approach, specifications are explicit system models constructed from either abstract or concrete primitives which are themselves well defined. In one such approach, the **Vienna Development Method** (VDM) [184], the primitives are mathematical abstractions such as sets and finite mappings. The system models consist of data objects constructed from these primitives representing inputs, outputs and the internal "state" of the system and operations that manipulate these data. Operations are specified either implicitly using pre- and post-conditions (the former is a predicate over inputs and initial state giving the conditions under which the operation produces a valid result, and the latter is a predicate over inputs, initial state, final state and outputs which defines the effect of the operation), or constructively with recursive functions.

The property-oriented approach defines a mathematical object in terms of relations among the operations defined over the object. Axioms define the relationships of the operators to each other and there is no explicit model. Algebraic specification is the best-known example of this type. In these methods, presentations of data types are formulated as heterogeneous algebras, a set of *sort* names, one for each sort of data involved and a set of declarations for *operation* symbols. The axioms in an algebraic specification are *equations,* that is pairs of terms which are supposed to denote the same value in every valid interpretation.

Cohen *et al* remark that the respective merits of both the model-oriented and property-oriented approaches are being increasingly recognized by the adherents of both schools and much research effort is being devoted to formalisms that allow specifications to be composed from smaller parts and with handling parameterized and partial specifications. In the algebraic approach, the work of Burstall and Goguen [151] on **Clear** is concerned with allowing specifications to be composed and with axioms other than equational ones. In the model-oriented approach, Z [178,199,204] can be seen as approaching similar objectives from a different direction.

The approaches described above deal adequately with sequential systems, but are much less attractive for describing concurrent system behaviour. There is still considerable research activity on theoretical approaches to handling concurrency, though much progress has been made. Barringer's book [148] is a good survey of this area. The books by Hoare [181] and Milner [191] describe particular approaches.

11.3 Applications to computer graphics

One of the earliest papers in this area is Guttag and Horning's [176] which describes the specification of a high-level interface to a display. Their approach combines algebraic specification with pre and post conditions. Systems are viewed as a state and a set of mechanisms (called *routines*) for changing and extracting information from that state. Actions of the "outside world" are also modelled as routines, so that the current state of a system is always the result of routines previously performed. States are defined algebraically by a set of function names, that can be used to refer to system states and a set of questions that can be asked about these states, and a set of equations designed to imply answers to the questions one can pose about states. The information contained in each state is thus defined indirectly in terms of replies to questions that may be asked about it.

In "pure" algebraic specification, the functions used to name states and to pose questions are identified with the set of mechanisms that would actually be used to interface with the system (or data type) being specified. In this paper, however, Guttag and Horning take a different approach and view the operators defined by the algebraic specification as purely mathematical abstractions. They may appear in specifications of programs or in reasoning about programs, but are not directly available to users of programs. Instead a set of routines is available to users. The routines deal with the dynamic behaviour of the system being specified and include mechanisms for establishing initial states, for transforming one state into another state, and for extracting information from the current state of the system. The specification of the routines depends upon the specification of the operators. If the routine is a function, it is defined by an equation relating it directly to the operators. If the routine is a declaration or a procedure, it is defined using pre- and post-conditions in which the algebraically defined functions may appear. The remainder of this paper is devoted to the design of a display interface. The user can simultaneously display several disjoint blocks of displayable information called *pictures*. A *view* is a spatial arrangement of pictures, which may overlap. The contents of a picture is a number (possibly zero) of components. Components are either text, figures or views. The idea is similar to windows and subwindows in a window management system [208].

A key idea in the specification is that of an *Appearance* function which takes a displayable object and a *coordinate* and returns the *Illumination* of the object at that point. Abstractly *Appearance* is a mapping from a point in space to an illumination value. Any given implementation will be an approximation to this abstract mapping, for example it might map discrete 2D Cartesian coordinates to RGB triples. Using this idea of an appearance function, the effect of combining pictures to form *Views* can be described. In their design the appearance of a particular point is determined by the front most picture that contains the coordinate. The idea of an appearance function gives a very natural way to describe this type of display system.

The paper presents a specification for the display system and then shows how it is possible to pose and answer questions about the design from the formal specification. For example it is shown that pictures are not transparent or translucent, i.e. if two pictures overlap, the bottom one has no effect on what one sees through the top one.

This paper made an important contribution by showing how specifications can be used for formal analysis and reasoning about a design.

Mallgren's paper [186] on formal specification of graphic data types is another important contribution. He identifies four general concepts which he uses as the basis for the specification of graphics data types, *region*, *picture*, *graphic transformation* and *hierarchical picture structure*. Each concept is treated as a collection of objects operated upon by well-defined operations.

A *region* corresponds to an area in two dimensions or a volume in three dimensions. Regions are defined as sets of points in some *universe U*. The definition is a very general one and can be applied at many levels, for example for the representation of continuous pictures the universe is either the entire plane or all of three-space. For modelling discrete pictures (e.g. raster graphics) it is convenient to let U consist of just the grid points.

For simplicity and without loss of generality, we follow Mallgren in confining discussion to two dimensions. As an example, the region consisting of the unit square at the origin can be written:

$$R_1 = \{(x_1, x_2) \mid 0 \le x_1 \le 1, 0 \le x_2 \le 1 \}$$

The important operations on regions are the normal set operations, intersection, union, difference and predicates for determining whether a region is empty or whether it contains another region.

Mallgren defines a picture as a function that assigns a value to each point in the plane. Pictures are defined as *partial* functions whose domain is a subset of the chosen universe. The functions are partial because they are only defined at those points in the universe covered by the picture. The values in the range can represent grey-scale intensities or colours. They are referred to in what follows as *colours*. Thus the diagonal line segment from the origin to the point $(1, 1)$ with colour 1 might be described by the partial function:

$$P_1 = \{ ((x_1, x_2), 1) \mid 0 \le x_1 \le 1, 0 \le x_2 \le 1, x_1 = x_2\}$$

The sum of two pictures P_1 and P_2 is defined as follows:

$$P_1 + P_2 = \{(p, P_0(p)) \mid p \in (\operatorname{\mathbf{dom}} P_1 \cup \operatorname{\mathbf{dom}} P_2)\}$$

where

$$P_0(q) = \begin{cases} P_1(q) & \forall\ q \in (\operatorname{\mathbf{dom}} P_1 - \operatorname{\mathbf{dom}} P_2) \\ P_2(q) & \forall\ q \in (\operatorname{\mathbf{dom}} P_2 - \operatorname{\mathbf{dom}} P_1) \\ P_1(q) + P_2(q) & \forall\ q \in (\operatorname{\mathbf{dom}} P_1 \cap \operatorname{\mathbf{dom}} P_2) \end{cases}$$

The appearance of $P_1 + P_2$ in the region of overlap is determined by the colour sum $P_1(q) + P_2(q)$ The precise interpretation of this depends on the kind of display system being considered.

Graphic transformations are modelled as functions mapping pictures to pictures. Transformations are also treated as objects on which operations are defined, for example composition. The composition of two graphic transformations T_1 and T_2 is:

$$T_1 \circ T_2 (P) = T_1 (T_2 (P))$$

The effect of a geometric transformation T^g on a picture P is defined as:

$$T^g (P) = \{ (G(p), P(p)) \mid p \in \textbf{dom } P \}$$

where G is the geometric function characterizing T^g (sometimes written $T^g < G >$).

Restriction transformations remove selected parts from a picture. A common example is the clipping operation which removes part of a picture outside a given region. The effect of a restriction transformation T^r on a picture P is defined by:

$$T^r (P) = \{ (p, P(p)) \mid p \in (R \cap \textbf{dom } P) \}$$

where R is the region characterizing T^r (sometimes written $T^r < R >$). It is shown that any series of graphic transformations can be reduced to a canonical form $T^g \circ T^r$. This can be achieved by the application of a series of general rules such as:

$$T^r < R > \circ\, T^g < G > = T^g < G > \circ\, T^r < G^{-1}(R) >$$

Hierarchically structured pictures are also treated, the key operation on which is the *display* operation which produces the resultant picture. The class of hierarchies considered can be represented as acyclic directed graphs. Transformations can be associated with nodes in the structure.

Mallgren then incorporates these concepts into abstract data types. His primary motivation for doing this is to provide a framework for the concepts needed in graphics programming languages. In the traditional approach graphic objects have been represented in the standard (general) data types provided by programming languages (e.g. *integer*, *real* and the two constructors *record* and *array*). The argument against this approach is that the graphics programmer has to work with abstractions that do not correspond to those used in graphics and in consequence has to be aware of representations at an inappropriate level of detail. Also responsibility for the integrity of the structures constructed rests with the programmer.

Mallgren describes graphical data types algebraically in the style of Guttag. The following is an extract from the data type *Point*.

Data Type Point
Operations
      point   real $\times$ real $\rightarrow$ point
      origin
$\rightarrow$ point
sum   point $\times$ point $\rightarrow$ point
      ...
Axioms
      origin = point(0 , 0)
      sum(point(x_1, x_2), point(x_3, x_4)) = point($x_1 + x_3$, $x_2 + x_4$)
      ...

To specify graphics operations a combination of algebraic and operational approaches is used. Operations on regions are specified in terms of equivalent operations on sets of points. The following extract illustrates the approach. The notation "$r \approx s$" means "region r corresponds to set s".

> nullregion $\rightarrow$ region
> lineseg   point $\times$ point $\rightarrow$ region
>
> ...
>
> *Definitions*
> nullregion $\approx$ { }
> lineseg(q_1 , q_2) $\approx$ {(x,y) | $x_1 \leq x \leq x_2$, $y_1 \leq y \leq y_2$,
> $$x (y_2 - y_1) - y (x_2 - x_1) = x_1 y_2 - x_2 y_1$$
> **where** x_1 = abscissa(q_1), y_1 = ordinate(q_1)
> x_2 = abscissa(q_2), y_2 = ordinate(q_2)
> }

Mallgren's paper then goes on to describe a simple graphics programming language and shows how it is possible to reason about programs in this language. These developments are beyond the scope of this paper. Mallgren's PhD dissertation [185] discusses the application of this technique to the specification of a part of the GSPC Core graphics system [19] and describes a technique for the specification of interaction.

Martins and Oliveira [188,189] have developed a notion of archetypes or generic objects and have given a specification for an editor which is parameterized on the class of object to be edited.

An early example of the application of formal specification techniques to graphics standards *per se* is the paper by Eckert [168] which explored the use of Parnas' trace technique as a basis for a GKS specification.

Formal approaches to the definition of graphics standards were considered at length in a series of workshops funded by the EEC on the Certification of Graphics Software [150,157] in 1981/82. An *ad hoc* subcommittee of the American National Standards Institute (ANSI) committee responsible for graphics (X3H3) also considered the problems of formally defining graphics systems. They examined a number of specification techniques which have been applied to programming languages, but concluded that none was adequate for specifying graphics systems [152,153]. Rosenthal [198] proposed the use of Pascal as a specification language, effectively by defining a reference implementation. This approach has many merits but suffers from the drawbacks that it is difficult to reason at that (low) level of abstraction, it unavoidably overspecifies how graphics primitives are to be processed and it requires the use of a particular language binding (functional graphics standards are defined independently of programming languages).

In parallel with the international development of GKS, the ANSI graphics group worked on a proposal for a minimal graphics system known as the **Programmer's Minimal Interface for Graphics** (PMIG [145]).

Although this system never became an ANSI standard (in fact the functionality of PMIG is contained in level *m* of the ANSI GKS standard), PMIG is important because Carson and Post gave a formal definition [152,153].

PMIG is specified in terms of an abstract picture in world coordinate space, the state of the overall system and a picture processing pipeline. Graphical functions are specified in a style similar to the "routine" approach of Guttag and Horning.

The creation of an abstract world coordinate picture by the application program is modelled by describing the effects of each graphics function on an abstract space (modelled on the Cartesian coordinate plane, with the addition of attributes associated with each point) and on the graphics state vector. The transformation from world coordinates to normalized device coordinates is given explicitly, and the clipping transformation is described in such a way that it can be applied either before or after the viewing operation.

The difficult part of any attempt to specify graphics systems is how to treat the rendering of primitives on a display. The difficulty is how to accommodate the range of physical display hardware in an abstract representation whilst being able to say something about how primitives should appear on the display surface. Some authors [187] have looked at the problem of specifying how primitives should appear when displayed. The difficulty here tends to be that these approaches are specific to a particular device class, for example raster displays. The approach taken by Carson is to model the output of a graphics system as abstract data types, and regard the display process as a binding of these abstract data types to a physical display device. This has the merit that the functionality of a graphics system can be specified, implemented and even certified without producing a single picture. The description of what a line should look like is regarded as a binding issue and not a specification issue.

The problem of how the display surface will change as the result of drawing an output primitive is treated through the idea of a combining function. This approach is adopted in recognition of the fact that if primitives overlap, the resulting image will depend on the properties of the display system. The idea of a combining function is that it describes precisely this effect. Combining functions are implementation dependent and are to be provided by the implementor as part of the system documentation. Each of these functions describes how the appearance of the display surface will change as the result of drawing some output primitive.

The abstract data type notation is adopted from Guttag and Horning. The data type *Picture* models the world coordinate space picture. This type is based on the two dimensional Cartesian coordinate plane. Attributes are associated with each point in the plane, which include *Colour*, *Linestyle*, and *Marker_symbol*. Attributes could be modelled by viewing each point as an element of a Cartesian product:

$$\mathbf{R} \times \mathbf{R} \times \textit{Colour} \times \textit{Linestyle} \times \textit{Marker\_symbol} \times \dots$$

but Carson and Post use a slightly more abstract approach using operators that provide these values as their results in the abstract data type that represents a picture. This is reminiscent of the *Appearance* function in Guttag and Horning's work.

When a blank picture is created, the attributes of each point in the plane are set to null or background values. As primitives are added the values of appropriate attributes are set.

The following extract of the PMIG specification illustrates these ideas.

---

type *Picture*
operators
    add_polyline : *Picture* × *ArrayOfPoint* → *Picture*
    clear : → *Picture*
    attributes : *Picture* × *Point* → *Colour* × *Linestyle* × *Marker_symbol*
                           × *Text_Attributes* × *Character*
      ...
axioms
For all *Pt* contained in polyline determined by *Point_Array*
    Linestyle(*add_polyline*(*Pic*, *Point_Array*), *Pt*) = *Current_Linestyle*
    Colour(*add_polyline*(*Pic*, *Point_Array*), *Pt*) = *Current_Colour*
    ...

The picture pipeline in PMIG is shown in figure 11.1.

Descriptions of each of the stages of the pipeline are given. Some have a simple form, for example transformations are specified as simple matrix operations. Clipping, however, is much more complicated, for example the clip operation for a polyline primitive is defined as producing a set of (possibly disjoint) polylines.

Gnatz's paper [173] describes a framework for the specification of graphics systems based on an algebraic approach, the CIP wide spectrum language of the Munich CIP project. The key idea here is that of transforming a specification by a series of correctness preserving transformations into an implementation.

Gnatz has a similar notion of combining functions to that of Carson, though the expression of it is both different and illuminating. The description is given in terms of a function *view* which maps a display element and its attributes into a viewgraph or transparent foil. Then the appearance of a display image (collection of primitives) is obtained from the superimposition of such transparent foils. The superimposition is formally described by a function *combine*. Different *combine* functions are needed for different classes of hardware, for example for colour raster displays *combine* is non-commutative, whereas for monochrome displays it is. It all depends what happens when primitives overlap.

Gnatz also goes on to discuss the specification of graphics metafiles for the transfer and storage of graphical information. His technique is an elegant one which uses the mathematical notion of "lifting" to model delayed evaluation. The idea is that the metafile corresponds to a sequence of graphical functions to which arguments are bound, but which have not been evaluated. The action of metafile interpretation is then modelled as evaluation and Gnatz is able to prove that two sequences of procedure calls are equivalent, the one generating graphical output directly, the other via intermediate generation and interpretation of a metafile. This paper, along with that by Richter [197] make the important point that considerations of syntax alone are not sufficient to define a graphics metafile. Semantics of the primitives also need to be given to ensure that when a primitive is stored in a metafile and subsequently interpreted, the original primitive is obtained. Generation and interpretation of metafiles are in this sense inverse operations.

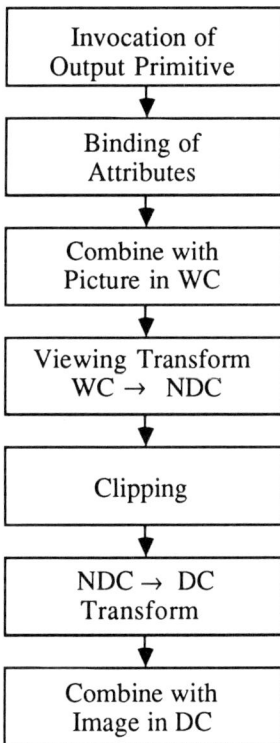

```
┌─────────────────────┐
│   Invocation of     │
│  Output Primitive   │
└─────────────────────┘
           │
           ▼
┌─────────────────────┐
│     Binding of      │
│     Attributes      │
└─────────────────────┘
           │
           ▼
┌─────────────────────┐
│   Combine with      │
│   Picture in WC     │
└─────────────────────┘
           │
           ▼
┌─────────────────────┐
│  Viewing Transform  │
│    WC → NDC         │
└─────────────────────┘
           │
           ▼
┌─────────────────────┐
│      Clipping       │
└─────────────────────┘
           │
           ▼
┌─────────────────────┐
│    NDC → DC         │
│    Transform        │
└─────────────────────┘
           │
           ▼
┌─────────────────────┐
│   Combine with      │
│   Image in DC       │
└─────────────────────┘
```

Figure 11.1 Picture pipeline for PMIG

The application of formal specification techniques to the Graphical Kernel System (GKS) and other emerging graphics standards is the subject of a research programme at Rutherford Appleton Laboratory and has resulted in a number of papers [147, 158-167]. The first paper in this series is [166]. This paper examines the GKS concept of implicit regeneration. A small subset of GKS is specified in the VDM notation and a proof is given that, under defined circumstances, the same picture is obtained regardless of whether a change is made by dynamic modification or implicit regeneration. The specification in this paper is developed in a number of stages and in more detail in [163]. In this specification, a single output primitive, polyline, and a single workstation are considered. The state of the system is described by the objects in figure 11.2.

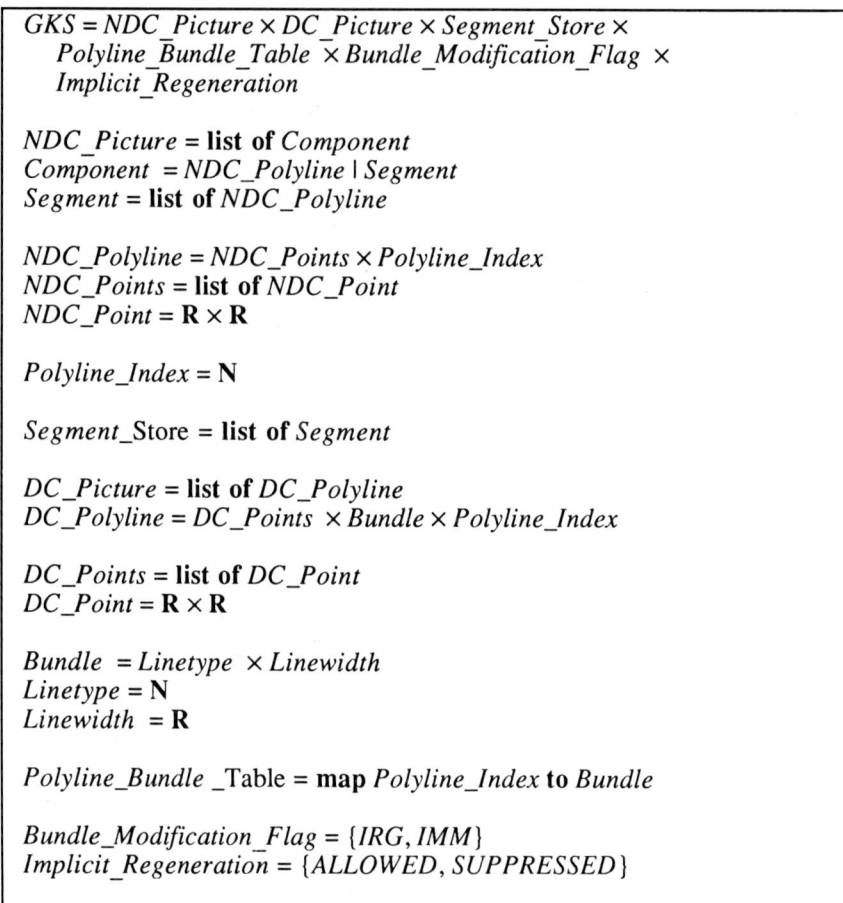

$GKS = NDC\_Picture \times DC\_Picture \times Segment\_Store \times$
  $Polyline\_Bundle\_Table \times Bundle\_Modification\_Flag \times$
  $Implicit\_Regeneration$

$NDC_Picture = $ **list of** $Component$
$Component = NDC\_Polyline \mid Segment$
$Segment = $ **list of** $NDC\_Polyline$

$NDC\_Polyline = NDC\_Points \times Polyline\_Index$
$NDC_Points = $ **list of** NDC_Point
$NDC\_Point = \mathbf{R} \times \mathbf{R}$

$Polyline\_Index = \mathbf{N}$

$Segment_Store = $ **list of** $Segment$

$DC_Picture = $ **list of** $DC\_Polyline$
$DC\_Polyline = DC\_Points \times Bundle \times Polyline\_Index$

$DC_Points = $ **list of** DC_Point
$DC\_Point = \mathbf{R} \times \mathbf{R}$

$Bundle = Linetype \times Linewidth$
$Linetype = \mathbf{N}$
$Linewidth = \mathbf{R}$

$Polyline_Bundle_Table = $ **map** $Polyline\_Index$ **to** $Bundle$

$Bundle\_Modification\_Flag = \{IRG, IMM\}$
$Implicit\_Regeneration = \{ALLOWED, SUPPRESSED\}$

Figure 11.2

Primitives are represented as ordered tuples, the first component representing the vertices of the polyline, the second the polyline index. Pictures are modelled as lists of primitives. A typical operation is *add_polyline* which is defined in figure 11.3.

  This operation is an abstraction from GKS functions. Its effect, described by the post-condition, is to create a polyline and add it to the NDC picture and to display a corresponding DC polyline by adding this to the DC picture. The function t maps normalized device coordinates to device coordinates. The DC picture is an abstraction from the physical picture that would be displayed on the display surface of the workstation. Like Carson, the rendering of a primitive on a physical display surface is regarded as a binding issue. The DC picture records the primitives to be displayed and data which characterize their appearance.

---

let $mk\_gks(ndcp, dcp, ss, pbt, bmf, ir) = gks$ **in**

$add\_polyline: GKS \times NDC\_Points \times Polyline\_Index \rightarrow GKS$
$add\_polyline(gks, pts, pi, gks') \triangleq$
pre $pi \in$ **dom** pbt
post $ndcp' = mk\_ndc\_polyline(pts, pi) :: ndcp \land$
$\quad dcp' = mk\_dc\_polyline(t(pts), pbt(pi), pi) :: dcp$

$t: NDC\_Points \rightarrow DC\_Points$

Figure 11.3

The formal specifications described so far only considered bundled specification of aspects. In [162] both mechanisms are formally specified, properties are formulated for the mechanisms and the specifications are proved to conform to them.

The specifications described so far have been in the model-oriented VDM notation. Reference [165] compares VDM with a property-oriented method, OBJ [146,155,171,174]. An example specification, roughly that in [163] is described in both techniques and comparisons are drawn. One of the main benefits of OBJ lies in the modularity constructs it provides, which enable the structure of the problem to be expressed more clearly. As already remarked, the Z specification language provides good facilities for structuring specifications, though Z was not examined in this particular study.

The work described so far has concentrated on what may be described as the control structures in GKS. The next paper in the series [164] gives definitions of the five main output primitives in GKS, polyline, polymarker, text, fill area and cell array. Primitives are described at three levels, corresponding to world coordinates (WC), normalized device coordinates (NDC), and device coordinates (DC). Essentially at WC level primitives are defined by their data. At NDC level attributes and a clipping rectangle are bound and at DC level aspects are bound. The geometry of primitives is represented by the set of points covered by the primitive. (Incidentally this makes clipping much easier to handle than in Carson's approach.)

At DC level primitives are modelled as relations between points and colours. Relations rather than functions are used for two reasons. First for the cell array primitive it is possible for more than one colour to be associated with a point (in particular the colour of points on the boundary between two cells is not clearly specified in GKS) and second the way in which primitives are combined to form pictures is loosely specified in GKS. Modelling primitives as relations enables the combination of primitives to be modelled as the union of the corresponding relations. This gives a picture which is expressed as a relation between points and colours. The relation is to be interpreted as meaning that a particular point may be displayed with any of the colours in the range of the relation corresponding to that point, or with any "combination" of those colours. These ideas are illustrated by the definitions of the polymarker primitive.

The polymarker primitive draws a sequence of points marked with the same symbol. The parameter associated with the primitive is a list of points. The world coordinate object is represented as the set of points to be marked.

Polymarker = **set of** *Point*

mk_Polymarker: **list of** *Point* → *Polymarker*
pre *mk_Polymarker*(*l*) $\triangleq$ *len l* ≥ *1*
mk_Polymarker(*l*) $\triangleq$ *vertices*(*l*)

vertices: **list of** *Point* → **set of** *Point*
vertices(*l*) $\triangleq$ { l$_i$ | *i* ∈ *1* .. *len l*}

The primitive at the NDC level is modelled as a tuple consisting of the set of points, the clipping rectangle and polymarker index associated with the primitive.

NDC_Polymarker = **set of** *Point* × *Clip_Rectangle* × *Polymarker_Index*

mk_NDC_Polymarker: *Polymarker* × *Window* × *Viewport*
                        × *Clip_Rectangle* × *Polymarker_Index*
                        → *NDC_Polymarker*
mk_NDC_Polymarker(*pm, w, v, cr, pmi*) $\triangleq$ (*normalize*(*w,v,pm*), *cr, pmi*
)

The display level primitive is modelled as a relation from a point to a colour index. The set of points constituting a positioned marker symbol is given by the function marker, which places the marker specified by the marker type and marker size scale factor arguments at a specified position. A marker is visible if, and only if, the marker position is within the clipping rectangle. It is workstation dependent how partially visible markers are clipped, and this is indicated by the operator $\cap_{wd}$. The definition is given in figure 11.4.

Arnold, Duce and Reynolds [147] is a first attempt to combine the ideas contained in the previous papers. The motivation for this paper came from the work of Arnold and Reynolds on configurable models of graphics systems [68]. This paper concentrates on a single output primitive, polyline, but should provide a general framework for a GKS specification. To demonstrate this is the subject of current work. The specification notation used is Z [199].

$Polymarker\_Bundle =$
$Marker\_Type \times Marker\_Size\_Scale\_Factor$
$\qquad\qquad\qquad \times Colour\_Index$
$DC\_Polymarker = Point \leftrightarrow Colour\_Index$

$marker : Point \times Marker\_Type \times Marker\_Size\_Scale\_Factor \rightarrow \textbf{set of} Point$

$mk\_DC\_Polymarker:$
$NDC\_Polymarker \times Window \times Viewport \times$
$\qquad\qquad\qquad Polymarker\_Bundle \rightarrow DC\_Polymarker$
$mk\_DC\_Polymarker(ndcpm, w, v, b) \triangleq$
$\quad \textbf{let}\quad ndcpm = (ndcpts, cr, pmi)$
$\quad \textbf{and}\quad b = (mt, msf, mci)$
$\quad \textbf{and}\quad s = \bigcup_{p \,\in\, cr \,\cap\, ndcpts} (marker(p, mt, msf) \cap_{wd} w)$
$\quad \textbf{in}\quad \{(p, mci) \mid p \in wstrans(w, v, s)\}$

Figure 11.4

The paper is based on the idea of a graphics pipeline. In this respect it resembles the PMIG specification of Carson and Post. However, the approach to the specification is different. An example of a graphics pipeline is given in figure 11.5.

Processes in the pipeline act on primitives and generate primitives. They also have an associated state that can be set by GKS functions. The first idea in this paper is how to represent primitives. The approach taken is based on the observation that not all the information associated with a primitive is known at every stage of the pipeline. Effectively the pipeline processes add to, subtract from, or otherwise modify the information contained in the primitive entering the process. This suggests associating a name or identifier with each kind of information and then modelling primitives as partial functions from these names to values of the information. Processes then have a fairly simple description in terms of these primitives. The effect of a pipeline is obtained by combining the effects of the operations in the pipeline in such a way that the output from one operation is identified with the input to the next. Z contains an operation combinator called "piping" for this purpose. Each pipeline process has an associated state and operations which modify this state can be readily written. The example in Annex D is based on this approach.

The benefits of this approach over those explored earlier is that the global system state can be partitioned between processes. This means that the descriptions of individual processes become simpler, because only the parts of the state that concern each process need to be considered. It also provides a mechanism for future expansion in that new processes can be easily added to the pipeline with their associated states. It is thought (though this has not yet been confirmed) that this framework is extensible to GKS-3D [15]. Essentially this should be achievable by replacing the transformation processes in the pipeline, but the attribute and aspect binding processes will remain unchanged, highlighting the fact that GKS and GKS-3D have the same attribute binding model.

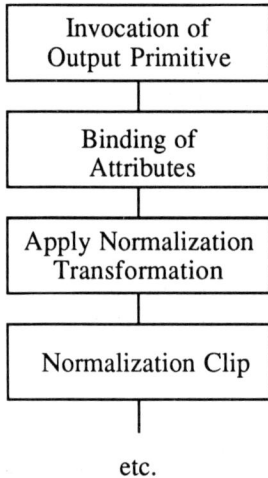

```
┌─────────────────────┐
│   Invocation of     │
│  Output Primitive   │
└──────────┬──────────┘
           │
┌──────────┴──────────┐
│    Binding of       │
│    Attributes       │
└──────────┬──────────┘
           │
┌──────────┴──────────┐
│ Apply Normalization │
│   Transformation    │
└──────────┬──────────┘
           │
┌──────────┴──────────┐
│  Normalization Clip │
└──────────┬──────────┘
           │

         etc.
```

Figure 11.5 Example of a graphics pipeline

The algebraic specification technique, OBJ, is again used in [161] which explores how formal specification techniques could be used to describe a family of graphics standards. The example developed is based on simplifications of GKS and PHIGS. A simple 2D output only system is described, which has a single output primitive, polyline, a single workstation, only bundled attributes and no segment storage. A PHIGS-like structure store is then defined with functions to open, close, and post structures, to set editing mode and the element pointer, and to create structure elements of the following types: 'polyline', 'polyline index', 'execute', 'global modelling transformation' and 'local modelling transformation'.

Graphical output is generated in the PHIGS-like system by traversal of the centralized structure store. The traversal operation is described in terms of the functions of the GKS-like system. Thus the definition of this system without structure storage is reused in the definition of the system with structure storage. This type of layering of descriptions is one form of compatibility between standards which might be felt to be desirable. As in all specifications, it is important to understand that the fact that a specification is structured in a certain way does not mean that the system must be implemented in that way. It is often the case that the decomposition employed in order to achieve a clear, concise specification, is inappropriate for achieving an efficient implementation.

A recent paper by Duce, ten Hagen and van Liere [167] considers how a formal description of the GKS input model can be given using Hoare's Communicating Sequential Processes (CSP) [181] notation. The paper goes on to discuss some possible extensions to the input model in the areas of composite devices, storage strategies (GKS, GKS-3D and PHIGS only have a single queuing strategy) and the interaction between input and output. There is more work to be done here.

Although not specifically concerned with the specification of graphics standards, the most coherent single body of work in the field of formal specification of graphics is contained in the very recent book by Fiume [170] which merits careful study by anyone interested in this field.

11.4   Formal descriptions of standards

ISO/IEC JTC1 encourages its subcommittees to explore the use of formal description techniques in the definition of standards. Three phases have been recognized for introducing formal descriptions into standards:

(1) *Phase 1.* In this phase, knowledge and experience of formal description techniques is lacking and the techniques themselves may be inadequate for describing particular standards. Standards are therefore defined using natural language approaches and the natural language description is the definitive standard.

In this phase, subcommittees are encouraged to experiment with formal description techniques and encourage the publication of formal descriptions, which faithfully represent significant parts of a standard, as ISO Technical Reports. Subcommittees are also encouraged to develop educational material to support the introduction of formal techniques.

(2) *Phase 2.* In this phase, knowledge and experience in formal descriptions is more widely available and it is feasible to support the production of a formal description of a standard, though it cannot be assumed that enough national bodies can review a description to enable a ballot to be held. Here the development of standards by conventional techniques is appropriate, but the developments should be accompanied and supported by the development of formal descriptions with a view to improving the consistency and correctness of the natural language description. Formal descriptions which are considered to represent faithfully a part of a standard or complete standard, would be published as informative annexes to the standard (i.e. would not be an integral part of the standard).

(3) *Phase 3.* In this phase, there is widespread knowledge of formal description techniques, and resources are available to produce and

review formal descriptions of standards. Subcommittees should be using formal description techniques routinely to develop standards and these descriptions would be a part of the standard along with natural language descriptions. Where there is more than one description of a standard, the document has to say which is definitive. Whenever a discrepancy between descriptions is detected, the conflict is to be resolved by changing or improving the descriptions without necessarily giving preference to the formal or natural language descriptions.

The use of formal description techniques in computer graphics standardization currently corresponds to phase 1 above. It is hoped that this chapter might assist in the education activity of this phase and encourage others to explore formal description techniques and their application to graphics standards.

Part 4
Refereeing

12
Validation and Testing

12.1 Introduction

The existence of any kind of standard immediately raises the important question of how one can know whether a product claiming to conform to the standard does in fact conform. Arguably standardization is a pointless activity if this question cannot be answered.

The general problem of deciding whether a software product corresponds to its specification is an active research area and is likely to remain so for some time to come. However, this does not mean that nothing can be done. The normal approach to software validation is through *testing*. The method is to subject the software to a collection of test cases and observe the results. If the results are not as expected, the software certainly does **not** conform to the specification. If the software does produce the expected results, then all that can really be said is that the software performs correctly in that particular instance. There are no grounds for concluding that it will perform correctly under all circumstances. To quote Dijkstra's famous remark — "testing can show the presence of bugs, never their absence". Testing approaches to validation are termed *falsification* methods. The belief underlying our faith in software testing is that programs have a regular structure and if the results are correct for one carefully chosen test case, the correct results will be obtained for a class of similar cases. The question remains of course as to how wide the class of similar cases is and how to choose the test cases in order to give confidence that correct results will be obtained for a practically useful range of cases.

Least the above remarks should sound too negative, it has to be said that falsification methods are the best methods currently available for validating large pieces of software. The confidence that can be placed in assessments obtained by such methods depends largely on the skill with which the test cases are constructed. These methods have been used widely in compiler validation. The book by Wichman and Ciechanowicz gives a good account of applications to Pascal compiler validation [144]. The approach has also been followed extensively for Fortran, Cobol and Ada compiler validation.

Before work in the computer graphics area is discussed, it is helpful to establish some terminology that will be used in the remainder of this chapter. This is necessary because the vocabulary is formal and intuitive meanings given to words can be misleading.

12.2 Terminology

The terminology introduced here is taken from the working draft of the standard on conformance testing [129]. This standard will contain general concepts and guidelines for conformance testing of the range of graphics standards. Although this standard is at a very early stage of processing, the terminology introduced here is widely accepted terminology within ISO/IEC.

Validation is a method to determine the correctness of a *candidate implementation* (an implementation that is being tested for conformance to a given standard). *Conformance* is the adherence of an implementation to the specification of a standard. *Conformance testing* is a testing method to determine the adherence of an implementation to a standard.

A *test suite* is a set of test programs and corresponding documentation that are used for conformance testing. A *test program* comprises a set of *test cases*. A *test case* is the smallest unit of a test program that tests one feature of a candidate implementation. The output of a test case is a *test result*. A *test script* is a document describing the test suite and its various test cases for operator guidance and decision support.

The results of running the test suite on a candidate implementation is a *test report* - a document containing information about the conformance of a candidate implementation including configuration description and detected errors.

A *test service* is a service offered by a *testing laboratory* - an institution offering a conformance testing service.

If a candidate implementation passes the conformance tests for a given standard, a *certificate* (a document officially recognizing that a candidate implementation has passed the conformance testing for a given standard) is issued. The procedure to issue a certificate is called *certification*.

An institute that can issue certificates is called a *certification authority*. *Accreditation* is the procedure by which testing laboratories are assessed. An *accreditation authority* is an institution that provides accreditations.

The next section discusses the problems of constructing test suites for graphics standards. A subsequent section discusses the status of certification for graphics standards.

12.3 Conformance testing of graphics standards

GKS being the first standard for computer graphics was the testbed on which ideas for conformance testing of graphics standards were worked out. The strategy for conformance testing of GKS was developed in the early 1980's. The Commission of the European Community sponsored a workshop held in

Rixensart, Belgium, which brought together parties interested in contributing to the development of a test suite for GKS. The test programs were developed by the University of Leicester in the U.K. and the Technical University of Darmstadt in West Germany. The approach taken is described in some detail in the papers by Brodlie [135] and Brodlie, Maguire and Pfaff [137].

The simplest model of a falsification procedure is one in which the test programs are applied to the candidate implementation and the test results are compared automatically with reference results. This approach is used in some forms of compiler testing. It has also been used very successfully in validating implementations of the NAG numerical algorithms library. The installation tape includes the library, a test suite and a set of reference results, plus a program to run the test suite and compare the test results against the reference results and report any discrepancies.

Unfortunately this approach is not adequate for computer graphics standards, because the results of graphics standards include pictures and validation has to include judgements of test results in the form of pictures against reference pictures. The test programs generating pictures required very careful design [140].

There are two interfaces across which stimuli can be sent and responses observed, the *application interface* and the *operator interface.*

Some parts of the application interface tests can be automated. Functions which set or inquire entries in state lists are well-suited to automated testing. One part of the test suite is devoted to testing the effect of each GKS function on the state lists. Checking of the test results is automated. GKS also has a well-defined error reporting mechanism and another part of the test suite is concerned with checking the response of each function in the error situations identified in the standard.

Response at the operator interface is far more difficult, and is compounded by the number of workstation and implementation dependencies allowed in GKS, for example, whether linetype is continuous or restarted at the start of a polyline, at the start of a clipped piece of polyline or at each vertex of a polyline.

The operator interface part of the test suite consists of a set of test programs which generate visual images, or require the operator to perform some action with a physical input device. The human tester then has to compare the images generated by the candidate implementation against the reference images or reference responses to the input action. The tester has to judge whether the results are adequate and for the reasons stated above, this can call for difficult judgements. The test script points out allowable differences, but checking is still a difficult and time-consuming operation. Not surprisingly, there have been calls from the operators of GKS Testing Services for the number of workstation and installation dependencies in GKS to be reduced when GKS is reviewed.

A great deal of care was taken in the design of the operator interface tests to design images which check large amounts of GKS with a small amount of visual effort. The images are carefully annotated to aid the tester;

for example, a test of fill area interior style can attempt to produce the four styles, HOLLOW, PATTERN, SOLID and HATCH, and then label each to indicate which it is, or is not, mandatory for the workstation to display.

The test suite does have a lot of structure to it, for example, the output tests are organized into classes including simple control, output, primitive attributes, normalization transformations and clipping, workstations and workstation attributes and workstation transformations.

GKS is defined independently of programming languages. It is not quite so easy to do this for the test suite and in terms of validation of a GKS implementation, it is the combination of language binding and GKS that is of interest to someone purchasing a GKS implementation. The GKS test suite was initially coded for the Fortran language binding. A C version is being prepared and versions for other languages are under discussion.

Metafile testing was the subject of a workshop held in Disley, U.K., in March 1987. One of the difficulties with metafile testing is that the conformance statement in the CGM standard only requires that a file conforms to the metafile syntax. There are no requirements placed on generators and interpreters of metafiles. Test suites for CGM are starting to appear. CGM Technology Software in the USA offer products called Metaview and Metacheck. The latter checks that datafiles conform to the (ANSI) CGM standard. Metaview interprets a CGM and displays the resulting picture. The National Computer Centre Ltd in the UK are starting to set up a CGM Testing Service. A prototype testing tool was demonstrated at the Eurographics UK Chapter Conference and CGM Demonstration in March 1989. The tool is being developed by System Simulation Ltd (London) and includes tools to check metafiles for conformance, translate between the different encodings, and generate CGM test data. It is intended that the CGM Test Tool will be available for purchase as a useful aid to development.

The Integrate'88 CGM demonstration [98] held at NCGA'88 in March 1988 did much to improve the quality of a number of products using CGM. Some of the metafiles used in that demonstration have been collected by Bono and Henderson[1]. Integrate'88 used only the binary CGM encoding (see Chapter 10) and a CGM profile close to that being incorporated in MAP/TOP.

The problems of testing the CGI were discussed at a workshop held in Heppenheim, West Germany, in May 1988 [133]. The Commission of the European Community is sponsoring a project aimed at establishing a CGI conformance testing service. The Heppenheim workshop was intended to occupy a similar position in this endeavour to that occupied by the Rixensart workshop in the establishment of the GKS Conformance Testing Service, notably in gathering together international experts to discuss ideas on what form conformance testing for this standard might take.

Although CGI is only at the 2nd DP stage at the present time and thus could change in technical content before it becomes an International

---

[1]For details, contact CGM Technology Software, P.O. Box 648, Gales Ferry, Connecticut, USA.

Standard, there are characteristics of this type of interface which are sufficiently different to API's such as GKS, that it is worthwhile to start to address the conformance testing issues now.

The first problem concerns the diversity of bindings for CGI and is nicely expressed in the paper by Guy and Hewitt [139]. CGI functions are independent of the API standards and programming languages. It is planned that language bindings including single entry point bindings will be defined for Fortran, Pascal, Ada and C. In addition, however, three data stream encodings (clear text, character and binary) are also planned and have to be tested. Taking a simple-minded approach would lead to a plethora of test suites, one for each language binding/ encoding. Maintaining such a volume of software would be difficult, and the chances of inadvertently introducing subtly different behaviour between different versions would be very high. The GKS test suite was initially written in Fortran and has been translated, with a sophisticated translation tool, into C; but such general purpose translation tools do not provide a complete answer. Guy and Hewitt (and others also) advocate an approach based on automatic generation of language / encoding specific modules from a language-independent "pseudo-code" source.

A paper by Vanderschel [143] in the same workshop, considers the problems that arise because CGI will be used in distributed environments. His paper contains a good characterization of the kinds of CGI components (meaning software entities that can accept calls for a CGI procedural language binding, make calls to a CGI language binding, interpret data records which encode CGI functions, or generate data records encoding CGI functions). The most fundamental interface to be addressed is the "My box speaks CGI: plug in here!" interface, but other component types, for example those presenting procedural interfaces, cannot be excluded.

As mentioned earlier, one of the fundamental problems in validation of graphics standards is how to decide if a picture produced on a device is adequate. Human judgement has been used until now and is likely to continue to be used, but papers by Arnold [134] and Brodlie [136] argue that image understanding techniques should at least be explored for this role, though this is clearly a long-term research topic.

The standard on conformance testing of implementations of graphics standards will endeavour to lay down requirements which test suites have to satisfy, but it is as yet premature to say what form these will take.

12.4 Conformance testing services

12.4.1 Test suites

The previous section addressed some of the technical issues and resolutions adopted that arise in conformance testing. This section discusses briefly some of the administrative issues which arise in the operation of a testing service.

There are five issues that have to be addressed before a test service can be established:

(1)   acceptance of the test suite;
(2)   establishment of test procedures;
(3)   acceptance of a test report format;
(4)   issue of licences;
(5)   maintenance procedures.

The first stage in establishing a testing service is to establish test tools. Obviously the test tools have to be of impeccable quality as the confidence one places in the testing service depends crucially on the quality of the tools. The GINO-F graphics package is distributed with a good test suite which consists of a number of programs and the output each should generate. This serves as a valuable aid for installers of the package. The GKS Test Suite was developed in the main by two laboratories and was then submitted to extensive review by the organizations intending to operate the initial test service and by other organizations involved in the development of GKS.

Once the tools have been developed, they are put forward for accreditation as the versions to be used by all testing laboratories operating the testing service. Accreditation is discussed later.

Equally important to the test suite are the procedures under which the test suite is used and the testing procedures operated. The first consideration here is that of maintenance of the test suite. It is in the nature of things that someone will submit an implementation for testing; it will fail some test case and the argument will be advanced that the implementation is right and the reference result of the test case wrong. It is also in the nature of things that sometimes this 'someone' will be right! It is important to have in place procedures to deal with the resolution of such queries, which will often hinge around subtle interpretations of what is specified in the International Standard.

The approach to dealing with the problem is to set up a Control Board whose membership includes a representative from each laboratory operating the testing service and a representative from ISO/IEC JTC1/SC24. Control Boards are charged with resolving disputes. Such a body has the authority to withdraw specific tests on the grounds that they are deemed to be faulty, and authorize reinstatement in a subsequent version of the test suite once the errors have been corrected. Control Boards may also rule that a test case is inapplicable to a specific candidate implementation.

Test suites are developed by a test suite developer who then licences the test suite to accredited testing laboratories and to clients of the testing service.

12.4.2 Testing procedures

Procedures have also to be set up for testing candidate implementations. The GKS Testing Service operates along the following lines. Clients of the testing laboratory may purchase copies of the test suite (under licence) for their own usage. Prior to on-site testing, a client is required to run the test suite and may be required to supply the results to the testing laboratory, including a description of how the test suite was installed and details of initialization values used. Graphics test suites in general will have to be configured for the candidate implementation, for example, in respect of the names of the workstation types supported by the implementation. In the GKS test suite such configuration issues are managed by a configuration program which is part of the test suite and delivers a version of the test suite configured according to the parameters supplied.

On-site testing is conducted by personnel from the testing laboratory. A fresh copy of the test suite is used for this purpose. If any changes are made to the software environment during testing, the results have to be discarded and the procedures restarted from the beginning. All output produced is collected and inspected. Photographic evidence of test results may also be gathered. Journal listings of procedures carried out are also obtained if possible. For the GKS Testing Service, there are comprehensive check lists to ensure that each test case has been run correctly. It will be clear that on-site testing is a time-consuming business.

If conformance problems are encountered during testing, the client either accepts that the errors will be noted in the test report, or testing is abandoned until the errors have been corrected. In the latter case, the entire testing procedure begins again from the start.

When the procedures are complete, a draft Test Report summarizing the procedures followed and the results is produced. This is then sent to the client and the Control Board for comment. The Official Test Report is produced as soon as agreement has been reached, and is signed on behalf of the testing laboratory.

If the implementation has satisfied the conditions prescribed by the Certification Body (see Section 12.4.3), a Conformance Certificate will be issued, and the implementation will be added to the list of certified implementations maintained by the Certification Body.

It is worth noting that in the case of the GKS Testing Service, the Certificates issued are (obviously) very specific in terms of the environment in which the candidate implementation was tested. For example, operating system and more importantly, the types of workstation tested. Certificates are issued with respect to specific workstation (in the GKS sense) configurations. The labour involved in testing may mean that it is not possible to test an implementation against all the workstation types it supports. Labour saving approaches in the area of the operator tests are much needed.

12.4.3 Organizations

There are four kinds of organizations whose roles need to be defined

(1) Certification Authority;
(2) Accreditation Authority;

(3) Client;
(4) Testing Laboratory.

A Certification Body is essentially the body that issues certificates. Accreditation Bodies are bodies that assert that a particular testing laboratory is competent to carry out specific tests or types of tests. In some countries the Certification Body and Accreditation Body are the same organization, in other countries the two are different. There is international cooperation between Certification Bodies towards mutual recognition of test results. Certificates are only issued in respect of testing by an accredited testing laboratory using approved test methods.

A client is an organization which employs a testing laboratory. Testing is carried out on the basis of a contract agreed between client and testing laboratory.

12.5 Current status of testing services

Within Europe a GKS Testing Service is operated by testing laboratories in France, West Germany and the U.K. Certificates are issued under the CENCER Certification Scheme (see Section 4.4.2). The National Institute of Science and Technology (NIST) in the U.S.A. is operating a GKS Testing Service.

There is international cooperation working towards the establishment of testing services for CGM, GKS-3D and PHIGS. As noted earlier, there is a European initiative to produce test methods for CGI. Validation tests for PHIGS are being developed by NIST and a preliminary version is scheduled to be available by the end of 1989.

13
Registration of Graphical Items

13.1 Introduction

As explained in Chapter 3, there are some quantities which it is not reasonable to completely standardize in any particular standard, perhaps because it is not possible to foresee all the examples that will be required at the time the standard is made. An example of this is the linetype aspect of the polyline primitive. There are many different linetypes that can be imagined. Values are given to linetypes 1 to 4 in GKS; 1 is solid, 2, dashed line, 3 dotted line and 4 dashed-dotted line. Values <0 are reserved for implementation dependent linetypes and values ≥5 for values assigned by registration.

It was realized long ago that the way to handle standardization of such quantities is to standardize a small number of examples in a particular standard and allow the set of standardized examples to be extended by a registration mechanism. Registration can be thought of as a name server: once it is agreed that an example of some quantity can be registered, a value or identifier is allocated to that example of the quantity within the name space for the quantity.

When items have been registered, an implementation of a standard providing a value which has been defined by registration has to implement the registered definition.

The questions immediately arise as to what quantities can be handled in this way, how should it be decided whether a particular proposal for registration should be accepted, how should items for registration be specified?

Registration initially deals with the following elements:

(1) generalized drawing primitive function definitions;
(2) escape function definitions;
(3) linetypes;
(4) marker types;
(5) hatchstyles;
(6) text font appearance;
(7) prompt and echo types;
(8) error messages.

The next section looks at procedures that have been established for Registration.

13.2 Registration procedures

It has taken something like three years to agree procedures for the registration of graphical items. At the time of writing, the final text of ISO Technical Report, TR 9973 [132] had been circulated but publication was still awaited. Why should it have taken so long?

The ISO Directives [2] contain some general guidelines on registration procedures, but much flesh has to be hung onto this skeleton. The Register of Graphical Items was initiated under SC21, and was the first set of registration procedures to be devised by that Sub-Committee. The project progressed slowly because it was realized that the procedures devised would be adopted in other areas also and so it was important that they be sound and generalizable.

The Registration process is illustrated in figure 13.1. The key elements in this process are:

(1)   the submitter;

(2)   the Sponsoring Authority;

(3)   the Registration Authority;

(4)   SC24;

(5)   the Register of Graphical Items.

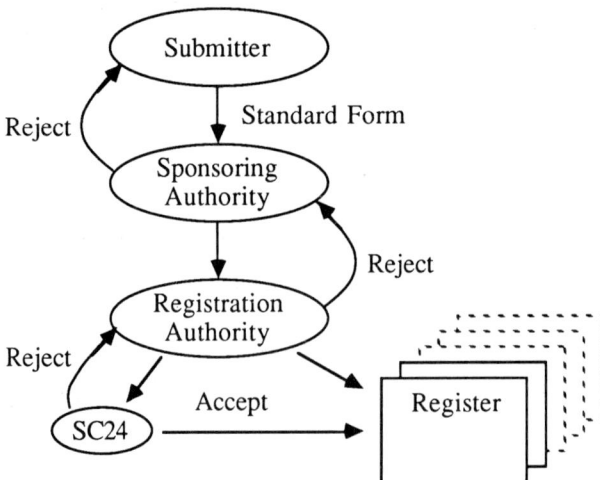

Figure 13.1 The Registration process

The *submitter* submits proposals for registration to a *Sponsoring Authority*. The opportunity to submit registration proposals to a Sponsoring Authority is open to all. A Sponsoring Authority is any of the following organizations:

(1)   any ISO or IEC Technical Committee or Sub-Committee;

(2)   any P-member or O-member of ISO/IEC JTC1 or ISO/IEC JTC1/SC24;

(3)   any international organization having Category A liaison status with ISO/IEC JTC1 or ISO/IEC JTC1/SC24.

Sponsoring Authorities then have to decide whether proposals referred to them should be forwarded for further processing or rejected. This is done by a vote. Criteria for rejection of a proposal include:

(1)   incomplete or incomprehensible definition of the graphical item;

(2)   inadequate language binding or data encoding;

(3)   existence of an identical or similar item in the register;

(4)   not a permitted graphical item;

(5)   non-conformance to existing standards;

(6)   inadequate justification for inclusion in the register.

Proposals which pass this hurdle are then forwarded to the *Registration Authority*.

For the Register of Graphical Items, the National Institute of Science and Technology in the U.S.A. is the Registration Authority. The Registration Authority receives proposals from Sponsoring Authorities and circulates them to the secretariat of ISO/IEC JTC1/SC24 for vote within the Sub-Committee. Criteria for rejection are the same as at the Sponsoring Authority level.

For items which are accepted for registration, the Registration Authority then assigns a value or identifier to the item and incorporates the item in the register.

Proposals may also be made that items be deleted from the Register. These are treated in a similar manner.

13.3 Proposal forms

Proposals for items for registration are made on standard forms. Some examples are included in Section 13.5.

Proposals for the registration of graphical items such as generalized drawing primitives and escapes also have to be accompanied by proposed language bindings. TR 9973 [132] contains guidelines on the generation of such language bindings. These include:

(1)   consistent abbreviations should be used;

(2)   existing datatypes should be used as far as possible;

(3)   existing enumeration types should be used where such exist.

13.4 Status of registration

At the time of writing, no graphical items have actually been accepted for registration. Some graphical items have been submitted for registration as a test of the procedures and already some difficulties have emerged.

These concern, for example, the level of specification required in a proposal. For example, the dashed-dotted-dotted linetype proposal at the end of the chapter, does not state how much bigger the second and third line segments must be than the first. Is any multiplier >1 acceptable?

Another example is a proposal that some hatch styles used in civil engineering drawing to represent different types of materials should be registered. There are several issues here. Can this be construed as an attempt to standardize certain items that should properly fall within the remit of a different part of the ISO structure? There is also an issue of the preciseness of specification which can be given to a hatch style. The proposals are still under discussion.

In future it is likely that registration will extend into other areas, for example CGI Profiles. The principles of registration are sound, but the mechanisms need to be made to work.

13.5 Examples of proposals for registration

The following example of a possible proposal is meant to illustrate the form that proposals take. It must be stressed that at the present time, no proposals have been accepted for inclusion in the Register of Graphical Items.

Proposal Number	1

Date of Presentation	24 July 1989
Sponsoring Authority	DIN
Class of Graphical Item	Linetype
Name	dashed-dotted-dotted

Description

A repeating pattern of three line segments and three gaps, in which the first line segment is larger than the second and third line segments and the second and third line segments are equal in length. The gaps are equal in length. The intended visual representation is illustrated below:

Additional Comments

Justification for Inclusion

This linetype is already present in the CGM. The same linetype value should be registered for use by other graphics standards.

Relationship to Standards

1) ISO 7942 (GKS) - Specifies a registered linetype to supplement those defined in subclause 5.4.1 of ISO 7942.

2) ISO 8632 (CGM) - Specifies a registered linetype to supplement those defined in subclause 5.7.2 of ISO 8632. It should be noted that this linetype is present in CGM as linetype 5.

Part 5
The Result

14

Current Status and Future Directions

14.1 Introduction

In this chapter we examine where the effort towards producing a compatible family of standards has reached, and the directions being taken in directing the efforts planned for the next period. We are mindful of the fact highlighted in the preface that this book is being drafted 10 years to the month after the Editorial Board meeting in Amsterdam, which attempted to draw together some of the ideas of the GSPC (developing the Core proposal) and of the DIN group (developing GKS).

We are assisted in this task by the introspection which occurred within SC24 during the period after its first meeting in Berlin in December 1987. There was general concern then that manpower did not seem to match the workload which was implied for the increasing number of potential new areas for standardization. It was decided therefore that a Special Working Group (SWG) should be established for one meeting to consider the problems of the next five years and make suggestions as to alternative methods of working and for covering the areas to be standardized.

There was also a general feeling that the projects which had been spawned by the initial impetus of the early and mid 70's were largely drawing to a reasonably well defined conclusion with a number of full ISO standards about to appear and the technical work completed. However, while there might be a brief respite which would allow some introspection, the ISO process requires quinquennial reviews of all standards and, with GKS published in 1985, this process would soon be upon the group. In addition a number of new areas were beginning to put pressure on the group, notably the perceived urgent need for standards in the windowing area and in extending the capabilities of the newly agreed PHIGS standard in the area of rendering.

This Chapter will therefore begin examining the status of currently active projects, and then consider the results of the Special Working Group which was held in Blakeney, Norfolk, England in April 1988. We will then examine the impact of the recommendations of the Special Working Group on the planning of future projects which took place at the SC24 meeting in Tucson in July 1988, and the range of projects which has subsequently been initiated.

14.2 The current state of SC24 projects

The status of current SC24 work is summarized in Table 14.1, which shows all the active Work Items and completed projects. The range of new activities will be summarized in later sections.

There are a number of features to this range of projects which should be noted. The main point to note is that due to the interactions with other ISO/IEC work some of the projects cannot progress until other actions are taken by other ISO/IEC committees. Most notable of these interactions is the relationship to ISO/IEC JTC1/SC22, which is concerned with Programming Language Standards. SC22 is currently engaged in two projects having a direct impact on SC24 work; the standardization of firstly the C language and secondly Extended Pascal. In both of these areas SC24/WG4 has been somewhat in advance of the language standard itself getting agreement, knowing how they would wish to use the language before SC22 have decided the exact wording of the standard. This is affecting Part 4 of all the language binding standards and Part 2 of the PHIGS language binding.

Where project timescales are known to depend upon target dates (recorded in SC24/N188) which have already been missed, or where other circumstances have changed we have attempted to record a realistic estimate for new timescales. From past experience it is noticeable that targets are rarely other than earliest times.

14.3   Special Working Group on future planning

The Special Working Group on Future Planning for SC24 met at Blakeney in Norfolk, England in April 1988 under the Chairmanship of Steve Carson (US). The objectives of the meeting were to produce advice to SC24 for the planning of its work over a five year period. As part of formulating that advice the group felt that it was necessary to try and draw together:

- feelings on the experiences of the previous work on producing what has become to be known as "the first generation" of graphics standards;
- suggestions for new ways of structuring the work and the projects;
- predictions about the likely new project topics and their relative importance;
- opinions about the importance of an underlying reference model for graphics systems and standards;
- predictions about other outside pressures on the process (including available manpower, the expectations of standards users, the requirements for liaison with other parts of ISO/IEC, etc.);
- the requirements for enforceable conformance.

Table 14.1 Current Status of ISO/IEC JTC1/SC24 Projects (as at June 1989)

Project	Document Reference	WD	DP	DIS	IS
GKS	ISO 7942				IS (1985)
GKS Addendum 1	ISO 7942/ADD.1			10/88	10/89
GKS Language Bindings					
Fortran	ISO 8651-1				IS (1988)
Pascal	ISO 8651-2				IS (1988)
Ada	ISO 8651-3				IS (1988)
C	SC24/N180	7/88			
GKS-3D	ISO 8805				IS (1988)
GKS-3D Language Bindings					
Fortran	DIS 8806-1				4/89
Pascal	SC24/N190	7/88			
Ada	SC24/N189	7/88	2/89	6/90	
C	SC24/N181	7/88	3/89	12/89	
PHIGS					
Functional description	ISO 9592-1				IS (1989)
Archive file format	ISO 9592-2				IS (1989)
Archive file clear text encoding	ISO 9592-3				IS (1989)
PHIGS PLUS	ISO 9592-4	6/89	10/89		
PHIGS Language Bindings					
Fortran	ISO 9593-1				12/88
Extended Pascal	DP 9593-2		5/89	12/89	
Ada	DIS 9593-3		9/87	1/89	8/89
C	DP 9593-4		5/89	12/89	
CGM					
Functional description	ISO 8632-1				IS (1987)
Character encoding	ISO 8632-2				IS (1987)
Binary encoding	ISO 8632-3				IS (1987)
Clear text encoding	ISO 8632-4				IS (1987)
CGM Addendum 1					
Functional description	ISO 8632-1/ADD.1			10/88	10/89
Character encoding	ISO 8632-2/ADD.1			10/88	10/89
Binary encoding	ISO 8632-3/ADD.1			10/88	10/89
Clear text encoding	ISO 8632-4/ADD.1			10/88	10/89
CGM Addendum 2					
Functional description	ISO 8632-1/ADD.2	3/88	5/89	10/89	10/90
Character encoding	ISO 8632-2/ADD.2	10/89			
Binary encoding	ISO 8632-3/ADD.2	10/89			
Clear text encoding	ISO 8632-4/ADD.2	10/89			
CGI Parts 1-6	DP 9636		11/88	10/89	2/91
CGI Character encoding	SC24/N209	3/89	10/89		
CGI Binary encoding	SC24/N210	3/89	10/89		
CGI Library language binding					
Fortran	SC24/N192	1/89	8/89	4/90	6/91
C	SC24/N191	1/89	8/89	4/90	6/91
Conformity Testing	SC24/N185	7/88	3/89	12/89	10/90
Reference Model	SC24/N177	2/89	9/89		

Gathering this list of opinions provoked wide ranging discussions and lead to the production of a report to SC24 entitled "Towards a Five Year Plan for SC24 [222]" and a series of formal recommendations [215]. The major lessons learnt were listed as follows:

(1)   There should be fewer implementation dependencies in SC24 standards. It was felt that the levels of implementation dependency in current SC24 standards had made it very difficult to define tests for conformance and had impacted the usefulness of statements that a particular implementation conformed.

(2)   The precise scope and goals of a work item need to be agreed before the development starts on a New Work Item and that this precision should be used to try and prevent the enhancement of a project's scope as personnel involved on a particular project changed.

(3)   Continuity of staffing on a particular project cannot be guaranteed throughout a standards activity. Project management techniques therefore have to be evolved which expect the personnel to change rather than rely on accumulated experience of a fixed body of experts. This will involve international acceptance of the need to prevent continual reopening of the same technical issues, in order to assist the discussions in converging in a reasonable time, along with proper recording of the decisions taken and the reasons for them.

(4)   Existing methods lead to too long a timescale for the development of standards, causing pressure for *de facto* standards to be adopted. The long timescale has compounded the problems under (2). It was felt that a well thought out reference model would have greatly eased the problems of developing the first generation of graphics standards and would be equally necessary in ensuring efficient processing of the second generation.

(5)   There were acknowledged deficiencies in the areas of the text and input models used in the first generation of graphics standards.

There were a number of future trends which were felt to have undoubted and urgent implications for the projects over the planning period.

(1)   Windowing technology cannot be ignored, ought to be standardized and has fundamental implications not only for future projects, but potentially for the usefulness of the first generation standards and the feasibility of combining conforming implementations of graphics standards with windowed environments.

(2)   This is one aspect of the wider issues of integration of the graphics standards with a broad range of other work, for example databases in distributed environments. It is also part of the increasing and accelerating trend to use graphics in more diverse application areas, involving many groups who are relatively unfamiliar with the concepts of the first generation systems, and who are (correctly) not interested in becoming graphics experts.

(3) As an extrapolation of the previous point there is a strong expectation that domain specific standards will need to evolve, although these might be formulated by tying down some of the aspects which have been left implementation dependent in more general standards.

(4) Expected increase in the pressure for adoption of *de facto* standards as the products appear to be widely available in the market.

In considering solutions to these problems the Group reviewed a number of alternative strategies, varying from stopping any internal projects and becoming a body which only influenced and ratified *de facto* standards, to doing nothing to improve the progression of the projects. Out of these discussions two strategies emerged as leading contenders for improving the processing of SC24 projects. Both involved the acceleration of work on a reference model for computer graphics.

The first alternative was based on a proposal from the UK to formulate a basic reference model in a rapid and well staffed project, in order to get agreement to a reasonably advanced stage in time for the 1989 SC24 meeting. At that time any projects not at DIS stage would be expected to be reformulated to directly address the new reference model. In the meantime no projects would be allowed to progress to DP status (although work would continue on the definition of the projects and the formulation of New Work Items and on the refinement of Initial and Working Drafts). Work on the Reference Model would be viewed as an essential prerequisite to the GKS review.

The second alternative was very similar except that the basis of the Reference Model work was suggested as needing to encompass a new technique for the definition of standards, which might well also impact the process of standardization. This technique is called Components and Frameworks [127] and proposes that SC24 adopt a toolkit approach to the creation of new standards. In this approach items such as sets of datatypes and operations would be considered as "components" which would be brought together with interrelations defined in a "framework" to compose the overall system. Thus a range of primitives might be considered as a component (e.g. the GKS set of primitives) and combined with only those parts of the transformation pipeline which were at the workstation level to define a new output only device with no storage capability. The approach was seen as having a number of advantages:

- Groups could work on component sets to a large extent independent of, but with liaison to, other groups. This partitioning of the work should help lead to smaller projects with advantages in speed of processing and in the enhanced ability to manage the work.

- The method would help stop the "creeping functionality" problems experienced in the development of first generation standards. Since one group would have responsibility for the update of component sets of a particular type the situation (cf Chapter 5) where one group adds "just one more primitive" to a standard might be avoided with more explicit version control over primitive sets. In addition it should be possible for a framework group to adopt an updated version of component sets leading to the possibility of simplified standards maintenance.

• Incorporating the same components into a number of frameworks should enhance the compatibility between standards.

The Special Working Group recommended that one of the two options be adopted by SC24, whilst a meeting of the BSI reference model group a week after the Special Working Group, produced a report demonstrating that the two approaches were not incompatible [127]. The documents from the Special Working Group were discussed further at the Tucson meeting of SC24 in July 1988. SC24/WG1 considered a number of new areas of functionality and instituted a number of new groups to examine the level of requirement for standards in each area.

14.4 Study Periods and Special Rapporteur Groups

In July 1988 SC24/WG1 recommended the formation of a number of groups to study areas of potential new work within SC24's area of work.

Special Rapporteur Groups

Improved Graphical Text Model [218]

Impact of Windowing on Graphics Standards [221]

Improved Graphics Input Model [219]

Product Data Geometry [220]

Extensions to PHIGS

Study Periods

New Application Program Interface Standards – following on from the results of the GKS Review [215]

Windowing Environments [216]

An API for Imaging

Extensions to the CGM Static Picture Capture Capabilities

Extensions to PHIGS [17]

The Special Rapporteur Groups are each charged with producing a report for the next SC24 meeting addressing the particular topic of the group, whereas the Study Periods are established to define the terms of reference for expected New Work Item proposals to be considered for sponsorship by SC24. The output of these groups is due to reviewed by SC24 at their plenary in October 1989 at which time the directions to be taken in each area should become rather clearer.

The main objectives of the groups are to promote greater harmonization between various areas such as windowing and the SC24 standards; the model and techniques for handling text; and the integration of graphics and product data. In addition the groups are looking at new functional areas (the Imaging API and the windowing system proposal) or additions and revisions to existing standards (the extension to PHIGS to incorporate basic rendering facilities and the review of GKS).

14.5 PHIGS PLUS

A New Work Item proposal has been prepared for a project to extend PHIGS by incorporating new primitives for defining curves and surfaces together with lighting models and shading. A base document has been developed in the U.S.A. and at the time of writing the NWI ballot was about to commence.

The intention is that PHIGS PLUS should be produced as a new Part (4) to ISO/IEC 9592:1989 and a set of Amendments to the three existing parts [17]. It is premature in ISO terms to discuss the technical content of the proposals at this time.

14.6 GKS review

There is an ISO rule that International Standards must be reviewed at not more than five-yearly intervals, with a view to deciding whether they should be confirmed, revised or withdrawn. GKS was published in 1985 and the formal review process is just starting. An informal review of GKS took place in 1987 at a workshop organized by the Eurographics Association [213,217]. The results of this were fed into the ISO/IEC process.

The review of a standard follows the same stages as the creation of a new standard, starting with a New Work Item proposal. A New Work Item proposal for the GKS review was drafted at the Tucson meeting of SC24 in July 1988 and was circulated within SC24 for comment. The comments were addressed by a GKS Maintenance Rapporteur Group meeting held in March 1989 and a revised New Work Item proposal has been submitted to the secretariat for letter ballot within JTC1. At the time of writing, the letter ballot had not been completed.

Revision of an International Standard is a difficult process, for it raises the vexed question of the extent to which application programs which run on the existing standard should, or should not, continue to run unmodified on the revised standard. These problems and some approaches to their solution are familiar from programming language standardization.

The scope of the New Work Item proposal [214] envisages changes to GKS under the following headings, though it must be stressed that these are subject to change as the proposal has not yet been approved.

(1)   Correct editorial mistakes.

(2)   Clarify.

(3)   Remove inconsistencies and technical errors.

(4)   Reduce implementation dependencies.

(5)   Reduce workstation dependencies.

(6)   Review error reporting.

(7)   Improve verifiability.

(8)   Review interworking in window environments.

(9)   Add new functionality.

(10)   Review inquiry functions.

(11)   Review study period output.

(12)   Review special workstation categories.

(13)   Review level structure.

The most open ended of these categories would seem at first sight to be (9), but constraints have been placed on this to limit discussion to new primitives and attributes (including precise appearance control mentioned briefly in Section 5.3), consideration of the output from the special rapporteur groups and improved interworking with metafiles.

There is a strong desire in some quarters, most notably the U.K., to see the emergence of a new slimline GKS based on a small set of well-defined concepts with clear relationships to other standards such as CGM and the emerging CGI. The functionality of ISO 7942:1985 would be provided by a layer on top of this.

It is clear that users of GKS wish to see the number of workstation and implementation dependencies drastically reduced and also to see some toolkit-like facilities for extension of the standard by users in well-defined and controlled ways, for example in the provision of user-defined input device classes and prompt/echoing techniques. Users also want to see the standard take account of modern graphics hardware.

There is much discussion still to take place, but some clear requirements and directions for technical work are emerging.

Part 6
The Reserves

A
Bibliography

A.1 Standards bodies

(1)   *CEN Information Package*, CEN, Rue Brederode 2, BTE 5-1000, Bruxelles, Belgium (1988).

(2)   *Directives for the Work of ISO Technical Committees*, International Organization for Standardization, ISO Central Secretariat, Geneva, Switzerland.

(3)   *ITU Information Package*, International Telecommunication Union, Place des Nations, CH-1211 Geneva 20, Switzerland (1988).

(4)   *Memento 1989*, European Computer Manufacturers Association, 114 Rue du Rhône, CH-1204 Geneva, Switzerland (1989).

A.2 Application Program Interface standards

(5)   BSI, *GKS-3D*, OIS/5/Graphics/230 (January 1984).

(6)   BSI, *Graphical Kernel System (GKS) Functional Description*, Version 3, DPS 13/WG5/25 (December 1978).

(7)   DIN, *Graphical Kernel System (GKS)*, Version 5.0 (1979).

(8)   DIN, *Graphical Kernel System (GKS)*, Version 5.2, NI-9/26-79, DIN (1979).

(9)   ISO, *Graphical Kernel System (GKS)*, Version 6.2 (1981).

(10)   ISO, *Graphical Kernel System (GKS)*, Version 6.6 (1981).

(11)   Rutherford Appleton Laboratory, 'The Graphical Kernel System', RAL 82-007, (January 1982).

(12)   ISO, *ISO/DIS 7942 Information Processing - Graphical Kernel System (GKS) - Functional Description: GKS Version 7.2*, ISO/TC97/SC5/WG2 N163 (1982).

(13)   ISO, *Information processing systems - Computer graphics - Graphical Kernel System (GKS) functional description*, ISO 7942, ISO Central Secretariat, Geneva, Switzerland (August 1985).

(14)   ISO, *Information processing systems - Computer graphics - Graphical Kernel System (GKS) functional description Addendum 1*, ISO 7942/DAD.1, ISO Central Secretariat, Geneva, Switzerland (October 1988).

(15)   ISO, *Information processing systems - Computer graphics - Graphical Kernel System for Three Dimensions (GKS-3D) functional description*, ISO 8805, ISO Central Secretariat, Geneva, Switzerland (1988).

(16)   ISO, *Information processing systems - Computer graphics - Programmer's Hierarchical Interactive Graphics System (PHIGS)*, ISO 9592, ISO Central Secretariat, Geneva, Switzerland (1988).

(17)   ISO, *PHIGS PLUS*, ISO/IEC JTC1/SC24/WG2 N18 (March 1989).

(18)   ACM SIGGRAPH, 'Status Report of the Graphic Standards Planning Committee', *Computer Graphics* **11**(3) (1977).

(19)   ACM SIGGRAPH, 'Status Report on the Graphic Standards Planning Committee', *Computer Graphics* **13**(3) (1979).

(20)   S.S. Abi-Ezzi and A.J. Bunshaft, 'An Implementor's View of PHIGS', *IEEE Computer Graphics and Applications* **6**(2) (1986).

(21)   D.B. Arnold, G.Hall and G.J. Reynolds, 'Proposals for Configurable Models of Graphics Systems', *Computer Graphics Forum* **3**(3), pp. 201-208 (1984).

(22)   D. B. Arnold, G. Hall and G.J. Reynolds, 'GKS Programming in a PHIGS Environment', *Computer Graphics Forum* **4**(4), pp. 349-358 (1985).

(23)   D.B. Arnold and M.R. Hinds, 'On Implementing Parallel GKS', *Computer Graphics Forum* **8**(1), pp. 13-20 (1989).

(24)   R. Bettarini, G. Faconti and L. Moltedo, 'Extending GKS to a Distributed Architecture', in *Proceedings of Eurographics '85*, Ed. C.E. Vandoni, North-Holland (1985).

(25)   R.D. Bergeron, P.R. Bono and J.D. Foley, 'Graphics programming using the Core system', *Computing Surveys* **10**(4), pp. 389-443 (December 1978).

(26)   P.R. Bono, J. Encarnacao, F.R.A. Hopgood and P.J.W. ten Hagen, 'GKS - The First Graphics Standard', *IEEE Computer Graphics and Applications*, pp. 9-23 (July 1982).

(27)   P.R. Bono and I. Herman, *GKS Theory and Practice*, Springer-Verlag (1987).

(28) K.W. Brodlie and G. Pfaff, 'An Algorithmic Interpretation of the GKS TEXT Primitive', *Computer Graphics Forum* **2**(4), pp. 233-241 (1983).

(29) K.W. Brodlie, D.L. Fisher, G.G. Tolton and T.W. Lambert, 'The Development of the NAG Graphical Supplement', *Computer Graphics Forum* **1**(3), pp. 133-142 (1982).

(30) K.W. Brodlie, 'A Better Structure for GKS Programs', in *Proceedings of the GKS Review Meeting*, Eurographics Association (September 1987).

(31) M.D. Brown and M. Heck, *Understanding PHIGS*, Template, San Diego (1985).

(32) R. Buhtz, 'Common Graphics Manager (CGM) - Concepts and their Realization' in *GKS Theory and Practice*, Ed. P.R. Bono and I. Herman, Springer-Verlag (1987).

(33) I. Carlbom and J. Paciorek, 'Planar Geometric Projections and Viewing Transformations', *Computing Surveys* **10**(4), pp. 465-502 (December 1978).

(34) Computer Aided Design Centre, *GINO-F Users' Manual* (1976).

(35) I. Cotton, 'Network Graphic Attention Handling' *Online 72 International Conference*, Brunel University, Uxbridge, England, pp. 465-490 (1972).

(36) D.A. Duce and F.R.A. Hopgood, 'Multiple Inputs in REQUEST mode in GKS', IST/21/2 working paper, Rutherford Appleton Laboratory (1986).

(37) D.A. Duce, 'Concerning the Compatibility of PHIGS and GKS', Informatics Division, Rutherford Appleton Laboratory, Chilton, Didcot, OXON OX11 0QX (1987).

(38) D.A. Duce, 'Configurable Input Devices - A Discussion Paper', in *Proceedings of the GKS Review Meeting*, Eurographics Association (September 1987).

(39) D.A. Duce and F.R.A. Hopgood, 'The Graphical Kernel System (GKS)', *Computer-Aided Design* **19**(8), pp. 396-409 (1987).

(40) A. Ducrot , A. Lemaire and H. Watkins, 'A GKS Implementation for Meteorological Applications', in *Proceedings of Eurographics '81*, Ed. J.L. Encarnacao, North-Holland (1981).

(41) C. Egelhaaf and G. Schumann, 'GOCS - The GKS-oriented Communications System', in *Proceedings of Eurographics '87*, Ed. G. Maréchal, North-Holland (1987).

(42) G. Enderle, K. Kansy and G. Pfaff, *Computer Graphics Programming, GKS - The Graphics Standard*, Second Edition, Springer-Verlag (1987).

(43)　J.D. Foley and V.L. Wallace, 'The Art of Natural Graphic Man-Machine Conversation', *Proceedings IEEE* **62**(4), pp. 462-470 (April 1974).

(44)　J.R. Gallop and C.D. Osland, 'Experiences with implementing GKS on a PERQ and other computers', *Computers and Graphics* **9**(1) (1985).

(45)　R.A. Guedj and H.A. Tucker (Eds), *Methodology in Computer Graphics*, North-Holland, Amsterdam (1979).

(46)　P.J.W. ten Hagen and F.R.A. Hopgood, 'Towards Compatible Graphics Standards', Report 17/79, Stichting Mathematisch Centrum (now CWI), Amsterdam (February 1979).

(47)　I. Herman, *Projective Geometry and Computer Graphics*, Eurographics '88 Tutorial Notes, Eurographics Association, P.O. Box 16, 1288 Aire-la-Ville, Switzerland (1988).

(48)　I. Herman, '2.5 Dimensional Graphics Systems' in *Proceedings of Eurographics '89*, Ed. F.R.A. Hopgood and W. Strasser, North-Holland (1989).

(49)　I. Herman and J. Reviczky, 'A General Device Driver for GKS', in *GKS Theory and Practice*, Ed. P.R. Bono and I. Herman, Springer-Verlag (1987).

(50)　I. Herman and J. Reviczky, 'A Means to Improve the GKS 3D/PHIGS Output Pipeline Implementation', in *Proceedings of EUROGRAPHICS '87*, Ed. G. Maréchal, North-Holland (1987).

(51)　I. Herman and J. Reviczky, 'Some Remarks on the Modelling Clip Problem', *Computer Graphics Forum* **7**(4), pp. 265-271 (1988).

(52)　I. Herman, T. Tolnay-Knefely and A. Vincze, 'A Concept for a GKS Machine', in *Proceedings of Eurographics '85*, Ed. C.E. Vandoni, North-Holland (1985).

(53)　I. Herman, T. Tolnay-Knefely and A. Vincze, 'XGKS - A Multitask Implementation of GKS', in *GKS Theory and Practice*, Ed. P.R. Bono and I. Herman, Springer-Verlag (1987).

(54)　F.R.A. Hopgood and D.A. Duce, 'Graphics Standards - The Current State', Report RAL-86-081, Rutherford Appleton Laboratory, Chilton, Didcot, OXON OX11 0QX, U.K. (1986).

(55)　F.R.A. Hopgood and D.A. Duce, 'GKS-3D and Filters', IST/121/2/3: 20 (August 1986).

(56)　F.R.A. Hopgood, D.A. Duce, E.V.C. Fielding, K. Robinson and A.S. Williams, *Methodology of Window Management*, Springer-Verlag (1985).

(57)　F.R.A. Hopgood, D.A. Duce, J.R. Gallop and D.C. Sutcliffe, *Introduction to the Graphical Kernel System (GKS)*, Second Edition, Academic Press (1986).

(58)   T.L.J. Howard, 'A Shareable Centralised Database for KRT³ - A Hierarchical Graphics System based on PHIGS', in *Proceedings of Eurographics '87*, Ed. G. Maréchal, North-Holland (1987).

(59)   T.L.J. Howard, 'An Annotated PHIGS Bibliography', *Computer Graphics Forum* **8**(3), pp. 262-265 (1989).

(60)   R.J. Hubbold and W.T. Hewitt, 'GKS-3D and PHIGS - Theory and Practice', Eurographics '88 Tutorial Notes, Eurographics Association, P.O. Box 16, 1288 Aire-la-Ville, Switzerland (1988).

(61)   G. Krammer, 'Notes on the Mathematics of the PHIGS Viewing Pipeline', *Computer Graphics Forum* **8**(3), pp. 219-226 (1989).

(62)   L. McKay, *GKS Primer*, Nova Graphics International, Austin, Texas (1984).

(63)   V. Milanese, 'A Proposal for a Distributed Model of GKS Based on Prolog', *Computer Graphics Forum* **7**(3), pp. 203-213 (1988).

(64)   W.M Newman, 'A System for Interactive Graphical Programming', *SJCC 1968*, Thompson Books, Washington, D.C., p. 47-54 (1968).

(65)   C.D. Osland, 'Case Study of GKS Development', in *Eurographics Tutorials '83*, Ed. P.J.W. ten Hagen, Springer-Verlag (1983).

(66)   M.A. Penna and R.R. Patterson, *Projective geometry and its applications to computer graphics*, Prentice-Hall (1986).

(67)   R.F. Puk and J.I. McConnell, 'GKS-3D: A Three-Dimensional Extension to the Graphical Kernel System', *IEEE Computer Graphics and Applications* **6**(8), pp. 42-49 (1986).

(68)   G.J. Reynolds, 'A Token Based Graphics System', *Computer Graphics Forum* **5**(2), pp. 139-146 (1986).

(69)   D.S.H. Rosenthal and P.J.W. ten Hagen, 'GKS in C', in *Proceedings of Eurographics '81*, Ed. J.L. Encarnacao, North-Holland (1981).

(70)   D.S.H. Rosenthal, J.C. Michener, G. Pfaff, R. Kessener and M. Sabin, 'The Detailed Semantics of Graphics Input Devices', *Computer Graphics* **16**(3), pp. 33-38 (July 1982).

(71)   R. Salmon and M.Slater, *Computer Graphics: Systems and Concepts*, Addison-Wesley (1987).

(72)   D. Shuey, 'PHIGS: a graphics platform for CAD application development', *Computer-Aided Design* **9**(8), pp. 410 - 417(1986).

(73)   D. Shuey, D. Bailey and T.P. Morrissey, 'PHIGS: A Standard, Dynamic, Interactive Graphics Interface', *IEEE Computer Graphics and Applications* **6**(8), pp. 50-57 (1986).

(74)   R.W. Simons, 'Minimal GKS', *Computer Graphics* **17**(3), pp. 183-190 (1983).

(75)   K. Singleton, 'An Implementation of the GKS-3D/PHIGS Viewing Pipeline' in *GKS Theory and Practice*, Ed. I. Herman and P.R. Bono, Springer-Verlag (1987).

(76)   M. Slater and R.J. Baker, 'GRAPH: An Interactive Program based on the Graphical Kernel System', in *Proceedings of Eurographics '82*, Ed. D.S. Greenaway and E.A. Warman, North-Holland (1982).

(77)   D.C. Sutcliffe, 'Attribute Handling in GKS', *Proceedings of Eurographics 82*, Ed. D. S. Greenaway and E. A. Warman, North-Holland (1982).

(78)   UK Experts, 'Compatibility between GKS-3D and PHIGS', IST/21/2/3: 15 (August 1986).

(79)   UK Experts, 'Extensions to the GKS Input Model', BSI IST/21/2: 378 (1987).

(80)   C.N. Waggoner, C. Tucker and C.J. Nelson, 'NOVA*GKS A Distributed Implementation of the Graphical Kernel System', *Computer Graphics*, **18**(3), pp. 275-282 (1984).

(81)   V.L. Wallace, 'The Semantics of Graphic Input Devices', *Computer Graphics* **10**(1), pp. 61-65 (April 1976).

(82)   A.S. Williams, 'An Architecture for User Interface R&D', *IEEE Computer Graphics and Applications* (July 1986).

(83)   K.M. Wyrwas and W.T. Hewitt, 'A Survey of GKS and PHIGS Implementations', *Computer Graphics Forum* **8**(1), pp. 49-59 (1989).

(84)   M. Zachrisen, 'Yet Another Remark on the Modelling Clip Problem', *Computer Graphics Forum* **8**(3), pp. 237-238 (1989).

A.3 Metafile and Archive standards

(85)   ISO, *Information processing systems - Computer graphics - Metafile for the storage and transfer of picture description information*, ISO 8632 Parts 1 to 4, ISO Central Secretariat, Geneva (1987).

(86)   ISO, *Information processing systems - Computer graphics - Metafile for the storage and transfer of picture description information Addendum 1*, ISO 8632 /DAD.1 Parts 1 to 4, ISO Central Secretariat, Geneva (1988).

(87)   ISO, *Information processing systems - Computer graphics - Metafile for the storage and transfer of picture description information Addendum 2*, Working Draft, ISO/IEC JTC1/SC24/N219-222.

(88)   D.B. Arnold, 'The Importance of a Correct Approach to the Design of Metafile Standards', in *Proceedings of Eurographics '82*, Ed. D.S. Greenaway and E.A. Warman, North-Holland (1982).

(89)   D.B. Arnold and P.R. Bono, *CGM and CGI: Metafile and Interface Standards for Computer Graphics*, Springer-Verlag (1988).

(90)   P. Bono, 'A Survey of Graphics Standards and their Role in Information Interchange', *IEEE Computer* **18**(10), pp. 63-75 (1985).

(91)   K.W. Brodlie, L. R. Henderson and A. M. Mumford, 'The CGM a metafile for GKS?', *Computer Graphics Forum* **6**(2), pp. 87-90 (1987).

(92)   F.R. Dawson, 'The Computer Graphics Metafile Implementation at McDonnell Douglas', *Computer-Aided Design* **9**(8), pp. 431-435 (1987).

(93)   L. Henderson, M. Journey and C.D. Osland, 'The Computer Graphics Metafile', *IEEE Computer Graphics and Applications* **6**(8), pp. 24-32 (1986).

(94)   F.R.A. Hopgood, R.J. Hubbold and D.A. Duce (Eds), *Advances in Computer Graphics II*, Springer-Verlag (1986).

(95)   L. McKay, *CGI/CGM Primer*, Nova Graphics International, Austin, Texas (1984).

(96)   A. Mumford, 'Why care about the Computer Graphics Metafile?', *Computer-Aided Design*, **9**(8), pp. 425-430 (1987).

(97)   A.M. Mumford, 'Application Profiles for Computer Graphics Standards', in *Proceedings of Eurographics '88*, Ed. D.A. Duce and P. Jancene, North-Holland (1988).

(98)   A.M. Mumford, 'Integrating at NCGA', *Computer Graphics Forum* **7**(3), pp. 229-230 (1988).

(99)   A.M. Mumford, 'The CGM Today and Tomorrow', *Computer Graphics Forum* **8**(2), pp. 125-128 (1989).

(100)   A.M. Mumford and L. Henderson, *The Computer Graphics Metafile*, Butterworth Scientific Ltd (To be published).

(101)   A.M. Mumford and M.K. Skall, *CGM in the Real World*, Springer-Verlag (1988).

(102)   A.M.Mumford, 'The CGM Today and Tomorrow', *Computer Graphics Forum* **8**(2), pp. 125-128 (1989).

A.4 Device Interface standards

(103)   ISO, *Information processing systems - Computer graphics - Interfacing techniques for dialogues with graphical devices*, 2nd DP 9636 (February 1989).

(104) ISO, *Information processing systems - Computer graphics - Interfacing techniques for dialogues with graphical devices data stream encoding - Character encoding*, ISO/IEC JTC1/SC24 N209.

(105) ISO, *Information processing systems - Computer graphics - Interfacing techniques for dialogues with graphical devices data stream encoding - Binary encoding*, ISO/IEC JTC1/SC24 N210.

(106) D.B. Arnold, 'Computer Graphics Interface and CAD Applications', *Computer-Aided Design* **9**(8), pp. 444-450 (1987).

(107) D.B. Arnold and P.R. Bono, *CGM and CGI: Metafile and Interface Standards for Computer Graphics*, Springer-Verlag (1988).

(108) T. Powers, A. Frankel and D.B. Arnold, 'The Computer Graphics Virtual Device Interface', *IEEE Computer Graphics and Applications* **6**(8), pp. 33-41 (1986).

(109) K.S. Vecchiet, 'Computer Graphics Interface: a developer's perspective', *Computer-Aided Design* **9**(8), pp. 451-455 (1987).

A.5 Language binding standards

(110) ISO, *Information processing systems - Computer graphics - Graphical Kernel System (GKS) language bindings - Part 1: Fortran ISO 8651-1 (1988) Part 2: Pascal ISO 8651-2 (1988) Part 3: Ada ISO 8651-3 (1988)*, ISO Central Secretariat, Geneva, Switzerland.

(111) ISO, *Information processing systems - Computer graphics - Graphical Kernel System (GKS) language bindings - Part 4: C*, ISO/IEC JTC1/SC24 N180.

(112) ISO, *Information processing systems - Computer graphics - Graphical Kernel System for Three Dimensions (GKS)-3D language bindings - Part 1: Fortran*, DIS 8806-1, ISO Central Secretariat, Geneva, Switzerland.

(113) ISO, *Information processing systems - Computer graphics - Graphical Kernel System for Three Dimensions (GKS)-3D language bindings - Part 2: Pascal* ISO/IEC JTC1/SC24 N190, ISO Central Secretariat, Geneva, Switzerland.

(114) ISO, *Information processing systems - Computer graphics - Graphical Kernel System for Three Dimensions (GKS)-3D language bindings - Part 3: Ada*, ISO/IEC JTC1/SC24 N189, ISO Central Secretariat, Geneva, Switzerland.

(115) ISO, *Information processing systems - Computer graphics - Graphical Kernel System for Three Dimensions (GKS)-3D language bindings - Part 4: C*, ISO/IEC JTC1/SC24 N181, ISO Central Secretariat, Geneva, Switzerland.

(116) ISO, *Information processing systems - Computer graphics - Interfacing techniques for dialogues with graphical devices library language binding - Fortran*, ISO/IEC JTC1/SC24 N192.

(117) ISO, *Information processing systems - Computer graphics - Interfacing techniques for dialogues with graphical devices library language binding - C*, ISO/IEC JTC1/SC24 N191.

(118) ISO, *Information processing systems - Computer graphics - Programmer's Hierarchical Interactive Graphics System (PHIGS) language bindings - Part 1: Fortran ISO 9593-1 (to be published)*, ISO Central Secretariat, Geneva, Switzerland.

(119) ISO, *Information processing systems - Computer graphics - Programmer's Hierarchical Interactive Graphics System (PHIGS) language bindings - Part 2: Extended Pascal*, DP 9592-2, ISO Central Secretariat, Geneva, Switzerland.

(120) ISO, *Information processing systems - Computer graphics - Programmer's Hierarchical Interactive Graphics System (PHIGS) language bindings - Part 3: Ada*, DIS 9592-3, ISO Central Secretariat, Geneva, Switzerland.

(121) ISO, *Information processing systems - Computer graphics - Programmer's Hierarchical Interactive Graphics System (PHIGS) language bindings - Part 4: C*, ISO/IEC JTC1/SC24 N66.

(122) D.B.Arnold and M.R. Hinds, 'GKS Occam Binding', Version 2, School of Information Systems, UEA, Norwich NR4 7TJ, UK (1988).

(123) W. Hübner and Z.I. Markov, 'GKS-based Graphic Programming in Prolog', in *GKS Theory and Practice*, Ed. P.R. Bono and I. Herman, Springer-Verlag (1987).

(124) D.S.H. Rosenthal and P.J.W. ten Hagen, 'GKS in C', in *Proceedings of Eurographics '82*, Ed. D.S. Greenaway and E.A. Warman, North-Holland (1982).

(125) M.R. Sparks and J.R. Gallop, 'Language Bindings for Computer Graphics Standards', *Computer Graphics and Applications* 6(8), pp. 58-65 (1986).

(126) M.R. Sparks and J.R. Gallop, 'Computer graphics language bindings: programmer interface standards', *Computer-Aided Design* 19(8), pp. 418-424 (1987).

A.6 Framework standards

(127) BSI, 'BSI Contribution on a Computer Graphics Reference Model', ISO/IEC JTC1/SC24 N111 (April 1988).

(128) ISO, 'Component Process for Development of Standards', ISO/IEC JTC1/SC24 N139 (April 1988).

(129) ISO, *Information processing systems - Computer graphics - Conformance testing of implementations of graphics standards*, ISO/IEC JTC1/SC24 N185 (March 1989).

(130) ISO, *Information processing systems - Computer graphics - Reference Model of Computer Graphics*, Interim Draft, ISO/IEC JTC1/SC24/WG1 N49 (1989).

(131) ISO, *Information processing systems - Open systems interconnection - Basic reference model*, ISO 7498, ISO Central Secretariat, Geneva (1984).

(132) ISO, 'Procedures for the Registration of Graphical Items', ISO/TR 9973, ISO Central Secretariat, Geneva, Switzerland (1988).

(133) Eurographics, 'Report on the CGI Conformance Testing Workshop', *Computer Graphics Forum* **7**(3), pp. 231 (1988). (Position papers available as Computer Graphics (Device) Interfaces - Applications and Test Methods for CGI - contact Eurographics Association, P.O. Box 16, 1288 Aire-la-Ville, Switzerland.)

(134) D.B. Arnold, 'Image Analysis Techniques in Certification', University of East Anglia, U.K. (May 1988). (Position paper included in Computer Graphics (Device) Interfaces - Applications and Test Methods for CGI - contact Eurographics Association, P.O. Box 16, 1288 Aire-la-Ville, Switzerland.)

(135) K.W. Brodlie, 'GKS Certification - An Overview', *Computers and Graphics*, **8**(1), pp.5-12 (1984).

(136) K.W. Brodlie, 'Comparison of Pictures', University of Leeds, Leeds, U.K. (May 1988). (Position paper included in Computer Graphics (Device) Interfaces - Applications and Test Methods for CGI - contact Eurographics Association, P.O. Box 16, 1288 Aire-la-Ville, Switzerland.)

(137) K.W. Brodlie, M.C. Maguire and G.E. Pfaff, 'A Practical Strategy for Certifying GKS Implementations', *Computers and Graphics* **8**(2), pp.125-134 (1984). (Also included in *GKS Theory and Practice*, Ed. P.R. Bono and I. Herman, Springer-Verlag (1987).)

(138) G.S. Carson and E. McGinnis, 'The Reference Model for Computer Graphics', *IEEE Computer Graphics and Applications* **6**(8), pp. 17-23 (August 1986).

(139) G.J. Guy and W.T. Hewitt, 'Conformance Testing at the Computer Graphics Interface', NCC and University of Manchester, Manchester, U.K. (May 1988). (Position paper included in Computer Graphics (Device) Interfaces - Applications and Test Methods for CGI - contact Eurographics Association, P.O. Box 16, 1288 Aire-la-Ville, Switzerland.)

(140) M.C. Maguire, 'Visual Testing of GKS at the Human Interface', *Computers and Graphics* **8**(1), pp. 19-28 (1984).

(141) A.M. Mumford, 'Application Profiles for Computer Graphics Standards', in *Proceedings of Eurographics '88*, Ed. D.A. Duce and P. Jancene, North-Holland (1988).

(142) M.W. Skall, 'NBS's Role in Computer Graphics Standards', *IEEE Computer Graphics and Applications* **6**(8), pp. 50-57 (1986).

(143) D. Vanderschel, 'CGI Components in a Distributed Environment', Nova Graphics Corp., USA (April 1988). (Position paper included in Computer Graphics (Device) Interfaces - Applications and Test Methods for CGI - contact Eurographics Association, P.O. Box 16, 1288 Aire-la-Ville, Switzerland.)

(144) B.A. Wichman and Z.J. Ciechanowicz, *Pascal Compiler Validation*, Wiley (1983).

A.7 Formal specification

(145) ANSI, 'American National Standard Functional Specification of the Programmer's Minimal Interface for Graphics', X3H3/82-15rl, ANSI Document (1982).

(146) Gerrard Software Ltd, *ObjEx Reference Manual*, (1987).

(147) D. B. Arnold, D. A. Duce and G. J. Reynolds, 'An Approach to the Formal Specification of Configurable Models of Graphics Systems', in *Proceedings of Eurographics 87*, Ed. G. Maréchal, North-Holland (1987).

(148) H. Barringer, 'A Survey of Verification Techniques for Parallel Programs', in *Lecture Notes in Computer Science Volume 191*, Springer-Verlag (1985).

(149) D. Bjorner and C. B. Jones, *Formal Specification and Software Development*, Prentice-Hall (1982).

(150) K.W. Brodlie and G.E. Pfaff, 'Report on the EEC Workshop on Graphics Certification', *Computer Graphics Forum* **1**(3), pp. 88-90 (1982).

(151) R.M. Burstall and J.A. Goguen, 'An Informal Introduction to Specifications Using Clear', in *The Correctness Problem in Computer Science*, Ed. R.S. Boyer and J.S. Moore, Academic Press (1981).

(152) G.S. Carson, 'The Specification of Computer Graphics Systems', *IEEE Computer Graphics and Applications*, pp. 27-41 (September 1983).

(153) G.S. Carson and E. Post, 'The Formal Specification of a Computer Graphics System', TR 83-6, GSC Associates (1983).

(154) B. Cohen, W.T. Harwood and M.I. Jackson, *The Specification of Complex Systems,* Addison-Wesley Publishing Company (1986).

(155) D. Coleman and R.M. Gallimore, 'Software Engineering Using Executable Specifications', Dept. of Computation, UMIST, U.K. (1984).

(156) P. Dickman, 'Definition of Interior Points in CGI, CGM, GKS-3D and PHIGS', Laser Scan Ltd., U.K. (June 1985).

(157) D.A. Duce, 'The EEC Workshop on Formal Specification of Graphics Software Standards', *Computer Graphics Forum* **1**(3), pp. 92-95 (1982).

(158) D.A. Duce, 'A Simple Example from GKS in Z', RAL-86-082, Rutherford Appleton Laboratory (1986).

(159) D.A. Duce, 'Formal Specification of Graphics Software', in *Proceedings of CIL'87*, Barcelona, Spain (March 1987).

(160) D.A. Duce, 'Formal Specification of Graphics Software', in *Theoretical Foundations of Computer Graphics and CAD*, Ed. R.A. Earnshaw, Springer-Verlag (1988).

(161) D.A. Duce, 'GKS, Structures and Formal Specification', in *Proceedings of Eurographics '89*, Ed. F.R.A. Hopgood and W. Strasser, North-Holland (1989).

(162) D.A. Duce and E.V.C. Fielding, 'Better Understanding through Formal Specification', *Computer Graphics Forum* **4**(4), pp. 333-348 (1985).

(163) D.A. Duce and E.V.C. Fielding, 'Formal Specification - A Simple Example', *ICL Technical Journal*, pp. 96-111 (May 1986).

(164) D.A. Duce and E.V.C. Fielding, 'Towards a Formal Specification of the GKS Output Primitives', in *Proceedings of Eurographics '86*, Ed. A.A.G. Requicha, North-Holland (1986).

(165) D.A. Duce and E.V.C. Fielding, 'Formal Specification - A Comparison of Two Techniques', *Computer Journal* **30**(4), pp. 316-327 (1987).

(166) D.A. Duce, E.V.C. Fielding and L.S. Marshall, 'Formal Specification of a Small Example Based on GKS' *Transactions on Graphics* **7**(3), pp. 180-197 (1988).

(167) D.A. Duce, P.J.W. ten Hagen and R. van Liere, 'Components, Frameworks and GKS Input', in *Proceedings of Eurographics '89*, Ed. F.R.A. Hopgood and W. Strasser, North-Holland (1989).

(168) R. Eckert, 'Specification of Graphics Systems', in *Methodology of Interaction,* Ed. R.A. Guedj, P.J.W. ten Hagen, F.R.A. Hopgood, H. Tucker and D.A. Duce, North-Holland (1980).

(169) Elizabeth Fielding, 'The Specification of Abstract Mappings and their Implementation as B+-Trees', Technical Monograph PRG-18, Oxford University Computing Laboratory, Programming Research Group (September 1980).

(170) E. Fiume, *The Mathematical Structure of Raster Graphics,* Academic Press (1989).

(171) K. Futatsugi, J. A. Goguen, J.-P. Jouannaud and J. Meseguer, 'Principles of OBJ2', *Proceedings of the 1985 Symposium on Principles of Programming Languages* (1985).

(172) N.Gehani and A.D. McGettrick, *Software Specification Techniques,* Addison-Wesley Publishing Company (1986).

(173) R. Gnatz, 'An Algebraic Approach to the Standardization and the Certification of Graphics Software', *Computer Graphics Forum* **2**(2/3), pp. 153-166 (1983). (Also in I. Herman and P.R. Bono (Eds.), *GKS Theory and Practice*, Springer-Verlag (1987).)

(174) J. Goguen and J. Meseguer, 'Rapid Prototyping in the OBJ Executable Specification Language', *ACM Sigsoft Software Engineering Notes* **7**(5), pp. 75 (1982).

(175) J.A. Goguen, J.W. Thatcher and E.G. Wagner, 'An Initial Algebra Approach to the Specification, Correctness, and Implementation of Abstract Data Types', in *Current Trends in Programming Methodology Volume IV*, Ed. R. T. Yeh, Prentice-Hall (1978).

(176) J. Guttag and J.J. Horning, 'Formal Specification as a Design Tool', *Proceedings of the Seventh Annual ACM Symposium on Principles of Programming Languages* (1980).

(177) J. V. Guttag, E. Horowitz and D. R. Musser, 'The Design of Data Type Specifications', in *Current Trends in Programming Methodology Volume IV*, Ed R. T. Yeh, Prentice-Hall (1978).

(178) I. Hayes, 'Examples of Specification using Mathematics', Programming Research Group, Oxford (1985).

(179) P. Henderson, 'me too - a language for software specification and model building - preliminary report', Computing Science FPN-9, University of Stirling (1984).

(180) P. Henderson, 'Specifications and Programs', in *Software; Requirements, Specifications and Testing*, Ed. T. Anderson, Blackwell Scientific Publications.

(181) C.A.R. Hoare, *Communicating Sequential Processes,* Prentice-Hall (1985).

(182) C.B. Jones, 'Systematic Program Development', Department of Computer Science, University of Manchester (1984).

(183) C.B. Jones, *Software Development: A Rigorous Approach*, Prentice-Hall (1980).

(184) C.B. Jones, *Software Development Using VDM,* Prentice-Hall (1986).

(185) W.R. Mallgren, 'Formal Specification of Interactive Graphics Programming Languages', Technical Report 81-09-01, PhD Dissertation, Department of Computer Science, University of Washington, Seattle (September 1981). (Also published by ACM-MIT Press Distinguished Dissertation Series in June 1983.)

(186) W.R. Mallgren, 'Formal Specification of Graphic Data Types', *ACM Transactions on Programming Languages and Systems* 4(4), pp. 687-710 (October 1982).

(187) L.S. Marshall, 'A Formal Specification of Line Representations on Graphics Devices', in *Lecture Notes in Computer Science Volume 186,* Springer-Verlag (1985).

(188) M. Martins and J.N. Oliveira, 'Graphics Programming with Archetypes', in *Proceedings of Eurographics '85*, Ed. C. E. Vandoni, North-Holland (1985).

(189) M. Martins and J.N. Oliveira, 'On the Specification of Archetype Oriented Graphics Editors', Universidade do Minho, Braga, Portugal (1986).

(190) M.D. McGettrick, *The Definition of Programming Languages,* Cambridge University Press (1980).

(191) A.J.R.G. Milner, *A Calculus of Communicating Systems,* Lecture Notes in Computer Science Volume 92, Springer-Verlag (1980).

(192) C. Minkowitz, 'A Methodology for the Prototyping of Software Design' Department of Computer Science, University of Stirling, Scotland (1984).

(193) C. Minkowitz, 'Specification to Prototype - A comparison of two formal methods of software design' Department of Computer Science, University of Stirling, Scotland (1984).

(194) C. Morgan, 'The Schema Language' Programming Research Group, Oxford (1984).

(195) T. Onodera and S. Kawai, 'A formalization for the specification and systematic generation of computer graphics systems', *The Visual Computer* 2, pp. 112-126 (1986).

(196) F.G. Pagan, *Formal Specification of Programming Languages,* Prentice-Hall (1981).

(197) D. Richter, 'Mappings between Product Data Definitions' in *Proceedings of Eurographics '86,* Ed. A.A.G. Requicha, North-Holland (1986).

(198) D.S.H. Rosenthal, 'A Framework for Specifying GKS' X3H3/80-63, ANSI Document (1980).

(199)   J.M. Spivey, *The Z Notation: A Reference Manual*, Prentice-Hall (1988).

(200)   J. E. Stoy, *Denotational Semantics*, The MIT Press (1977).

(201)   B. Sufrin, 'Notes for a Z Handbook. Part 1: The Mathematical Language', Software Engineering Working Paper, Programming Research Group, Oxford (1984).

(202)   B. Sufrin, 'Towards a formal specification of the ICL Data Dictionary' *ICL Technical Journal*, pp. 195-217 (November 1984).

(203)   K.J. Turner, 'Towards better specifications', *ICL Technical Journal*, pp. 33-49 (May 1984).

(204)   J.C.P. Woodcock and M. Loomes, *Software Engineering Mathematics*, Pitman (1988).

A.8 UIMS and Window Systems

(205)   ACM SIGGRAPH, Special Issues on User Interface Software, *Transactions on Graphics* **5**(2-4) (1986).

(206)   W.H. Clifford, J.I. McConnell and J.S. Saltz, 'The Development of PEX, a 3D Graphics Extension to X11', in *Proceedings of Eurographics '88*, Ed. D.A. Duce and P. Jancene, North-Holland (1988).

(207)   H.I.M. Hartelt, L.P. Magalhaes and B.M. Daltrini, 'A Window Management System on Top of GKS', in *Proceedings of Eurographics '87*, Ed. G. Maréchal, North-Holland (1987).

(208)   F.R.A. Hopgood, D.A. Duce, E.V.C. Fielding, K. Robinson and A.S. Williams, *Methodology of Window Management*, Springer-Verlag (1985).

(209)   M. Prime, 'User Interface Management Systems - A Current Product Review', RAL-88-028, Rutherford Appleton Laboratory, U.K. (1988).

(210)   W. Roberts, M. Slater, K. Drake, A. Simmins, A. Davison and P. Williams, 'First Impressions of NeWS', *Computer Graphics Forum* **7**(1), pp. 39-57 (1988).

(211)   D.S.H. Rosenthal, 'Window System Implementations', Eurographics UK Chapter Conference '87 Tutorial Notes, Eurographics Association, P.O. Box 16, 1288 Aire-la-Ville, Switzerland (1987).

(212)   R.W. Scheifler and J. Gettys, 'The X Window System', *Transactions on Graphics* **5**(2), pp. 79-109 (1986).

A.9 Future work

(213) Eurographics, 'GKS Review Workshop', *Computer Graphics Forum* **6**(4), pp. 367-369 (1987).

(214) ISO, 'GKS Revision NWI', ISO/IEC JTC1/SC24/WG1 N68 (March 1989).

(215) ISO, 'Recommendations of the Special Working Group on Future Planning', ISO/IEC JTC1/SC24 N140 (April 1988).

(216) ISO, 'Report on the Eurographics/SC24 joint workshop on the Impact of Windowing Systems on Graphics Standards', Copenhagen (November 1988).

(217) Eurographics, *Proceedings of the GKS Review*, Eurographics Association, P.O. Box 16, 1288 Aire-la-Ville, Switzerland (September 1987).

(218) ISO, 'Terms of Reference for Improved Graphics Text Model', ISO/IEC JTC1/SC24 N172 (July 1988).

(219) ISO, 'Terms of Reference for Studying an Improved Graphics Input Model', ISO/IEC JTC1/SC24 N173 (July 1988).

(220) ISO, 'Terms of Reference for Studying Product Data Geometry', ISO/IEC JTC1/SC24 N173 (July 1988).

(221) ISO, 'Terms of Reference for Studying the Impact of Windowing on Graphics Standards', ISO/IEC JTC1/SC24 N174 (July 1988).

(222) ISO, 'Towards a Five Year Plan for SC24', ISO/IEC JTC1/SC24 N136 (April 1988).

(223) P. Bono, 'Software Standards: Which Ones are Here to Stay?', *The S. Klein Computer Graphics Review*, Inaugural Issue, pp. 94-100 (Spring 1986).

(224) I.D. Hill and B.L. Meek, *Programming Language Standardisation*, Ellis and Horwood (1980).

B
Glossary

ACM	Association for Computing Machinery
AD	Addendum
ANSI	American National Standards Institute
ANSI X3H3	ANSI Computer Graphics Working Group
ASF	Aspect Source Flag
BSI	British Standards Institution
CCITT	International Telegraph and Telecommunications Committee (of ITU)
CEN	European Committee for Standardization
CENCER	CEN Certification scheme
CENELEC	European Committee for Electrical Standardization
CEPT	European Conference of Postal and Telecommunications Administrations
CGM	Computer Graphics Metafile (ISO 8632)
CGI	Computer Graphics Interface (2nd DP 9693)
CSS	Centralized Structure Store (PHIGS)
DAD	Draft Addendum
DC	Device Coordinates
DIN	Deutsches Institut für Normung, the West German National Standards Body
DIS	Draft International Standard
DP	Draft Proposal
ECMA	European Computer Manufacturers' Association
EMUG	European Map Users' Group
EN	European Standard
ENV	European Pre-Standard
EWOS	European Workshop on Open Systems
GDP	Generalized Drawing Primitive
GINO	Graphical INput/ Output (graphics package)
GKS	Graphical Kernel System (ISO 7942)
GKS-3D	Graphical Kernel System for Three Dimensions (ISO 8805)
GPGS	General Purpose Graphic System
GSPC	Graphic Standards Planning Committee
IDIGS	Interactive Device Independent Graphic System
IEC	International Electrotechnical Commission
IFIP	International Federation for Information Processing
IFIP WG5.2	IFIP CAD/CAM Working Group

ISO	International Organization for Standardization
IT	Information Technology
ITSTC	Information Technology Steering Committee
ITU	International Telecommunications Union
MAP	Manufacturing Automation Protocols
NDC	Normalized Device Coordinates
NPC	Normalized Projection Coordinates
OSI	Open Systems Interconnection
PDAD	Proposed Draft Addendum
PHIGS	Programmer's Hierarchical Interactive Graphics System (ISO 9652)
SIGGRAPH	ACM Special Interest Group on Computer Graphics
SPAG	Standards Promotion and Applications Group
TOP	Technical Office Protocols
VRC	View Reference Coordinates
WC	World Coordinates
WD	Working Draft
WDSS	Workstation Dependent Segment Storage
WISS	Workstation Independent Segment Storage
X3H3	Contraction of ANSI X3H3

C

Standardization Bodies

C.1 National Bodies

ABNT/CB-21
Av. 13 de Maio, 13-S/2007
BR - 20.031 - Rio de Janeiro-RJ   Phone   +55 21 240 25 99/553 3376
BRASIL   Telex   38 (21) 34.333 ABNT BR

AFNOR
Division Informatique
Tour Europe - Cedex 7   Phone   +33 1 42 91 57 06
F - 92080 Paris La Defense   Telefax +33 1 42 91 56 56
FRANCE   Telex   611 974 AFNOR F

ANSI
1430 Broadway   Phone   +1 212 642 4934
USA - New York, N.Y. 10018   Telefax +1 212 302 1286
U S A   Telex   023 / 42 42 96

BSI
British Standards Institution
2 Park Street   Phone   +44 1 629 90 00
GB - London W1A 2BS   Telefax +44 1 629 05 06
GREAT BRITAIN   Telex   266 933 BSILON G

Dansk Standardiseringsraad DS
Aurehojvej 12 - Postboks 77   Phone   +45 1 62 32 00
DK - 2900 Hellerup   Telefax +45 1 62 30 77
DENMARK   Telex   15 615 DANSTA DK

DIN
Burggrafenstr. 6 - Postfach 11 07   Phone   +49 3026011
D-1000 Berlin 30   Telefax +49 302601231
F.R. GERMANY   Telex   184273 DIN D

Institut Belge de Normalisation (IBN)
Av. de la Brabanconne, 29
B - 1040 Bruxelles   Phone   +32 02 734 92 05
BELGIUM   Telex   23 877 BENOR B

Japanese Industrial Standards Committee (JISC)
c/o Standards Department
1-3-1, Kasumigaseki, Chiyodaku   Phone   +81 3 431 2808
J - Tokyo 100   Telefax +81 3 431 6493
JAPAN   Telex   02 32 53 40 IPSJ J

Magyar Szabvanyügyi Hivatal (MSZH)
P.O. Box 24
H - 1450 Budapest 9
HUNGARY

Nederlands Normalisatie Instituut (NNI)
Kalfjeslaan 2
Postfach 50 59   Phone   +31 15 61 1061
NL - 2600 GB Delft   Telefax +31 15 69 0390
NEDERLANDS   Telex   3 81 44 nni nl

Österr. Normungsinstitut (ONORM)
Heinestr. 38
Postfach 130
A - 1021 Wien 2   Phone   +43 222 26 75 35
AUSTRIA   Telex   115 960

SNV
Kirchenweg 4 - Postfach
CH - 8032 Zürich
SWITZERLAND

Standardiseringskommissionen i Sverige (SIS)
Box 3295 Tégnergatan 11   Phone   +46 8 23 04 00
S - 10366 Stockholm 6   Telefax +46 8 11 70 35
SWEDEN   Telex   17 453 sis s

UNIPREA
Ente di Unificazione
Federato all'UNI
Via Montevecchio, 29
I - 10128 Torino   Phone   +39 11-53 17 12-51 31 46
ITALY   Telex   216 825 unipto i

Urad pro normalizaci a mereni
(CSN)
Vaclavske namesti 19
CS - 113 47 Praha 1
CZECHOSLOVAKIA

USSR State Committee for Standards (GOST)
Leninsky Prospekt 9
SU - Moskva 117049
SOVIET UNION

BDS State Committee for
Science and Technological Progress
Standards Office
21, 6th September Street
BG - 1000 Sofia
BULGARIA

Standards Council of Canada (SCC)
International Standards Branch
350 Sparks Street, Suite 1200 Phone +1 613 238 3222
CDN - Ottawa, Ontario KIP7 S8 Telefax +1 613 995 4564
CANADA   Telex 0 53 4403

SFS
Bulevardi 5 A 7
Postfach 205
SF - 00121 Helsinki 12   Phone +35 8 64 56 01
FINLAND   Telex 122 303 stand sf

Korean Bureau of Standards
Indust. Advancement Administr.
2, Chungang-dong, Kwachon-city Phone +82 25 03 79 28
ROK - Kyonggi-do 171-11   Telefax +82 25 03 79 41
REPUBLIC KOREA   Telex 28 456 FINCEN K

PKNMiJ Polish Committee for Standardization
Measures and Quality Control
UL. Elektoralna 2
PL - 00-139 Warsaw
POLAND

Standards Association of Australia (SAA)
Standards House
80-86 Arthur Street   Phone +61 2 963 4111
AUS - North Sydney - N.S.W. 2060 Telefax +61 2 959 3896
AUSTRALIA   Telex 26 514 ASTAN AA

C.2 International organizations

CEN
Rue Brederode 2   Phone   +32 25196811
BTE 5-1000 Bruxelles   Telefax +32 25196819
BELGIUM   Telex   26257 CENLEC B

ECMA
114 Rue du Rhône   Phone   +41 22 7353634
CH-1204 Geneva   Telefax +41 22 7865231
SWITZERLAND   Telex   413237

ISO
Case postale 56   Phone   +41 22 341240
CH-1211 Geneva 26   Telex   23887
SWITZERLAND

ITU
Place des Nations   Phone   +41 22 995111
CH-1211 Geneva   Telefax +41 22 337256
SWITZERLAND   Telex   421000 UIT CH

D
Formal Specification
An Example from GKS

D.1 Overview

This section contains a formal specification of a part of GKS. It is included to give an idea of what a formal specification of GKS would look like. The example is based on the approach in the paper by Arnold *et al* [147] but considers the polymarker primitive instead of polyline. A simplified graphics pipeline is considered which excludes segment storage. The model system is equivalent to GKS output level 0 in this respect. In addition some control aspects of GKS, for example considerations of dynamic modification, are not addressed. These issues are peripheral to this book and their consideration does not change the output pipeline. A formal specification of dynamic modification has been given elsewhere [166]. The definitions of the following GKS functions are considered:

POLYMARKER   SET COLOUR REPRESENTATION
SET POLYMARKER INDEX   SELECT NORMALIZATION
                                      TRANSFORMATION
SET MARKER TYPE   SET WINDOW
SET MARKER SIZE SCALE FACTOR   SET VIEWPORT
SET POLYMARKER COLOUR INDEX   SET CLIPPING INDICATOR
SET POLYMARKER REPRESENTATION   SET WORKSTATION VIEWPORT
SET ASPECT SOURCE FLAG   SET WORKSTATION WINDOW

The following processes are described:

Application Interface
mk_wc_polymarker   describes the geometry of the primitive in world
          coordinates

Transformation Strand
apply_norm_trans   applies the current normalization transformation
apply_ws_trans   applies the current workstation transformation

Clipping Strand
bind_cr   binds the clip rectangle
apply_norm_clip   clips the geometry to the bound clip rectangle
apply_ws_clip   clips to the workstation window

Attribute Strand

bind_pm_asf	binds the aspect source flags
bind_ind_values	binds the values of individually specified aspects
bind_ws_bundle	binds the values of aspects specified by bundles
bind_colour	binds the representation of the colour index
elaborate	renders the primitive

Device Interface

mk_dc_polymarker	describes the primitive in display space
add_dcp	adds the primitive to the DC picture

The pipeline is shown in figure D.1.

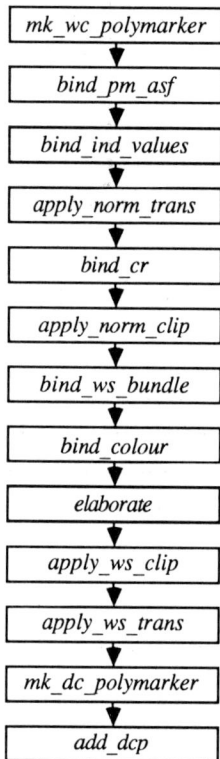

```
┌─────────────────────┐
│  mk_wc_polymarker   │
└─────────────────────┘
           ▼
┌─────────────────────┐
│    bind_pm_asf      │
└─────────────────────┘
           ▼
┌─────────────────────┐
│   bind_ind_values   │
└─────────────────────┘
           ▼
┌─────────────────────┐
│   apply_norm_trans  │
└─────────────────────┘
           ▼
┌─────────────────────┐
│      bind_cr        │
└─────────────────────┘
           ▼
┌─────────────────────┐
│   apply_norm_clip   │
└─────────────────────┘
           ▼
┌─────────────────────┐
│   bind_ws_bundle    │
└─────────────────────┘
           ▼
┌─────────────────────┐
│    bind_colour      │
└─────────────────────┘
           ▼
┌─────────────────────┐
│     elaborate       │
└─────────────────────┘
           ▼
┌─────────────────────┐
│   apply_ws_clip     │
└─────────────────────┘
           ▼
┌─────────────────────┐
│   apply_ws_trans    │
└─────────────────────┘
           ▼
┌─────────────────────┐
│  mk_dc_polymarker   │
└─────────────────────┘
           ▼
┌─────────────────────┐
│      add_dcp        │
└─────────────────────┘
```

Figure D.1 Pipeline for the example

There is nothing absolute about this set of processes. It has been chosen for the purposes of illustration; there are obvious alternative decompositions with both coarser and finer granularity. The order in which the processes are composed is discussed in section D.3.

Primitives are represented by functions. The type of functions used are called *finite functions* because the argument of the function only takes a finite number of values. Not all the possible information associated with a primitive is known at every stage of the pipeline, hence the functions representing primitives are in fact *partial functions*, that is functions which are not necessarily defined for every possible value of their arguments. The domain of the partial function is the set of values of the argument for which the function is defined.

The usual representation for finite functions is as a set of ordered pairs. The first element of the pair is a value in the domain of the function and the second is the value in the range to which it is mapped by the function. Thus:

$$p = \{NDCG \mapsto ndcg, PIND \mapsto pmi \}$$

is the finite function for which $p(NDCG) = ndcg$ and $p(PIND) = pmi$. The symbol "$\mapsto$" is read as "maps to".

Primitives then will be represented by finite partial functions of type *PRIM* whose domain is of type *IDENTIFIER* and range of type *VALUE*. In the Z notation this is expressed as:

PRIM _____
| IDENTIFIER ↦ VALUE _____

Table D.1 gives the complete set of identifiers for a polymarker, a description of the information and its type. In the definitions of types, the symbol "$\rightarrow$" denotes a function and the symbol "**P**" (powerset) denotes a set of the following type. Thus $POINT \rightarrow COLOUR$ is a function from *POINT* to *COLOUR* and **P** *POINT* is a set of *POINT*.

Table D.1 Primitive identifiers

Identifier	Description	Type of Information
ASF	aspect source flags	$ASPECT \rightarrow ASF\_VALUE$
ASP	aspects	$ASPECT \rightarrow ASP\_VALUE$
COL	colour	COLOUR
DCG	geometry in device coordinate space	**P** POINT
DCP	device coordinate primitive after rendering	$POINT \twoheadrightarrow COLOUR$
NCR	clip rectangle for normalization clip	RECTANGLE
NDCG	geometry in normalized device coordinate space	**P** POINT
PIND	polymarker index	PMI
WCG	geometry in world coordinate space	**P** POINT

The type IDENTIFIER is thus:

IDENTIFIER _____
| ASF | ASP | COL | DCG | DCP | NCR | NDCG | PIND | WCG

The arrows between processes in figure D.2 (in Section D.4) are labelled with the domain of the function representing the primitive at each stage in the pipeline. The domain is equivalent to the information known about the primitive at each stage.

The type of the range of the partial functions representing polymarkers needs to include all the types in the table above. The type *VALUE* is then the disjoint union of these types. This is expressed in Z as follows.

VALUE ::=   *mkasf*<< *ASPECT* → *ASF_VALUE* >> |
                 mkasp<< *ASPECT* → *ASP_VALUE* >> |
                 mkcol<<*COLOUR*>> |
                 mkps<< **P** *POINT* >> |
                 mkdcp<< *POINT* ⇸ *COLOUR* >> |
                 mkr<<*RECTANGLE*>> |
                 mkpind<< *PMI* >>

The symbols *mkasf* etc are constructor functions for the type. The inverse functions (*mkasp*[-1] etc) map from the type *VALUE* to the component types of the disjoint union. Occurrences of these functions are often intrusive in the specification, but they may be ignored by the reader as their purpose is purely to map between types to ensure correct typing of the specification. Thus if *ps* denotes a variable of type **P** *POINT*, the corresponding value of type *VALUE* is *v* = *mkps* (*ps*) and also *ps* = *mkasp*[-1](*v*).

The processes are described in strand order rather than the order of occurrence in the pipeline. Thus the transformation processes are described together rather than interspersed between other processes. It is one of the strengths of this approach that it is possible to separate concerns in this way.

D.2 The pipeline

D.2.1 Application interface

mk_wc_polymarker
This is the first process in the pipeline. A polymarker primitive draws a sequence of points marked with the same symbol. The parameter associated with the primitive is the sequence (with length greater than 1) of points. The world coordinate object is represented as the set of points to be marked. The result is an object representing the geometry of the world coordinate primitive defined by the application as a set of points. Points are represented by the type *POINT*:

POINT _____
| $x : \mathbf{R}$
| $y : \mathbf{R}$

A point is a tuple with selectors *x* and *y*. Thus *p.x* denotes the *x* coordinate of the point *p* and *p.y* the *y* coordinate.

The operation *mk_wc_polymarker* defines the world coordinate geometry of the primitive. The input parameter to *mk_wc_polymarker* is a sequence (with length greater than 1) of points in the real plane.

---

mk_wc_polymarker _____

 pts? : seq_1 *POINT*
 p! : *PRIM*

---

 p! = { *WCG* $\mapsto$ *mkps*(ran *pts?*) }

The notation calls for some explanation. The operation *mk_wc_polymarker* is described by a *schema*. Schemas consist of two parts: the declarations (above the centre line) in which variables to be used in the schema are declared, and a predicate (below the centre line) containing predicates giving properties of and relating those variables. By convention variables which are inputs to an operation are given names ending in "?" and outputs are given names ending in "!". The input to the operation is a set of points represented by the variable *pts?* of type seq_1 *POINT*, and the output is a primitive represented by the variable *p!* of type *PRIM*. The only information known about the primitive is its world coordinate geometry and so the partial function *p!* has just one identifier in its domain (*WCG*) whose value is the set of points to be marked.

The operator *ran* applied to a sequence delivers the set of objects which are elements of the sequence.

ran s = { $i : 1 .. \#s \cdot s(i)$ }

The operator '#' returns the number of elements in a set. For completeness, the definition of seq_1 of any type X is:

$seq_1 X == \{ f : seq\ X \mid \#f > 1 \}$

The input parameter to this operation corresponds to the two input parameters to the GKS POLYMARKER function. The use of a more abstract datatype (seq_1 *POINT*) has simplified the definition of the operation.

D.2.2 Transformation strand

apply_norm_trans
Normalization transformations are functions from points to points. The exact definition is given in section D.4.2.

T_N : *POINT* $\rightarrow$ *POINT*

The operation *apply_norm_trans* has an associated state, represented by the variable T_N, which denotes the value of the normalization transformation to be applied. To perform the operation we apply the transformation to all the world coordinate points in the primitive and remove the world coordinate geometry from the primitive's definition.

*apply_norm_trans*_____
> $p?$: *PRIM*
> T_N : *POINT* → *POINT*
> T_N' : *POINT* → *POINT*
> $p!$: *PRIM*
> _____
> $T_N' = T_N$
> $WCG \in \mathbf{dom}\ p?$
> $p! = p? \backslash WCG \oplus \{\ NDCG \mapsto mkps(T_N\ (|\ mkps^{-1}\ (p?(WCG))\ |)\ )\ \}$

The resulting NDC geometry is a represented as a set of points.

The notation needs some more explanation. Variables whose names do not end with either "?" or "!" denote components of the state. A further convention is that names decorated with a prime (′) denote components of the state after the operation has been performed and the corresponding undecorated variables denote the values of the state before the operation. In the example above, the value of the current normalization transformation (denoted by the variables T_N and T_N') is not changed by the operation (T_N' =T_N). The NDC geometry is bound to the primitive. This is expressed by the predicate:

$$p! = p? \oplus \{\ NDCG \mapsto mkps(T_N\ (|\ mkps^{-1}\ (p?(WCG))\ |)\ \}$$

The operator "$\oplus$" adds

$$NDCG \mapsto mkps(T_N\ (|\ mkps^{-1}\ (p?(WCG))\ |)\ \}$$

to the finite function $p?$, overriding any previous value associated with $NDCG$. For convenience, long predicates may be broken at conjunctions ("$\wedge$"), and written on several lines with the conjunction signs omitted.

The operator "$\backslash$" denotes domain corestriction. In the example above, $p? \backslash WCG$ is the function $p?$ with WCG removed from its domain.

The function T_N is of type *POINT* → *POINT*. It has to be applied here to each point in a set of points. The brackets (| and |) enclose an argument of type set of points and apply the function to each of the points in the set. This is commonly known as *generalized application*.

The schema notation in Z gives a powerful mechanism for structuring specifications. If *NORM_TRANS* is the schema:

*NORM_TRANS*_____
> T_N : *POINT* → *POINT*

the statements

> T_N : *POINT* → *POINT*
> T_N' : *POINT* → *POINT*
> _____
> $T_N' = T_N$

can be replaced by the schema $\Xi\ NORM\_TRANS$ and thus *apply_norm_trans* can be written as:

*apply_norm_trans*_____
  $p?$: *PRIM*
  Ξ *NORM_TRANS*
  $p!$: *PRIM*
_____
  $WCG \in$ **dom** $p?$
  $p! = p? \setminus WCG \oplus \{ NDCG \mapsto mkps(T_N \;(\mathsf{l} \; mkps^{-1} \; (p?(WCG)) \; \mathsf{l}) \;) \}$

More generally, Ξ *Schema* duplicates the variables declared in *Schema* with their decorated counterparts and includes the predicate that corresponding decorated and undecorated variables have equal values. Thus Ξ *NORM_TRANS* denotes the schema:

Ξ *NORM_TRANS*_____
  T_N : *POINT* $\rightarrow$ *POINT*
  $T_N{}'$: *POINT* $\rightarrow$ *POINT*
_____
  $T_N{}' = T_N$

The effect of referring to a schema in the definition of another (for example Ξ *NORM_TRANS* in the definition of *apply_norm_trans*) is to include the definitions of the referred to schema in the declarations part, and to "and" together the predicates part with that of the outer schema. Thus the expansion of *apply_norm_trans* is exactly the definition first given in this section.

Later the notation Δ *Schema* is used. This denotes the same schema as Ξ *Schema* but excludes the predicate that corresponding decorated and undecorated variables have equal values. Thus Δ *NORM_TRANS* denotes the schema:

Δ *NORM_TRANS*_____
  T_N : *POINT* $\rightarrow$ *POINT*
  $T_N{}'$: *POINT* $\rightarrow$ *POINT*
_____

apply_ws_trans
This operation applies the current workstation transformation to the NDC geometry bound to the primitive. The result is a set of points in device coordinate space addressed by the identifier *DCG*. This operation is identical in form to *apply_norm_trans*. Workstation transformations are functions from points to points.

*WS_TRANS*_____
  T_{WS} : *POINT* $\rightarrow$ *POINT*

```
apply_ws_trans _____
  p? : PRIM
  Ξ WS_TRANS
  p! : PRIM
_____

  NDCG ∈ dom p?
  p! = p? \NDCG ⊕ { DCG ↦ mkps(T_WS (⏐ mkps⁻¹ (p?(NDCG)) ⏐) ) }
```

D.2.3 Clipping strand

bind_cr
This operation binds the clipping rectangle to the primitive and is defined by
the schema:

```
CR _____
  curcr : RECTANGLE
_____
```

```
bind_cr _____
  p? : PRIM
  Ξ CR
  p! : PRIM
_____
  p! = p? ⊕ {NCR ↦ mkr(curcr) }
```

RECTANGLE is a tuple type whose components are the points representing
the bottom left hand (selector *min*) and top right hand (selector *max*)
corners of the rectangular region.

apply_norm_clip
This operation applies the normalization clip. The clipping operation is
modelled by set intersection, a clipped object is represented by the set of
points covered by the object which is also covered by the clipping region.
This idea is captured in the following schemas.

```
clip _____
  λ ps, cr : P POINT • (ps ∩ cr)
_____
```

Lambda notation [200] is used in the definition of functions. Thus *clip* is a
function of two parameters *ps* and *cr*, both of type **P** *POINT* . The symbol
"•" is used a separator between the definition of the parameters of a function
and its body.

Clipping rectangles have been represented by a pair of points, the lower
left and top right hand corners of the rectangular region. The function *rect*
delivers the set of points covered by the rectangular viewport *v*.

rect _____
  $\lambda\ v : RECTANGLE \bullet (\ \{\ v.min + p\ \bullet\ a, b : \mathbf{R} \mid 0 \le a, b \le 1$
    where $p = \mu\ POINT \mid p.x = a\ (v.max.x - v.min.x)$
       $\wedge\ p.y = b\ (v.max.y - v.min.y)$
    $\})$
_____

The operation *apply_norm_clip* removes the clip rectangle from the
primitive's definition and defines the NDC geometry of the output primitive
as that portion of the NDC geometry of the input primitive which is covered
by the clipping region.

apply_norm_clip _____
  p? : PRIM
  p! : PRIM
_____
  $NDCG \in \mathbf{dom}\ p?\ \wedge NCR \in \mathbf{dom}\ p?$
  $p! = (p?\ \backslash NCR) \oplus \{\ NDCG \mapsto mkps(clip\ (\ mkps^{-1}\ (p?\ (NDCG)),$
                     $rect(mkr^{-1}\ (p?\ (NCR)))))\ \}$
_____

apply_ws_clip
The workstation clip is described by the following schema. The primitive is
clipped to the current workstation window. Windows are also rectangular
regions and are also represented by the type *RECTANGLE*.

WS_CR _____
  | *wsw* : *RECTANGLE*
  _____

apply_ws_clip _____
  p? : PRIM
  Ξ WS_CR
  p! : PRIM
_____
  $NDCG \in \mathbf{dom}\ p?$
  $p! = p?\ \oplus\ \{\ NDCG \mapsto mkps(clip\ (\ mkps^{-1}\ (p?\ (NDCG)), rect(wsw)))\ \}$
_____

D.2.4 Attribute strand

bind_pm_asf
This operation binds aspect source flags to a polymarker. Aspect source
flags are modelled as a finite function from aspects to values (*ASPECT* $\rightarrow$
ASF_VALUE). The aspects of the polymarker primitive are marker type,
marker size scale factor and polymarker colour index (*PmType*, *PmSF* and
PmColi, respectively). An aspect source flag can take just the values
INDIVIDUAL and *BUNDLED*.

```
ASPECT_____
| PmType | PmSF | PmColi
```

```
ASF_VALUE_____
| INDIVIDUAL | BUNDLED
```

```
ASFS_____
| asfs : ASPECT → ASF_VALUE
```

```
bind_pm_asf_____
  p? : PRIM
  Ξ ASFS
  p! : PRIM
_____
  p! = p?  ⊕  { ASF ↦ mkasf(asfs) }
```

bind_ind_values

This operation binds individual attribute values to the primitive, for those aspects which are specified individually. The current polymarker index is also bound to the primitive. There is a distinction in GKS between attribute names and aspect names. In this book the values of individual attributes are modelled as a finite function from the corresponding aspect names to values.

```
INDIV_____
  indiv : ASPECT → ASP_VALUE
  curpmi : PMI
_____
```

ASP_VALUE is a disjoint union of the types of each of the aspects. In this specification, the only constructor function that needs to be referred to is that for the polymarker colour index, $mkpmci \ll CIND \gg$.

The definition of bind_ind_values is given below. Effectively this binds to the primitive a function of type: $ASPECT \rightarrow ASP\_VALUE$ which contains the values of all the individually specified aspects. This function is addressed by the identifier ASP. The domain of the function is the set of aspects whose aspect source flags have the value INDIVIDUAL. Recall that the aspect source flags of a primitive are represented as a function of type $ASPECT \rightarrow ASP\_VALUE$ The expression $mkasf^{-1} (p? (ASF))$ gives the aspect source flags bound to the primitive p? and $mkasf^{-1} (p? (ASF)) (n)$ is the value of the aspect source flag for the aspect n.

The current polymarker index is also bound to the primitive by this operation.

*bind_ind_values*_____
| $p?$: *PRIM*
| Ξ *INDIV*
| $p!$: *PRIM*
|_____
| ASF $\in$ **dom** $p?$
| $p! = (p?$ $\oplus$ $\{$ *ASP* $\mapsto$ *mkasp(asp)* $\}$ $)$ $\oplus$ $\{$ *PIND* $\mapsto$ *mkpind(curpmi)*$\}$
| **where** asp : *ASPECT* $\rightarrow$ *ASP_VALUE* |
| $asp = \{n \mapsto v \cdot n$: *ASPECT*, v : *ASP_VALUE* |
| $(mkasf^{-1}$ $(p?$ $(ASF)))(n)$ = *INDIVIDUAL* $\wedge$ v = $indiv(n)$ $\}$

bind_ws_bundle

This operation binds in representations for the aspects of the primitives specified through a bundle table. Bundle tables are represented as partial functions from indices to bundles, a bundle being a function from aspects to aspect values. This is expressed by the schema *PBT*:

*PBT*_____
| pbt : *PMI* $\nrightarrow$ *ASPECT* $\rightarrow$ *ASP_VALUE*

A representation is always defined for polymarker index 1. Representing bundle tables as partial functions is a more elegant representation than the record collection approach in GKS.

The operation is defined by the schema *bind_ws_bundle*. This removes the polymarker index and aspect source flags from the primitive and adds to the definition of *ASP* mappings from *ASPECT* to *ASP_VALUE* for those aspects whose aspect source flags are set to *BUNDLED*. Note that $p?$ (*ASP*) is the set of mappings produced by *bind_ind_values* and $p!$ (*ASP*) now includes mappings for all the primitive's aspects.

*bind_ws_bundle*_____
| $p?$: *PRIM*
| Ξ *PBT*
| $p!$: *PRIM*
|_____
| ASF $\in$ **dom** $p?$ $\wedge$ PIND $\in$ **dom** $p?$ $\wedge$ ASP $\in$ **dom** $p?$
| $p! = p?$ \ASF\PIND $\oplus$ $\{$ ASP $\mapsto$ $(p?(ASP) \cup mkasp(asp))$ $\}$
| **where** asp : *ASPECT* $\rightarrow$ *ASP_VALUE* |
| $asp = \{$ $n \mapsto$ $v \cdot n$: *ASPECT*, v : *ASP_VALUE* |
| $(mkasf^{-1}$ $(p?(ASF)))(n)$ = *BUNDLED* $\wedge$
| v = $bundle(mkpind^{-1}$ $(p?(PIND)))(n)$ $\}$
| **where** $bundle$: *ASPECT* $\rightarrow$ *ASP_VALUE* $= \begin{cases} pbt(i) & i \in \textbf{dom } pbt \\ pbt(1) & i \notin \textbf{dom } pbt \end{cases}$
| **where** $i = \mu$*PMI* | i = $mkpind^{-1}$ ($p?$ (*PIND*))

If a representation is not defined for the polymarker index bound to the primitive, the representation of polymarker index 1 is used instead. A representation is always defined for this index.

bind_colour

This operation binds in the colour corresponding to the polymarker colour index aspect. Colours are defined in the colour table which is a function from colour index values to colours.

$$
\begin{array}{|l}
\hline
COLTAB \rule{3cm}{0.4pt} \\
\hline
coltab : CIND \rightarrow COLOUR \\
\hline
\end{array}
$$

The operation is defined by the schema *bind_colour*:

$$
\begin{array}{|l}
\hline
bind\_colour \rule{5cm}{0.4pt} \\
p? : PRIM \\
\Xi\ COLTAB \\
p! : PRIM \\
\hline
ASP \in \mathbf{dom}\ p? \wedge PmColi \in \mathbf{dom}\ mkasp^{-1}\ (p?(ASP)) \\
p! = p? \oplus \{\ COL \mapsto\ coltab(mkpmci^{-1}\ (mkasp^{-1}\ (p?(ASP))(PmColi)))\ \} \\
\hline
\end{array}
$$

elaborate

This operation applies the primitive aspects to the DC geometry and produces a set of points representing the rendered primitive. The set of points constituting a positioned marker symbol is given by the function *marker* which places the marker specified by the marker type and marker size scale factor arguments at a specified position.

The function *realized* performs the mapping from the aspect value specified by the application program to the nearest available value on the workstation. GKS does not specify the details of this and so the function is not further described here. The symbol "$\cup$" is distributed set union.

$$
\begin{array}{|l}
\hline
elaborate \rule{6cm}{0.4pt} \\
p? : PRIM \\
p! : PRIM \\
\hline
ASP \in \mathbf{dom}\ p? \wedge NDCG \in \mathbf{dom}\ p? \\
\qquad \wedge\ \{\ PmType, PmSF\ \} \subseteq \mathbf{dom}\ mkasp^{-1}\ (p?(ASP)) \\
p! = p?\ \oplus\ \{\ NDCG \mapsto \\
\\
\quad mkps\ (\ \bigcup_{pt:POINT\ \in\ mkps^{-1}(p?\ (NDCG\ ))}\ marker\ (realized(mkasp^{-1}(p?(ASP))(PmType)), \\
\qquad\qquad\qquad\qquad\qquad\qquad realized(mkasp^{-1}(p?(ASP))(PmSF)), pt) \\
\\
\quad) \\
\quad \} \\
\hline
\end{array}
$$

D.2.5 Device interface

mk_dc_polymarker
This operation converts a polymarker represented as a point set in DC space and a colour to a representation as a partial function from points to colours.

$$mk\_dc\_polymarker$$
$$p? : PRIM$$
$$p! : PRIM$$

$$DCG \in \textbf{dom}\ p? \wedge COL \in \textbf{dom}\ p?$$
$$p! = p? \setminus DCG \setminus COL \setminus ASP \oplus \{\ DCP \mapsto\ mkdcp(dcprim)\ \}$$
$$\textbf{where}\ dcprim : POINT \rightarrow COLOUR\ |$$
$$\{\ pt \mapsto\ mkcol^{-1}\ (p?(COL)) \bullet pt : POINT\ |\ pt \in mkps^{-1}\ (p?(DCG))\ \}$$

add_dcp
The DC picture is an abstraction of the picture actually displayed on the display surface of a workstation, and is defined over a region of the real plane. The representation of this abstract picture on a physical display surface (which is not in general discrete) is a further rendering issue which is not addressed here. The DC picture is modelled as a relation (rather than a function) whose domain represents the geometry of the picture and whose range is the colour with which the elements of the domain are to be displayed. A relation rather than a function is necessary because more than one colour may be associated with any one point, for example if the point is the intersection of two polymarkers of different colours. GKS does not define which of two overlapping primitives should take precedence (in general), the interpretation of the relation in this context is that an implementation of GKS is valid if the colour of the point is any of the allowed possibilities (or for some kinds of device a combination of the allowed possibilities). It is this representation of DC pictures that makes the previous operation *mk_dc_polymarker* necessary. Relations are indicated by the symbol ↔.

$$DCPIC$$
$$dcp : POINT \leftrightarrow COLOUR$$

$$add\_dcp$$
$$p? : PRIM$$
$$\Delta\ DCPIC$$

$$DCP \in \textbf{dom}\ p?$$
$$dcp' = dcp \cup mkdcp^{-1}\ (p?(DCP))$$

D.3 Constructing pipelines

The question which now arises is what is the effect of the operation *bind_cr* followed by the operation *apply_norm_clip* and how is this described in Z? There are many ways of combining schemas in the Z notation [194,199]. One of them, called *schema piping*, provides just what is needed in this case. We want to describe the effect of the pipeline:

This is given by the expression:

$$bind\_cr >> apply\_norm\_clip$$

The operator ">>" is the schema-piping operator. The schema S >> T is a schema in which the output variables of S (names with suffix "!") are identified with the input variables of T (names with suffix "?") that have the same base name (i.e. excluding the "?" and "!"). The expanded definition of *bind_cr >> apply_norm_clip* is the schema:

---
bind_cr >> apply_norm_clip _____

$p?$: *PRIM*
Ξ *CR*
$p!$: *PRIM*

$\exists\, p$: *PRIM* • p = $p? \oplus \{NCR \mapsto mkr(curcr)\} \wedge$
  $NDCG \in \textbf{dom }\ p \wedge NCR \in \textbf{dom }\ p \wedge$
  $p! = (p \setminus NCR) \oplus$
  $\{NDCG \mapsto mkps(clip\ (mkps^{-1}\ (p?(NDCG)), rect(mkr^{-1}\ (p?(NCR)))))\}$
---

which simplifies to:

---
bind_cr >> apply_norm_clip _____

$p?$: *PRIM*
Ξ *CR*
$p!$: *PRIM*

$NDCG \in \textbf{dom }\ p?$
$p! = p? \oplus \{NDCG \mapsto mkps(clip\ (\ mkps^{-1}\ (p?(NDCG)), rect(curcr)))\}$

Note that the operation defined is atomic. This model does not describe pipelines in which there is parallelism.

Figure D.1 describes one order in which the operations can be composed. This is not the only possible order, for example *apply_norm_trans* can occur before or after *bind_cr*. However, there are constraints, for example *bind_pm_asf* must be before *bind_ind_values*. This can be seen by examining the predicates of the two operations. *bind_ind_values* requires that *ASF* be in the domain of the input primitive. Only *bind_pm_asf* supplies this value and hence this operation must occur first.

In the later stages of the pipeline other considerations apply. The workstation clip takes place in NDC space. However a pipeline can be defined in which this clip takes place in DC space, after the workstation clip rectangle has been mapped from NDC to DC space. The paper by Onodera and Kawai [195] discusses this type of pipeline transformation in detail and presents an algorithm for generating the necessary compensating data transformations.

D.4 State control operations

D.4.1 Introduction

Some of the pipeline operations described in section D.2 have an associated internal state, for example the operation *apply_norm_trans* which applies the normalization transformation to a primitive has an internal state represented by the variable T_N which denotes the current normalization transformation. The purpose of this section is to describe where the values of these variables come from. There are in essence two kinds of operation in the system, operations which represent processes in the pipeline, and operations which modify the state of one or more pipeline processes.

Table D.2 lists the operations with internal state, the corresponding variables and the operations which set the internal state.

As will be seen shortly, additional variables representing state are introduced by the operations now to be defined. The schema structure for the state is shown in figure D.2.

D.4.2 Normalization transformation and clipping

A normalization transformation is a window to viewport mapping which maps a rectangular window in world coordinate space to a rectangular viewport in normalized device coordinate space.

A normalization transformation is a combination of scaling and translation operations. Functions defining translation, T_T, and scaling, T_S, are defined below in Curried form using lambda notation as described in [200]. The function definitions are Curried so that we can define a function that is the composition of translations and scales by specified amounts.

$$T_T$$
$$\lambda t? : POINT . \lambda p? : POINT \bullet (p? + t?)$$

T_S _____

$$\lambda s_x?,s_y? : \mathbf{R}.\lambda p?:POINT{\cdot}\mu r:POINT \mid (r.x = s_x? \times p?.x \wedge r.y = s_y? \times p?.y)$$

The expression $\mu\, S \mid E$ is defined only if there is a unique way to give values to the variables introduced by S such that the expression E is true. In the expression above the μ expression delivers the unique point with the specified property.

Table D.2 Operations with internal state

Operation	State	Set Operation
Transformations and Clipping		
apply_norm_trans	T_N	SET WINDOW
		SET VIEWPORT
		SELECT NORMALIZATION TRANSFORMATION
bind_cr	curcr	SET CLIPPING INDICATOR
		SET VIEWPORT
		SELECT NORMALIZATION TRANSFORMATION
apply_ws_trans	T_{WS}	SET WORKSTATION WINDOW
		SET WORKSTATION VIEWPORT
apply_ws_clip	wsw	SET WORKSTATION WINDOW
Aspects and Attributes		
bind_pm_asf	asfs	SET ASPECT SOURCE FLAGS
bind_ind_values	indiv	SET MARKER TYPE
		SET MARKER SIZE SCALE FACTOR
		SET POLYMARKER COLOUR INDEX
	curpmi	SET POLYMARKER INDEX
bind_ws_bundle	pbt	SET POLYMARKER REPRESENTATION
bind_colour	coltab	SET COLOUR REPRESENTATION

A normalization transformation, T_N, can be described as the composition of three transformations, a translation of the window to the origin, a scaling of the window to be the same size as the viewport, and a translation of the scaled window to the position occupied by the viewport. The symbol "$\circ$" denotes function composition.

T_{NORM} _____

$$\lambda w?,v?:RECTANGLE{\cdot}T_T(v?.min)\circ T_S(s_x,s_y)\circ T_T(-w?.min)$$
$$\text{where } s_x,s_y{:}\mathbf{R} \mid s_x=(v?.max.x-v?.min.x)/(w?.max.x-w?.min.x)\wedge$$
$$s_y=(v?.max.y-v?.min.y)/(w?.max.y-w?.min.y)$$

Normalization transformations are defined by a window and a viewport. GKS allows multiple normalization transformations to be defined, and one of the defined transformations to be selected as the current normalization transformation; which is applied to subsequently created primitives. The viewport of the currently selected normalization transformation also serves as the clipping rectangle when clipping is enabled. When clipping is disabled, the clipping rectangle is the unit square in NDC space. The schema *NORMALIZATION* captures these ideas.

State Schemas   **Pipeline Operations**

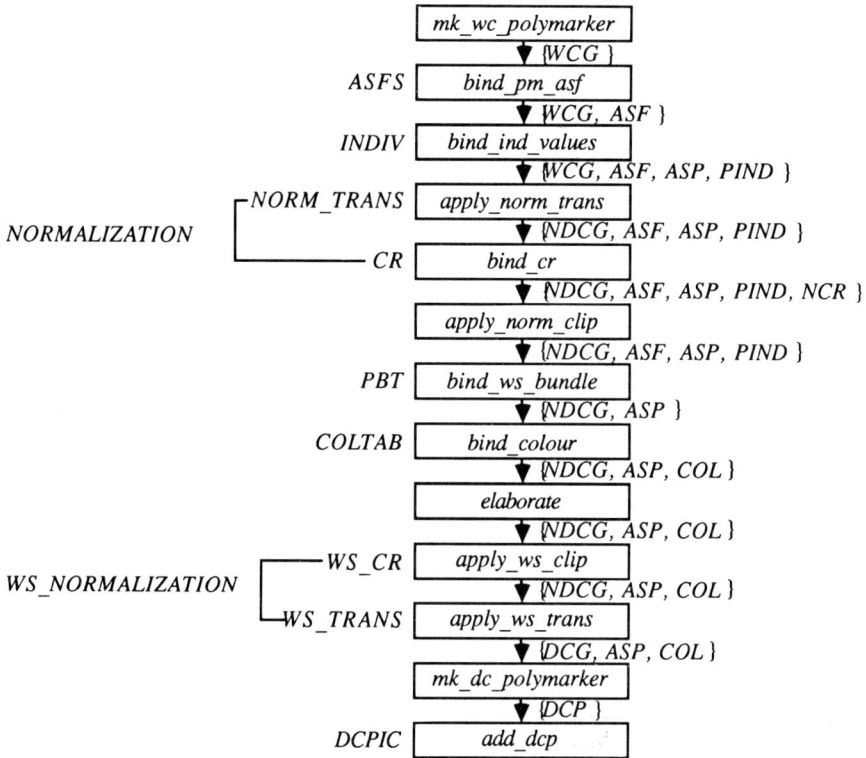

Figure D.2 Structure of state schemas

Multiple normalization transformations are modelled by a pair of functions of type $NT\_NO \rightarrow RECTANGLE$ representing windows and viewports. The type NT_NO represents normalization transformation numbers which are used to address the defined normalization transformations. The currently selected normalization transformation is represented by the variable *curcnt_no*. The current clipping rectangle is represented by the variable *curcr*, whose value is defined as above. The variable *curcind* denotes the current clipping indicator value. The variable T_N represents the currently selected normalization transformation and is a function of type $POINT \rightarrow POINT$. Initially all normalization transformations are set to a default, but initialization is not considered here. The schema *UNITVP* defines the unit square viewport.

```
CLIPIND_____
| CLIP | NOCLIP
```

```
UNITVP_____
| μv : VIEWPORT • (v.min.x = v.min.y = 0 ∧ v.max.x = v.max.y = 1)
```

```
NORMALIZATION_____
  NORM_TRANS
  CR
  ntw : NT_NO → RECTANGLE
  ntv : NT_NO → RECTANGLE
  curnt_no : NT_NO
  curcind : CLIPIND
  _____
  T_N = T_NORM ( ntw(curnt_no), ntv(curnt_no) )
  curcind = CLIP ⇒ curcr = ntv(curnt_no)
  curcind = NOCLIP ⇒ curcr = UNITVP
```

The operation to select a normalization transformation is defined by the schema:

```
Select_Normalization_Transformation _____
  n? : NT_NO
  Δ NORMALIZATION
  _____
  ntw' = ntw
  ntv' = ntv
  curnt_no' = n?
  curcind' = curcind
```

It may not be clear how a new normalization transformation is defined by this schema so a few words of explanation are in order. The currently selected normalization transformation after the operation is represented by the value of *curnt_no'* which is just *n?*, the value specified as an input to the operation. The normalization transformation after the operation is denoted by T_N', which by virtue of the predicate in Δ *NORMALIZATION* is

$$T_N' = T_{NORM} (ntw' (curnt\_no') , ntv' (curnt\_no'))$$
$$= T_{NORM} (ntw' (n?) , ntv' (n?))$$

Thus the transformation after the operation is that selected by the input to the operation.

The operations to set a window, set a viewport, and set the clipping indicator are defined and operate in a similar way. Only *Set_Window* is shown here.

Set_Window _____
| $n?$: NT_NO
| $w?$: $RECTANGLE$
| $\Delta\ NORMALIZATION$
_____
| $ntw'\ =\ ntw \oplus \{\ n? \mapsto\ w?\ \}$
| $ntv'\ =\ ntv$
| $curnt\_no'\ =\ curnt\_no$
| $curcind\_no'\ =\ curcind\_no$

D.4.3 Workstation transformation and clip

The workstation transformation is also a window to viewport mapping, but differs from the normalization transformation in that the aspect ratio of the workstation window is preserved. The window maps to the largest region of the viewport with the same aspect ratio.

The function $T_{WORKSTATION}$ defines the workstation transformation corresponding to a given window and viewport, using the functions T_T and T_S defined above.

$T_{WORKSTATION}$ _____
| $\lambda w?, v?$: $RECTANGLE \bullet T_T\ (\ v?.min\ ) \circ T_S\ (\ s\ ,\ s\ )\ \circ T_T\ (\ \text{-}\ w?.min\ )$
| **where** $s : R\ |\ \Delta\ w.y\ /\ \Delta\ w.x\ \geq \Delta\ v.y\ /\ \Delta\ v.x\ \Rightarrow s = \Delta\ v.y\ /\ \Delta\ w.y\ \wedge$
| $\Delta\ w.y\ /\ \Delta\ w.x\ <\ \Delta\ v.y\ /\ \Delta\ v.x\ \Rightarrow s = \Delta\ v.x\ /\ \Delta\ w.x$
| **where** $\Delta w, \Delta v : POINT\ |\ \Delta w = w?.max\ \text{-}\ w?.min\ \wedge$
| $\Delta v = v?.max\ \text{-}\ v?.min$

Here Δw and Δv correspond to the top right hand corner of the window and viewport respectively, when their bottom left hand corners are translated to the origin.

Each workstation has a single workstation transformation associated with it which defines the region of the NDC space to be viewed on the workstation and where on the workstation display surface it is to be placed. There is an additional complication in GKS that all the picture displayed on the workstation is derived from a single workstation transformation, thus if the workstation transformation is changed when the display surface is not empty, the new transformation will have a retrospective effect on the picture already displayed, or the new transformation will not take effect until the display surface is explicitly updated. The workstation's capabilities determine which case holds. These are complications which are not addressed in this present paper. Here we allow changes in the transformation to take immediate effect and not to affect primitives already processed by the pipeline.

The workstation transformation is modelled by a workstation window *wsw*, and workstation viewport, *wsv*. The workstation window also serves as a clip rectangle for the workstation clip. This clip cannot be disabled.

```
WS_TRANSFORMATION _____
  WS_TRANS
  WS_CR
  wsv : RECTANGLE
  _____
  T_WS = T_WORKSTATION  (wsw, wsv)
```

$$T_{WS} = T_{WORKSTATION} \ (wsw, wsv)$$

Operations *Set_Workstation_Window* and *Set_Workstation_Viewport* are provided to set the workstation window and viewport. Only *Set_Workstation_Window* is shown.

```
Set_Workstation_Window _____
  w? : RECTANGLE
  Δ WS_TRANSFORMATION
  _____
  wsw' = w? ∧ wsv' = wsv
```

$$wsw' = w? \land wsv' = wsv$$

D.4.4 Aspects and attributes

The operation, *Set_Aspect_Source_Flags*, is defined by the schema:

```
Set_Aspect_Source_Flags _____
  a? : ASPECT → ASF_VALUE
  ΔASFS
  _____
  asfs' = a?
```

The schema *ASFS* is defined in section D.2.4.

Operations to set the current polymarker index and individual attribute values may be readily defined. Only *Set_Polymarker_Index* and *Set_Polymarker_Colour_Index* are shown. The others are very similar.

```
Set_Polymarker_Index_____
  pmi? : PMI
  ΔINDIV
  _____
  indiv' = indiv ∧ curpmi' = pmi?
```

The problem alluded to in Section 11.1 of the behaviour of *Set_Polymarker_Index* when presented with an invalid polymarker index does not arise in this specification, because all values of the type are valid.

*Set_Polymarker_Colour_Index*_____

$ci?$: $CIND$
$\Delta INDIV$

―――――――――――――――――――――――――――――――

$indiv' = indiv \oplus \{\ PmColi \mapsto mkpmci(ci?)\ \} \wedge curpmi' = curpmi$

The schema *INDIV* is defined in section D.2.4.

    The GKS function SET POLYMARKER REPRESENTATION sets values for all the aspects associated with a specified polymarker index. It is defined by the schema:

Set_Polymarker_Representation _____

$pmi?$: PMI
$mt?$: MT
$ms?$: MS
$pmcoli?$: $CIND$
ΔPBT

―――――――――――――――――――――――――――――――

$pbt' = pbt \oplus \{\ pmi? \mapsto \{\ PmType \mapsto mkmt(mt?),$
$\qquad\qquad\qquad\qquad PmSF \mapsto mkms(ms?),$
$\qquad\qquad\qquad\qquad PmColi \mapsto mkpmci(pmcoli?)\ \}$
$\qquad\qquad \}$

The schema *PBT* is defined in section D.2.4. There is a complication in GKS that SET POLYMARKER REPRESENTATION can have a retrospective effect, but this is not considered in this paper.

    The GKS function SET COLOUR REPRESENTATION defines a colour to be associated with a specified colour index. Again there is a possibility of retrospective effects, but these are not considered here.

*Set_Colour_Representation*_____

$cind?$: $CIND$
$c?$: $COLOUR$
$\Delta COLTAB$

―――――――――――――――――――――――――――――――

$coltab' = coltab \oplus \{cind? \mapsto c?\ \}$

Index